Innovative Approaches in Teaching English Writing to Chinese Speakers

Trends in Applied Linguistics

Edited by
Ulrike Jessner

Volume 32

Innovative Approaches in Teaching English Writing to Chinese Speakers

Edited by
Barry Lee Reynolds, Mark Feng Teng

DE GRUYTER
MOUTON

ISBN 978-1-5015-2103-4
e-ISBN (PDF) 978-1-5015-1264-3
e-ISBN (EPUB) 978-1-5015-1244-5
ISSN 1868-6362

Library of Congress Control Number: 2020950141

Bibliographic information published by the Deutsche Nationalbibliothek
The Deutsche Nationalbibliothek lists this publication in the Deutsche Nationalbibliografie;
detailed bibliographic data are available on the Internet at http://dnb.dnb.de.

© 2022 Walter de Gruyter Inc., Boston/Berlin
This volume is text- and page-identical with the hardback published in 2021.
Typesetting: Integra Software Services Pvt. Ltd.
Printing and binding: CPI books GmbH, Leck

www.degruyter.com

Preface

Teaching English writing is tough. Innovating the teaching of English writing may be even tougher. This book synthesizes findings and ideas on innovating the teaching of English writing to Chinese speakers. Mark and I did not aim for this book to represent our own personal takes on what it means to innovate the teaching of English writing but instead encouraged contributors to advocate whatever approaches they felt were most suitable for the learners from their teaching and research contexts. While many colleagues may approach the teaching of English writing differently than some of the authors of the chapters in this book, we do feel that the book offers a number of alternative approaches for any teacher of English writing to consider. We never intended for this book to be a definitive guide to the teaching of second language writing. Instead, we wanted to offer a venue for the voices of second language writing teachers and researchers to share with others what they have been doing in their classrooms or what personal research problems they have been involved in tackling. We believe that this goal has been reached. We hope this book stimulates you to begin innovating approaches to the teaching of English writing in your classroom or is the catalyst for you to begin researching English writing instruction.

Barry Lee Reynolds
Taipa, Macau SAR
December 2019

Acknowledgements

As editors of the volume, we would like to express our gratitude to a number of people whose help has been invaluable in making this book a reality. Our thanks go to the chapter authors for their willingness to contribute and their continued persistence in revising throughout the review process. The chapters greatly benefitted from the expertise of a group of colleagues that kindly accepted taking on the job of reviewing. We are deeply indebted to these colleagues for their help.

Reviewers

Chingfen Chang, National Chiao Tung University, Taiwan
Shu-I Chang, National Chiayi University, Taiwan
Ru-Shan Chen, Chihlee University of Technology, Taiwan
Jun Scott Chen Hsieh, Asia University, Taiwan
Edsoulla Chung, The Open University of Hong Kong, Hong Kong SAR
David Coulson, Ritsumeikan University, Japan
Jenifer Ho, City University of Hong Kong, Hong Kong SAR
Shu-Chen Huang, National Chengchi University, Taiwan
Yun-Yin Huang, National Tsing Hua University, Taiwan
Chian-Wen Kao, Chihlee University of Technology, Taiwan
Miranda Sin I Ma, University of Macau, Macau SAR
Wei Ren, Beihang University, China
Barry Lee Reynolds, University of Macau, Macau SAR, China
Rustam Shadiev, Nanjing Normal University, China
(Mark) Feng Teng, University of Macau, Macau SAR, China
Claudia Wong, Simon Fraser University, Canada
Shizhou Yang, Payap University, Thailand
Shulin Yu, University of Macau, Macau SAR
Eric Yuan, University of Macau, Macau SAR
Xiaodong Zhang, Beijing Foreign Studies University, China
Cecilia Guanfang Zhao, University of Macau, Macau SAR
Yao Zheng, Chongqing University, China

Contents

Preface —— V

Acknowledgements —— VII

Contributors —— XI

Barry Lee Reynolds, Mark Feng Teng
Teaching English writing in Chinese speaking regions —— 1

Anisa Cheung
Integrating e-learning into process writing: The case of a primary school in Hong Kong —— 19

Amy Kong
A dual case study of perceptions of strategy-based training and peer review stances among Hong Kong secondary students: An activity theory perspective —— 43

Wilson Cheong Hin Hong
Improving English as a foreign language learners' writing using a minimal grammar approach of teaching dependent clauses: A case study of Macao secondary school students —— 67

Melissa H. Yu
A pedagogical inquiry into students' writing skills development from the perspective of English as a lingua franca: Insights from secondary and tertiary English language education in Taiwan —— 91

Maggie Ma, Mark Feng Teng
Metacognitive knowledge development of low proficiency Hong Kong English as a foreign language university students in a process-oriented writing course: An action research study —— 117

Dureshahwar Shari Lughmani, Dennis Foung
Metacognitive strategy-focused instruction in a writing across the curriculum programme in a Hong Kong university: The impact on writing performance —— 145

Anora Yu
A narrative inquiry into washback of high-stakes and low-stakes testing on second language English writing in Hong Kong higher education —— 179

(Luna) Jing Cai
Preparing Chinese novice writers for academia: An integrated genre-based approach for writing research articles —— 207

Yun-yin Huang, Hsiao-Hui Wua
Toward better English for research publication purposes practices through the lens of activity theory: A case study of a cross-disciplinary graduate writing course in Taiwan —— 233

Barry Lee Reynolds, Mark Feng Teng
Practice and future directions for developing Chinese speakers' English writing across different education levels —— 257

Index —— 271

Contributors

(Luna) Jing Cai is an associate professor at the School of English Language Education, Guangdong University of Foreign Studies, China. Her current research interests include English for Academic Purposes, genre-based theories, and lexical studies. She has published internationally on academic writing in Chinese tertiary contexts in journals such as *Journal of English for Academic Purposes*. She is dedicated to connecting research in EAP with pedagogy.

Anisa Cheung is currently Lecturer in the Center for Language Education, Hong Kong University of Science and Technology. She holds a doctorate in English Language Education from The University of Hong Kong. She has experience teaching English in a range of settings and has taught a range of courses related to linguistics and pedagogy. Her research interests include teacher cognition, second language teacher education and different aspects related to English language teaching and learning.

Dennis Foung is Teaching Fellow at the Hong Kong Polytechnic University. He holds a doctorate in language education and has been teaching English to different tertiary students in Hong Kong. Having a keen interest in genre-based pedagogy, he is involved in various writing across the curriculum programmes. Other than WAC, his research interests include CALL, learning analytics, classroom discourse, and teacher behaviors.

Wilson Cheong Hin Hong is an Education PhD candidate at University College London and an MA graduate in Linguistics from Newcastle University in the UK. He is interested in EFL/ESL pronunciation, writing pedagogy and student errors. Mr. Hong is currently a full-time lecturer at the Macao Institute for Tourism Studies and a former lecturer at City University of Macau and the Macao Polytechnic Institute. He has experience teaching EFL/ESL students of different ages and nationality backgrounds.

Yun-yin Huang is an assistant professor of Language Center, National Tsing Hwa University (NTHU) in Taiwan. She currently serves as the coordinator of the graduate EAP courses. She has taught a wide variety of ESL courses at (under) graduate levels for over 10 years in Taiwan and New York City. She specializes in incorporating technologies in second language instructions, with a strong track record in qualitative analysis. Her current research interests include second language writing, English for research publication purposes (ERPP), and digital literacy/-cies.

Amy Kong is Senior Lecturer in the Department of English, the Hang Seng University of Hong Kong. Dr. Kong worked on the topic of peer review in the ESL writing classroom for her PhD dissertation. Her recent work includes a "Reader Stances and Writer Responses in L2 Peer Review: A Study of L2 Writing Literacy among Hong Kong Secondary School Students" published in *The Asian EFL Journal*. Dr. Kong is also interested in oral feedback. She has recently published an article "Disambiguating Recasts with Prosodic and Extra-Linguistic Cues in Task-based Interactions among Young Learners" in *Language Teaching for Young Learners*.

Dureshahwar Lughmani coordinates a collaborative WAC programme at the English Language Centre of The Hong Kong Polytechnic University. Her research interests include genre-based and L2 writing pedagogy and academic literacies. She teaches EAP, ESP, and Creative Writing.

Maggie Ma is Assistant Professor in the English Department of the Hang Seng University of Hong Kong. Her research interests include second language writing and formative assessment.

Barry Lee Reynolds is Assistant Professor of English Education in the Faculty of Education at the University of Macau. Dr. Reynolds has taught English for General Purposes, English for Academic Purposes, English for Specific Purposes, and trained language teachers at thirteen institutions in the USA, Taiwan, and Macau. He conducts interdisciplinary applied linguistics research in the areas of vocabulary acquisition, second language literacy education, and computer assisted language learning. His work has been published in numerous flagship international journals.

(Mark) Feng Teng is an active researcher in the TESOL community. He has extensive teaching and teacher education experience in mainland China. His research programme spans cognitive, and developmental factors in writing development, metacognition, self-regulated learning (SRL) and writing development in L2 and EFL contexts, vocabulary acquisition, and language teacher education. He was the recipient of the 2017 Best Paper Award from the Hong Kong Association for Applied Linguistics (HAAL), as well as the Teaching Excellence Awards in mainland China. He has published more than 40 articles in international flagship journals, including *Computers & Education, TESOL Quarterly, Language Teaching Research, Computer Assisted Language Learning, Applied Linguistics Review, and Thinking Skills & Creativity*. His recent monographs were published by Springer and Bloomsbury.

Hsiao-Hui Wu, Ed.D., is an assistant professor the in Department of Applied English at Tainan University of Technology in Taiwan. She has taught EFL and ESP courses at the university level for 10 years. Her research interests focus on interdisciplinary academic research writing, English reading strategy, and EFL pedagogy.

Anora Yu holds an EdD from the University of Bristol, UK. Her research interests are in the areas of narrative inquiry, leadership in higher education, and washback in English language testing. Prior to her early retirement in 2019, she had held various key positions such as Head, Associate Head and Director of the English Language Teaching Programme in the Department of English at the Hang Seng University of Hong Kong.

Melissa H. Yu is currently a postdoctoral research fellow at the Faculty of Education, University of Macau. So far, she has completed and is carrying out several research projects at the faculty. Her main research interests include English as a lingua franca (ELF), TESOL, and ethnography. Before coming to the University of Macau, she was a secondary English language teacher in Taiwan and then worked as a part-time lecturer teaching TESOL teacher training and intercultural communication courses at the University of Southampton and Newcastle University in the UK.

Barry Lee Reynolds, Mark Feng Teng
Teaching English writing in Chinese speaking regions

Abstract: Whether discussing the teaching or learning of English writing, most educators and learners alike agree that it is the most challenging language skill to master. While contexts may differ in terms of purpose or motivation for learning to write in English, contexts may also share similar challenges. This is the exact situation with learners in Chinese speaking regions. From primary school to graduate school, learners are struggling with similar yet contextually unique difficulties in mastering English writing. These learners require instructional support informed by a multifaceted research literature covering the fields of second language acquisition, reading research, vocabulary research, bilingual processing, sociocultural factors, language assessment, and language policies. The complexity of English writing development was the seed of our attempt to characterize second language writing instruction for Chinese speakers in different yet historically related regions. This chapter juxtaposes the similarities and differences in English writing instruction in mainland China, Hong Kong SAR, Macau SAR, and Taiwan. With a focus on current innovative practices and research trends, this chapter provides a starting point for thinking about what is important to understand English writing instruction in the regions.

Keywords: Taiwan, Macau, Hong Kong, China, English Writing, Chinese

1 Introduction

English, the *de facto* lingua franca of the global world, is widely taught as a second/foreign language in primary schools, secondary schools, and universities (Reynolds and Teng 2019; Sharifian 2009). English writing, defined as a skill for learners to use symbols (e.g. letters of the alphabet, punctuation and spaces) to represent thoughts and ideas in a readable form has increasingly become as important as the spoken word (Teng and Reynolds 2019a, 2019b). Despite English writing being acknowledged as an essential skill for critical

---

Barry Lee Reynolds, Mark Feng Teng, University of Macau

https://doi.org/10.1515/9781501512643-001

thinking, learning, and expression, teaching writing itself is still a challenging task (Kao and Reynolds 2017). Most English as a foreign language (EFL) learners find themselves struggling when writing in English due to a lack of writing skills, content knowledge, writing strategies, intrinsic motivation, and fluency development practice (Teng 2016, 2019a). Likewise, English writing also presents challenges for EFL teachers in that they must have the knowhow to select reasoned approaches and make instructional decisions to address learners' poor writing skills and stagnant writing development (Nation 2009). The teachers must make these decisions without further widening the gap between theory and practice (Nation 2009).

Chinese speakers are the largest group of English language learners around the world (Cortazzi and Jin 1996; He and Teng 2019). Along with this wide acceptance of the importance in English language learning, education policies in Chinese speaking regions have further increased learners' exposure to English writing through compulsory writing courses at all stages of education (Teng and Reynolds 2019a, 2019b). Accordingly, the introduction of second/foreign language writing instruction is happening at an ever-increasing earlier age, resulting in English Language Teaching (ELT) researchers and practitioners seeking routes to enhance second language (L2) writing at all levels of education (Reynolds and Teng 2019). This edited volume, drawing upon collected studies targeted at primary, secondary, and tertiary-level education in mainland China, Hong Kong SAR, Macau SAR, and Taiwan, aims to provide teachers and practitioners with implications to enhance the English writing performance of first language (L1) Chinese speakers. As the main audience of this book is English writing teachers in Chinese speaking regions that teach Chinese speakers, our construals of *Chinese speakers* and *Chinese speaking regions* should be clearly operationalized. Below we first define Chinese speakers before moving on to a discussion of English writing teaching in Chinese speaking regions.

2 Chinese speakers

Chinese is a family of languages, not a single language (Norman 1988). However, a speaker of any of these varieties of Chinese is usually considered to be a native speaker of Chinese (Li and Thompson 1989). Two different varieties of Chinese may or may not be mutually intelligible (Norman, 1988). Discussing a particular Chinese variety requires specificity (Mair 1991). For example, Standard Chinese is the official language in mainland China and Taiwanese Mandarin is the official language in Taiwan (Adamson and Feng 2015; Baldauf and Kaplan 2000), both based on the Beijing dialect (Mair 1991). The two spoken varieties of Standard Chinese and Taiwanese Mandarin are mutually intelligible in a similar way that British English and American English are mutually intelligible (Normal 1988). Standard Cantonese, mutually unintelligible with Standard Chinese/Taiwanese Mandarin, is a de facto regional standard and the official language in the Hong Kong SAR and the Macau SAR (Norman 1988). Similarities between Standard Cantonese and Standard Mandarin lie in their use of similar formalized written forms (Mair 1991). Therefore, our use of *Chinese speakers* aimed at emphasizing the similarities in the L1 backgrounds of the learners discussed in the subsequent chapters. In doing so, we recognize that the Chinese speaking regions discussed below are multilingual societies and that learners in these contexts speak more than two languages. For example, English is also an official language in the Hong Kong SAR and many schools are adopting Standard Mandarin as a medium of instruction for particular courses while Standard Cantonese and English may be used for other courses (Wang and Kirkpatrick 2019). Similarly, in the Macau SAR, Portuguese is also an official language and English, Portuguese, and Standard Mandarin are often used as mediums of instruction along with Standard Cantonese (Ieong 2002). Other varieties of Chinese are also used in mainland China and Taiwan for varying purposes (Adamson and Feng 2015; Baldauf and Kaplan 2000). In sum, the use of *Chinese Speakers* is encompassing and not delimiting.

3 Chinese speaking regions

Second language writing teachers in Chinese speaking regions have a number of approaches in which to orient their classroom teaching. For example, teachers may focus on language structures, text functions, themes or topics, creative expression, composing processes, content, or genre and contexts of writing (Hyland 2003). While writing teachers have at their disposal a number of ways to implement the teaching of English writing, an overwhelming amount of evidence shows curricula should be eclectic and needs-based (Macalister and Nation 2010). With this thought in mind, we now turn our discussion to the current practice of writing instruction in mainland China, Hong Kong SAR, Macau SAR, and Taiwan – our operationalization of Chinese speaking regions. We have made effort to cite published research when providing descriptions of the teaching of English writing in the different regions; however, we acknowledge that our discussion may appear underdeveloped due to the lack of focused practical investigations currently available in the literature.

3.1 Mainland China

Accompanied with the globalization of writing theories and pedagogies in the western context, mainland China has imported knowledge in many areas, including writing pedagogies. After Wang (1986) introduced process-oriented writing pedagogy in mainland China, there was an increasing belief that writing is a process of discovery, and that writing is a complicated, recursive process. As a wakeup call to English writing teaching in mainland China, many classroom practitioners have called for innovative approaches, e.g., process-oriented writing, to enhance EFL students' writing proficiency. However, EFL teachers in mainland China have to confront many obstacles in helping their students learn to write. Obstacles have included large class size, disjunction between classroom instruction and test requirements, test-oriented teaching and learning styles, students' common low English proficiency, and teachers' own lack of English proficiency and training in the teaching of writing (You 2004a). Teachers also encounter other difficulties, for example, they lack a nationally unified syllabus, an awareness of understanding: student needs, effective instruction, teaching materials, and effective assessment. The teaching of EFL writing in mainland China is a result of the EFL education system in mainland China. As described by He and Teng (2019), teachers are facing immense pressure to help students achieve high passing rates in English tests. Some educational authorities have suggested that English should be an elective subject rather than a compulsory subject. Some even suggested that the teaching of English is a waste of money and labor in China. As argued by He and Teng (2019), English teachers in China have been trapped in an English teaching "tug-of-war" (p. 299). It is not surprising that teaching EFL writing in China is not an easy task.

The management style is a main difference between Chinese and western education cultures; the "top-down" system in mainland China controls power and decision-making, resulting in a sizeable number of teachers' stress (Hu et al. 2019). We also have to consider the gap that writing teachers need to bridge in linking theory with classroom practice (Nation 2009). The lack of effective writing assessment also leads to ineffective writing instruction (Icy Lee 2017). Major English tests in China include the National Matriculation English Test (NMET), College English Test (CET), and the Test for English Majors (TEM). These writing tests contain items that lack communicative elements, which result in negative backwash; teachers neglect to teach communicative English writing and students neglect to learn communicative English writing (Zhao 2014). Despite the increasing call for innovative writing approaches, the current writing approaches in mainland China have been characterized with the modes of "narration, description, exposition, and argumentation and an exclusive stylistic emphasis on correct form" (You 2004b, p. 98). English writing teachers need more support when facing challenges in facilitating writing teaching practices, handling students' needs in enhancing writing, and dealing with instructional constraints in local contexts.

When we flip through many language textbooks in mainland China, it is not surprising for us to find the majority are theme-based. The themes of the textbooks are about one aspect in our social life, and each unit is about one theme. Each unit commonly contains two passages. Following the two passages are some related grammar, vocabulary, translation and writing exercises. Examination of the textbooks show them to be a good example of a graded, controlled instruction that emphasizes the importance of correct grammar and vocabulary usage. One hidden agenda that can be uncovered from the analysis of these textbooks is that teachers may lead students to focus more on correct grammar and vocabulary usage, even for learning how to write. As documented by Yu and Reynolds (2018), few composition textbooks in mainland China have been specially developed for the needs of Chinese students; instead, most of the textbooks were so-called "integrated" textbooks. Only a few writing tasks are included, and they are rarely adopted as part of the compulsory modules. However, knowing how to write in English is far more than simply mastering grammar and vocabulary; L2 English writing requires practice through various writing tasks. Textbooks used for classroom instruction direct language teachers and students, but they should not be constrained by them. Teachers should adapt textbook materials based on students' language proficiency and customize the writing tasks to offer students more efficient and suitable writing practice (Yu 2018).

The situation of teaching English writing in mainland China deserves more attention. While writing teachers have to maneuver in a limited pedagogical space, students may just focus more on the correct form rather than how to develop thoughts. We acknowledge the increasing need to have more exposure to writing theories and approaches, and experiment with more writing pedagogies in mainland China. This will never be an easy road to travel; we need to reflect on how to make writing approaches innovative in mainland China, especially for young learners whose first influential experiences in English writing can either inspire or discourage these learners for years.

3.2 Hong Kong SAR

Hong Kong is a special administrative region (SAR) of the People's Republic of China with a different educational system from mainland China. Although the teaching of Putonghua was stressed after the handover in 1997, the English language is still commonly acknowledged as an important language in many areas, including business, government, higher education, and other professional sectors. Students start learning English when they enter kindergarten around the age of three. Teachers teach English as a compulsory subject from primary and throughout secondary education; English is the medium of instruction in higher education. In some primary and secondary schools, English is also the medium of instruction.

Despite the significant role of English, implementing innovative teaching approaches for English writing has never been easy. At the primary school level, the Education Bureau recommends five to eight periods of English instruction per week. Instruction focuses on several main components: providing greater opportunities for learners to use English for purposeful communication both inside and outside the classroom; making use of learner-centered instruction to encourage learner independence; making greater use of literary/imaginative texts to develop critical thinking and encourage free expression and creativity; and promoting strategies, values and attitudes that are conducive to effective, independent and life-long learning (Education Bureau 2001). Although the Hong Kong government promotes the use of a variety of resources in the teaching of English, most schools rely on commercially produced English language textbooks that focus mainly on the above-mentioned components. The Education Bureau has encouraged the use of information technology in the English curriculum to supplement the textbooks. However, innovative approaches in the teaching of English writing are still insufficient in many schools. When it comes to the secondary school level, the Education Bureau has increased English instruction periods to seven or eight periods from the recommended five to eight periods in primary education. However, instruction still focuses more on dictation, grammar, speaking, reading, and writing. Hence, given the limited time that is spent writing, teaching writing is not so satisfactory at either the primary or the secondary levels.

In addition, the Hong Kong education system is examination oriented. Despite the call for the teaching of process-oriented writing, traditional approaches to the teaching of writing still dominate which focus more on the product, i.e., the production of neat, grammatically correct pieces of writing (Cheung and Chan 1994). Product-oriented writing instruction is described as "one-shot effort by the teacher to evaluate the students' attempts" (Pennington and Cheung 1995: 20). It is easy to understand why many secondary English teachers adopt a product approach to the teaching of English writing: they are doing the best they can to prepare students for the examination to enter a good university. Form 6 secondary school students need to take the Hong Kong Diploma of Secondary

Education (HKDSE), which is the university entrance examination. In this examination, students' English proficiency is assessed at the micro level through the testing of the four traditional language skills: listening, speaking, reading, and writing. As argued by Lee (2005), an examination-oriented teaching system has a profound effect on the English curriculum, for which teachers have to prepare students with a heavy dosage of examination practice, model answers, and examination tips.

While the exam-oriented culture is for sure a major challenge for English writing teachers, another difficulty in implementing innovative writing instruction is students' passive attitude towards English learning. The teacher-centered instruction model of adopting knowledge transmission as their primary approach to the teaching of English writing may have caused the passive learning exhibited by learners. Another reason may be motivation. Students learning of English in Hong Kong mainly results from extrinsic motivation, i.e., getting higher scores in examinations (Man, Bui, and Teng 2018). This could explain why students often find learning to write unattractive, frustrating, and cognitively challenging (Lee 2005), at the tertiary level (Teng 2019a) and primary level (Teng 2019b).

In Hong Kong primary schools, the medium of instruction is mostly Cantonese. When it comes to secondary schools, the medium of instruction is "code-switching" between English and Cantonese, a product of the "biliterate and trilingual" policy in Hong Kong (Teng and Wang 2019). Commonly, teachers make a statement in English. Following this English statement will be explanation and elaboration in Cantonese. Students annotate between the lines and along the margins in Chinese, what each English word means. An overuse in teaching intensive reading will not help students develop proper reading skills (Nation 2013). Teng and Wang (2019) have argued that the "Biliterate and Trilingual" policy in Hong Kong is a political decision and teachers and students regard this policy as a source of conflict when trying to balance the use of English, Putonghua, and Cantonese. Without effective teaching practice, the decline of English standards among Hong Kong students has become a perennial issue in the past two decades (Bolton 2002). Hence, considering the constraints, implementing innovative approaches in teaching English writing in Hong Kong still has a long way to go.

In an attempt to enhance young learners' writing literacy, writing assessment has received much attention in Hong Kong. One of the features is the effortful promotion of learning-oriented assessment initiatives such as the adoption of assessment for learning (AfL) and assessment as learning (AaL). AfL refers to the effort of using assessment to support students' learning of writing through ongoing feedback and interactive pedagogical approaches. AaL refers to the facilitation of learners' active engagement in self-monitoring or self-evaluating progress in their writing development. Notwithstanding the potential of the two assessment approaches, writing teachers in Hong Kong have encountered some writing assessment challenges. Constraints have included teacher beliefs, lack of assessment training, and the exam-oriented education system (Lee, Mak, and Burns 2016). Based on a review of Hong Kong education policies, Lam (2019: 151) concluded the following L2 writing assessment strategies:

1. Emphasis on AaL and training pupils to be self-regulated
2. Promotion of e-learning and e-assessment (e.g., e-portfolios)
3. Use of standardized assessment data to improve teaching and learning (e.g., Hong Kong Diploma of Secondary Education Exam)
4. Enhancement of teacher assessment literacy.

Due to the exam-oriented culture, teachers seldom practice self- and peer assessment and self-regulated writing is not easy to implement despite the efforts of fostering self-regulated strategy training at the primary school level (Teng 2019b). Students in Hong Kong lack adequate support to brainstorm, draft, and revise their English writing. Students complete most of their writing individually through teacher instruction; however, students also need opportunities to experiment and improve their self-regulated and collaborative writing abilities. Unfortunately, they have few opportunities to experience this type of writing because of classroom management issues and large class sizes (Teng 2019b).

The development of the Hong Kong school curriculum has advanced into a new phase of ongoing renewal and updates. A new era for curriculum development to keep abreast of the macro and dynamic changes in various aspects in the local, regional and global landscapes in maintaining the competitiveness of Hong Kong. In future writing teaching practice, we need to think in what ways the teachers can use process writing to facilitate writing literacy development. For example, how teachers in an examination-oriented culture can guide students to brainstorm, draft, and edit a text. Another issue is how we can link the connection between the assessment policy and classroom practices, and how teachers can cross the hierarchy among policy makers and teaching practice and take initiatives to adopt a bottom-up approach to assessment innovations.

3.3 Macau SAR

Macau is the other SAR of the People's Republic of China. Searching the literature, one finds very little written about English language education in Macau and even less about the teaching of English writing. The existing research focuses mostly on how education policies have dictated that English be used as the medium of instruction and how such educational policies have affected students' foreign language learning (Bray and Koo 2004; Ieong 2002; Vong and Wu 2019; Young 2011; Ieong and Lau 2011). There are some interesting second language writing studies conducted at the tertiary level, mostly dealing with feedback issues (e.g. Icy Lee 2017), the incorporation of wikis for collaborative writing and translation (e.g. Biuk-aghai, Kelen, and Venkatesan 2008), and project based learning in English for academic purposes courses (e.g. Grant 2017). There is little research published about the primary education context in Macau, other than reporting on the efforts the government has made to encourage innovative teaching practices in English classrooms (e.g. Chan 2019). Primary and secondary schools in Macau have autonomy in selection and implementation of curriculum; one finds that each school has its own micro English language learning ecology (Moody 2008; Peng 2009). It is difficult to make general claims about the region as each school adopts either the curriculum setup by the Education and Youth Affairs Bureau or imports curriculum from Portugal, the United Kingdom, the United States, Hong Kong SAR, mainland China, or Taiwan (Ieong 2002; Moody 2008; Peng 2009; Young 2011).

Macau primary schools focus little on English writing instruction and students do little English writing; however, some private schools may focus more on the development of writing in addition to other language skills (Young 2011). Even in the higher primary grades, students may be found struggling with the task of writing a complete paragraph (Young 2011). Students in secondary schools practice lengthier academic writing (M. Wong, personal communication, September 17, 2019). It is up to the discretion of the individual schools in Macau whether teachers will emphasize writing more or less in their respective English curriculum (Young 2011).

When teachers provide writing instruction in secondary schools, it is often in the form of test preparation, for example writing to practice for the IELTS exam or the Macau higher education joint admissions exam. This has resulted in many of the writing tasks assigned to secondary school students having an obvious product-oriented feel to them (M. Wong, personal communication, September 17, 2019). Teachers may expect students to write a short paragraph on a topic introduced by a teacher that has only given them a title without a developed writing task (M. Wong, personal communication, September 17, 2019). Depending on the school, the teacher may or may not have the time to provide pre-writing brainstorming before the students get busy writing; if time permits, the teacher may be able to administer a round of editing before students turn in their final assignments (M. Wong, personal communication, September 17, 2019). Teachers also are found to struggle with how they should provide feedback on student writing, with most providing unfocused comprehensive feedback on all errors found in students' writing (M. Wong, personal communication, September 17, 2019). This is because many teachers emphasize accuracy, which runs the risk of stifling students' creativity (M. Wong, personal communication, September 17, 2019). While to a certain extent accuracy is important for writing, teachers should at least balance accuracy with the opportunities of providing students the chance to express their own ideas.

At the tertiary level, English writing instruction depends a lot on the university policy. To understand what type of English writing students are completing in universities requires one to have a look at the general education curriculum (Lee 2019). Some universities do provide writing instruction. This instruction is necessary for the students that are required to complete an undergraduate thesis. Other universities may provide English for general purposes instruction that may or may not include a writing element (Alice Shu-Ju Lee 2017; Young 2007). Although few generalizations can be made about English writing instruction in the Macau SAR (Young 2011), it is clear that there is a great need for not only innovation but also documentation of common practices in the English writing classroom at all levels of instruction. Otherwise, it is hard for scholars and practitioners alike to have a firm grasp of the current state of English writing instruction in Macau. English writing instruction and learning in Macau deserves investigation and innovation.

3.4 Taiwan

In Chen and Tsai's (2009) review of English teaching and learning research in Taiwan between 2004 and 2009, they dedicate a section to an overview of the English writing research conducted in the region. In their review, they indicate most of the English writing has been conducted at the tertiary level with a focus on either incorporating self/peer editing or information technology. There is an indication that researchers all incorporated process-oriented elements, but product-oriented activities still dominated. However, those studies that included process-oriented elements were not practically applied in the local schools. They also reviewed another group of studies, conducted under the English for Academic or Specific Purposes paradigm; these studies aimed at using corpus techniques either to compare Taiwanese students' writing to L1 English writers or to analyze the Taiwanese student writers' output to uncover some unique qualities of the writing produced by learners from the region. Lastly, they review a set of studies conducted under the computer assisted language-learning paradigm, which examined how the incorporation of information technology can have a positive effect on the Taiwanese writers' written language.

Chou and Hayes (2009) also conducted a systematic review, but unlike Chen and Tsai, their review focused only on English writing research conducted in Taiwan between 1989 and 2008. They found that the most frequently studied age group was university students. This could be due to the relative ease in obtaining informed consent from adult learner groups. Another reason could be that teachers emphasize spoken English in primary education in Taiwan, while grammar, vocabulary, reading, and writing is the focus of secondary English education classrooms (Chern 2002). In general, Taiwanese learners of English do not receive compulsory English education until the third grade and teachers are not permitted to teach English in Taiwanese kindergartens (Chern 2002). There are very few published studies that focus on Taiwanese English writing done in primary school (Chang, Chang, and Hsu 2019). There is a sizeable amount of English writing research for secondary school learners but this could be attributed to the need for the learners to prepare for the General English Proficiency Examination (GEPT) and also the college entrance exams (Yu 2019; Shih and Reynolds 2015, 2018a, 2018b). Looking only at the type of writing instruction that was received by learners, Chou and Hayes found secondary school, university, and adult learners have received the most attention. In agreement with Chen and Tsai's finding, Chou and Hayes found the incorporation of information technology into writing instruction to be a major focus of a large portion of the research. Lastly, they found that almost all the studies used qualitative methods for their investigation, indicating a need for more quantitative research.

Taking a cursory look at Taiwan's two most prestigious English language education academic journals, *English Teaching & Learning* and *Taiwan Journal of TESOL*, we found similar results of research published in these venues during the last ten years – a majority of the research has focused on tertiary level learners. In these studies, researchers apply corpus techniques to analyze learner writing and incorporate various technology into writing instruction – a small number of studies look into instruction issues such as critical thinking or learners' perceptions. While the research conducted by Taiwanese academics has focused a lot on secondary and university level learners, there has been less of a focus on the writing done at the primary level or in graduate school. In addition, it appears that technology has been a major focus. While we also believe technology has its part to play in the writing classroom (Reynolds 2013; Reynolds and Anderson 2015; Reynolds and Kao 2019), we also acknowledge that the incorporation of technology may not always be a feasible option for all language instructors (Snoder and Reynolds 2019). Instead, we hope that more research can come out of Taiwan that innovates in their approach to the teaching of writing rather than the use of technology for writing instruction.

The research literature can tell us only so much. Unless properly investigated, we do not know exactly why classroom English writing teachers do what they do. There is a need for research that can provide a clearer picture of what is taking place in classrooms at all levels of education. This will require not only examination of the teaching approaches but also materials and other resources used by teachers. For example, the course books used in primary and junior high education are at a much lower level compared to the senior high school textbooks. This requires students to make this rather large jump, often through after-school tutorial sessions or the attendance of "cram schools." The medium of instruction is very rarely English, even at secondary and tertiary levels (Kao and Yang 2011; Wu 2003). This is rather unfortunate because once students grasp the basics of the language, using English for instruction provides a readily available source of meaning-focused English input (Nation 2013). Most writing completed in senior high school is product-oriented (Song 2001) as the English teachers are simply preparing the learners to take the GEPT and college entrance examinations. As the above-reviewed research literature shows, instruction at the tertiary level is more innovative and varied, probably due to the amount of autonomy provided to university instructors and the privilege they enjoy of not needing to prepare learners for examinations. However, in recent years some universities have adopted a policy requiring learners to pass the GEPT or an equivalent international examination in order to meet graduation requirements (Chu and Yeh 2017). If this trend continues, it is sure to have a washback effect on tertiary level English language classrooms. It would not be an overstatement to say that the English writing instruction in Taiwan has not matured and there is much room for improvement.

4 Conclusion

While the benefits of introducing L2 writing to learners in early years are evident, recent economic, social, political, and educational developments have also made it clear to classroom practitioners and education researchers that there is still a need for change in the approaches used for the teaching of L2 English writing in Chinese speaking regions (He and Teng 2019; Wang 2019; Chern and Curran 2019, Vong and Wu 2019). There is agreement that writing instruction reform is needed, and this reform must be considered in connection to the common complaints that the current system of teaching writing in Chinese speaking regions is rigid, teacher-centered, and test-oriented (Kao and Reynolds 2017; Teng 2016, 2019a). There is not only a need for new approaches or techniques for teaching English writing, but also more research is needed to address whether these approaches or techniques can be implemented within the confines of current education systems. Academics and classroom teachers are well known for voicing complaints regarding the lack of English writing competency among L1 Chinese speakers (e.g. You, 2004a, 2004b). This book, responding to these needs, aims to draw a picture of the diverse teaching approaches in different Chinese-speaking regions so that educators can overcome the challenges they face. We have found that L2 English writing teachers are adopting a wide range of techniques from more traditional highly structured to more process-oriented, student-centered. Bearing the current situation regarding the diversity in the teaching of English writing to L1 Chinese speakers in mind, this book delineates innovative practices, serving as a useful supplementary descriptor of current trends in the development of writing pedagogy in these Chinese-speaking regions.

There is sure to be a difference in English writing education for non-Chinese speaking contexts, but we are certain that the pedagogical experiences of learners in Chinese speaking regions can still provide a valuable source of reference to all teachers of English writing. This is because the lack of English writing competency among students is not an isolated experience only found in Chinese speaking regions (Fox 1994). Enhancing effectiveness is a prime concern to language teacher educators in many countries and contexts throughout the world (Nation 2013). These insights are especially beneficial to Asian EFL contexts, where educators are eager to unchain themselves from sentence pattern oriented, textbook/worksheet driven, and teacher-dominated approaches (Thornsbury 2013). Even educators that put to use these antiquated techniques will acknowledge, when pushed, that learning to write is complex and difficult because it requires simultaneous and interactive cognitive activities, including content generation and organization, text organization, production, editing, and revision (Kao, Reynolds, and Teng 2019). This volume provides readers opportunities to engage with innovative approaches to the teaching of English writing through the voices of teacher-researchers that have raised questions about their teaching of L2 English writing.

References

Adamson, Bob, & Anwei Feng. 2015. Trilingualism in Education: Models and Challenges. In Anwei Feng & Bob Adamson (eds.), *Trilingualism in Education in China: Models and Challenges*, 243–258. Dordrecht: Springer.

Baldauf, Richard B. & Robert B. Kaplan (eds.). 2000. *Language planning in Nepal, Taiwan and Sweden*. Clevedon: Multilingual Matters Ltd.

Biuk-Aghai, Robert P., Christopher Kelen & Hari Venkatesan. 2008. Visualization of interactions in collaborative writing. In *2008 2nd IEEE International Conference on Digital Ecosystems and Technologies* (pp. 97–102). IEEE.

Bolton, Kingsley. 2002. Introduction. In Kingsley Bolton (ed.), *Hong Kong English: Autonomy and creativity*, 1–25. Hong Kong: Hong Kong University Press.

Bray, Mark & Ramsey Koo. 2004. Postcolonial patterns and paradoxes: Language and education in Hong Kong and Macao. *Comparative Education* 40 (2). 215–239.

Chan, Kan Kan. 2019. English literacy instruction in Macau primary education: What can we learn from the award scheme on instructional design? In Barry Lee Reynolds & Mark Feng Teng (eds.) *English Literacy Instruction for Chinese Speakers*, 95–108. Singapore: Palgrave Macmillan.

Chen, Suchiao & Yachin Tsai. 2009. Research on English teaching and learning: Taiwan (2004–2009). *Language Teaching* 45 (2). 180–201. Doi:10.1017/S0261444811000577

Chang, Fang-Chi, Shu-I Chang & Hsiu-Fen Hsu. 2019. Application of a visual organizer to improve English writing in a Taiwanese elementary school. *Asian EFL Journal* 23 (5). 28–54.

Chern, Chiou-lan. 2002. English language teaching in Taiwan today. *Asia Pacific Journal of Education* 22 (2). 97–105.

Chern, Chiou-lan & Jean E. Curran. 2019. Moving toward content-integrated English literacy instruction in Taiwan: Perspectives from stakeholders. In Barry Lee Reynolds & Mark Feng Teng (eds.) *English Literacy Instruction for Chinese Speakers*, 333–348. Singapore: Palgrave Macmillan.

Chou, Li-hua & Denis Michael Hayes. 2009. An overview of English writing research in Taiwan. *English Language Teaching* 2 (4). 215–225.

Cheung, Marie Yin Mei & A. Chan. 1994. *Teaching writing as a process*. Hong Kong: Education Department.

Chu, Hsin-yu & Hsi-nan Yeh. 2017. English benchmark policy for graduation in Taiwan's higher education: Investigation and reflection. Journal of Language Teaching and Research, 8(6), 1063–1072.

Cortazzi, Martin & Lixian Jin. 1996. English teaching and learning in China. *Language Teaching* 29 (2). 61–80.

Education Bureau. 2001. English language education. Retrieved from https://cd1.edb.hkedcity.net/cd/EN/Content_2908/e03/chapter3_36-39.pdf

Fox, Helen. 1994. *Listening to the world: Cultural issues in academic writing*. Urbana, Illinois: National Council of Teachers of English.

Grant, Sean. 2017. Implementing project-based language teaching in an Asian context: a university EAP writing course case study from Macau. *Asian-Pacific Journal of Second and Foreign Language Education* 2 (4). 1–13.

He, Fang, & Mark Feng Teng. 2019. Language tug-of-war: When English literacy education encounters the national matriculation English test policy in Mainland China. In Barry Lee Reynolds & Mark Feng Teng (eds.) *English Literacy Instruction for Chinese Speakers*, 299–316. Singapore: Palgrave Macmillan.

Hu, Bi Ying, Yuanhua Li, Chuang Wang, Barry Lee Reynolds, & Shuang Wang. 2019. The relation between school climate and preschool teacher stress: The mediating role of teachers' self-efficacy. *Journal of Educational Administration* 57 (6). 748–767.

Hyland, Ken 2003. *Second Language Writing*. Cambridge: Cambridge University Press.

Ieong, Sylvia S.L. 2002. Teaching and learning English in Macao. *Asian Englishes* 5 (1). 76–83.

Ieong, Sylvia S.L., & Sin Peng Lau. 2011. Quality input and sustainability in early immersion classrooms: A case study of an experimental school in Macao. *Frontiers of Education in China* 6 (1). 92–105.

Kao, Chian-Wen & Barry Lee Reynolds. 2017. A study on the relationship among Taiwanese college students' EFL writing strategy use, writing ability and writing difficulty. *English Teaching & Learning* 41 (4). 31–64.

Kao, Chian-Wen, Barry Lee Reynolds & (Mark) Feng Teng. 2019. What we need to know about student writers' grammar learning and correction. *Applied Linguistics Review*. doi:10.1515/applirev-2019-0016

Kao, Chian-Wen & Shu-ping Yang. 2011. Second language proficiency levels and learning strategy uses in persuasive writing tasks. *Providence Forum: Language and Humanities* 5. 89–124.

Lam, Ricky. 2019. Evolution of Writing Assessment in Hong Kong Secondary Schools: Policy, Practice and Implications for Literacy Development. In Barry Lee Reynolds & Mark Feng Teng (eds.), *English literacy instruction for Chinese speakers*, 143–158. Singapore: Palgrave Macmillan.

Lee, Icy, Pauline Mak & Anne Burns. 2016. EFL teachers' attempts at feedback innovation in the writing classroom. *Language Teaching Research* 20 2. 248–269.

Lee, Icy. 2005. Error Correction in the L2 Writing Classroom: What Do Students Think?. *TESL Canada Journal* 22 2. 1–16.

Lee, Icy. 2017. *Classroom assessment literacy for L2 writing teachers*. Springer, Singapore.

Lee, Alice Shu-Ju. 2019. A longitudinal study of second language literacy instruction through assignment design at the University of Macau. In Barry Lee Reynolds & Mark Feng Teng (eds.) *English Literacy Instruction for Chinese Speakers*, 281–296. Singapore: Palgrave Macmillan.

Lee, Alice Shu-Ju. 2017. *Multilingual Institutional Discourses of Negotiation and Intertextuality in Writing Center Interactions in Macao*. (Doctoral Dissertation) Retrieved from https://knowledge.library.iup.edu/etd/1555

Li, Charles N. & Sandra A. Thompson. 1989. *Mandarin Chinese : A Functional Reference Grammar*. Berkley: University of California Press.

Macalister, John & I.S. Paul Nation. 2010. *Language Curriculum Design*. New York: Routledge.

Mair, Victor H. 1991. What is a Chinese "dialect/topolect"?: Reflections on some key Sino-English linguistic terms. *Sino-Platonic Papers*, 29. 1–31.

Man, Laura, Gavin Bui & Mark Feng Teng. 2018. From second language to third language learning: Exploring a dual-motivation system among multilinguals. *Australian Review of Applied Linguistics* 41. 63–91.

Moody, Andrew. 2008. Macau English: Status, functions and forms. *English Today* 24 3. 3–15.

Nation, I. S. Paul. 2009. *Teaching ESL/EFL Reading and Writing*. New York: Routledge.

Nation, I. S. Paul. 2013. *What should every EFL teacher know?* Tokyo, Japan: Compass Publishing.

Norman, Jerry. 1988. *Chinese.* Cambridge: Cambridge University Press.

Peng, L.S. 2009. *A history of education in Macao.* Macau: University of Macau.

Pennington, Martha C. & Marie Cheung. 1995. Factors shaping the introduction of process writing in Hong Kong secondary schools. *Language, Culture and Curriculum* 8. 1–20.

Reynolds, Barry Lee. (2013). A web-based EFL writing environment as a bridge between academic advisers and junior researchers: A pilot study. *British Journal of Educational Technology* 44 (3). E77-E80.

Reynolds, Barry Lee. & Tom A.F. Anderson. (2015). Extra-dimensional in-class communications: Action research exploring text chat support of face-to-face writing. *Computers and Composition 35*. 52–64.

Reynolds, Barry Lee& Chian-Wen Kao. 2019. The effects of digital game-based instruction, teacher instruction, and direct focused written corrective feedback on the grammatical accuracy of English articles. *Computer Assisted Language Learning.* doi:10.1080/09588221.2019.1617747

Reynolds, Barry Lee& Mark Feng Teng. 2019. *English Literacy Instruction for Chinese Speakers.* Singapore: Palgrave Macmillan.

Sharifian, Farzad. (ed.). 2009. *English as an international language: Perspectives and pedagogical issues.* London: Multilingual Matters.

Shih, Ying-Chun & Barry Lee Reynolds. 2018a. Exploring strong and weak EFL readers' strategy use after a reading strategy and extensive reading instructional intervention: A think-aloud analysis. *Revista Española de Lingüística Aplicada/Spanish Journal of Applied Linguistics* 31 (1). 345–377.

Shih, Ying-Chun & Barry Lee Reynolds. 2018b. The effects of integrating goal setting and reading strategy instruction on English reading proficiency and learning motivation: A quasi-experimental study. *Applied Linguistics Review 9* (1). 35–62.

Shih, Ying-Chun & Barry Lee Reynolds. 2015. Teaching adolescents EFL by integrating Think-Pair-Share and reading strategy instruction: A quasi-experimental study. *RELC Journal: A Journal of Language Teaching and Research* 46 (3). 221–235.

Snoder, Per & Barry Lee Reynolds. 2019. How dictogloss can facilitate collocation learning in ELT. *ELT Journal 73* (1). 41–50.

Song, ShengYo. 2001. The effects of reasoning skills on vocational educational students' English writing. Unpublished master's thesis, Yunlin County, Taiwan, R.O.C: National Yunlin University of Science and Technology.

Teng, Feng. 2016. Immediate and delayed effects of embedded metacognitive instruction on Chinese EFL students' English writing and regulation of cognition. *Thinking Skills & Creativity* 22. 289–302.

Teng, Feng. 2019a. Tertiary-level students' English writing performance and metacognitive awareness: A group metacognitive support perspective. *Scandinavian Journal of Educational Research.* doi: 10.1080/00313831.2019.1595712

Teng, Feng. 2019b. A comparison of text structure and self-regulated strategy instruction for elementary school students' writing. *English Teaching: Practice and Critique.* doi:10.1108/ETPC-07-2018-0070

Teng, Feng & Barry Lee Reynolds. 2019a. English foreign and second language literacy development for Chinese speakers: What do we know? In Barry Lee Reynolds & Mark

Feng Teng (eds.) *English Literacy Instruction for Chinese Speakers*, 3–13. Singapore: Palgrave Macmillan.

Teng, Mark Feng & Barry Lee Reynolds. 2019b. English foreign and second language literacy instruction for Chinese speakers: Future directions and implications. In Barry Lee Reynolds & Mark Feng Teng (eds.) *English Literacy Instruction for Chinese Speakers*, 369–378. Singapore: Palgrave Macmillan.

Teng, Feng & Lixun Wang. 2019. *Identity, motivation, and multilingual education in Asian contexts*. London: Bloomsbury.

Thornbury, Scott. 2013. Resisting coursebooks. In John Gray (ed.) *Critical Perspectives on Language Teaching Materials*, 204–223. London: Palgrave Macmillan.

Vong, Sou-Kuan & Xiaomeng Wu. 2019. An examination of language planning and policy: Implications for language and literacy education in the Macau education system. In Barry Lee Reynolds & Mark Feng Teng (eds.) *English Literacy Instruction for Chinese Speakers*, 349–366. Singapore: Palgrave Macmillan.

Wang, Zhigang. 1986. Yingyu xiezuo lilun de xin fazhan [New developments in English writing theories]. *Waiguoyu [Foreign Languages]* 2 73–77.

Wang, Lixun. 2019. The "biliterate and trilingual" policy in Hong Kong primary school education. In Barry Lee Reynolds & Mark Feng Teng (eds.) *English Literacy Instruction for Chinese Speakers*, 317–332. Singapore: Palgrave Macmillan.

Wang, Lixun & Andy Kirkpatrick. 2019. *Trilingual Education in Hong Kong Primary Schools*. Cham: Springer.

Wu, Shu-jung Ruth. 2003. A comparison of learners' beliefs about writing in their first and second language: Taiwanese junior college business-major students studying English (Unpublished doctoral dissertation). The University of Texas at Austin, Austin, TX.

You, Xiaoye. 2004a. New directions in EFL writing: A report from China. *Journal of Second Language Writing* 13 (4). 253–256.

You, Xiaoye. 2004b. "The choice made from no choice": English writing instruction in a Chinese University. *Journal of Second Language Writing* 13 (2). 97–110.

Young, Ming Yee Carissa. 2011. English use and education in Macao. In Anwei Feng (Ed.) *English language education across greater China*, 114–130. Bristol, UK: Multilingual Matters.

Young, Ming Yee Carissa. 2007. English in postcolonial Macau: Functions and attitudes. *Asian Englishes*, 10 (1). 104–117.

Yu, Melissa H. 2018. Exploring the orientation and use of textbook lingua-cultural resources to teach and learn English for lingua franca communication. *The Asia-Pacific Researcher Education* 27 (4). 257–266. doi:10.1007/s40299-018-0381-6

Yu, Melissa H. 2019. Literacy skills education from the perspective of English as a lingua franca: A case study on Taiwanese secondary students' secondary English language education experience. In Barry Lee Reynolds & Mark Feng Teng (eds.) *English Literacy Instruction for Chinese Speakers*, 175–194. Singapore: Palgrave Macmillan.

Yu, Shulin & Barry Lee Reynolds. 2018. Investigating writing tasks in English textbooks for Chinese secondary students. *The Journal of Asia TEFL* 15 (4). 1114–1121.

Zhao, Huahui. 2014. Investigating teacher-supported peer assessment for EFL writing. *ELT journal* 68 (2). 155–168.

Anisa Cheung
Integrating e-learning into process writing: The case of a primary school in Hong Kong

Abstract: The advantages of a process writing approach to boost the written proficiency of second language learners are well-documented in literature. Recent advancements in technology has the potential of streamlining the stages of planning and revising for processing writing approaches to the teaching of second language writing. The present study explored how English teachers combined the benefits of process writing and e-learning tools to teach writing in a primary school in Hong Kong. They planned eight writing lessons for four Primary 5 classes. Two classes were taught to use the e-learning tools, namely Google Docs and Padlet, on iPads whilst the other two adopted the traditional paper-and-pencil approach. Findings from focus-group interviews, lesson observations, and student written products revealed that compared to their traditional writing counterparts, students in the e-learning classes, regardless of their language ability, were highly engaged in the lessons, showed an increased motivation to write in English and a decrease in grammatical mistakes. However, the teaching staff expressed concerns about time constraints and readiness of using e-learning tools, which may obscure successful implementation of this innovative approach in other settings. Implications of integrating process writing and e-learning tools into the local primary school English curriculum are discussed.

Keywords: process writing, written proficiency, e-learning tools, primary school, second language writing

1 Introduction

Writing is one of the most crucial skills needed to master a language. Frontline educators and academic researchers alike have been constantly searching for the best possible way to teach these skills to different cohorts of learners. Recent years have also seen the emergence of e-learning tools in language learning, due to their effectiveness in promoting autonomous learning (Lai 2017). How e-learning tools can be used to assist the pedagogy of writing would

Anisa Cheung, Hong Kong University of Science and Technology

https://doi.org/10.1515/9781501512643-002

therefore be a salient issue worthy of in-depth explorations. The present study is geared to exploring an innovative approach of teaching writing to English as a foreign language (EFL) students in a Hong Kong primary school by integrating two e-learning tools with process writing. In addition, it attempts to unveil how students interact during the writing lessons, as well as teacher perceptions on using e-learning tools to help students complete their writings.

1.1 Research on process writing

Studies on instructional strategies of writing skills have been well-documented in the literature for the past several decades. Earlier attempts to theorize the complex processes of producing a piece of writing focused primarily on decoding the linguistic and textual features of high-quality writings. The pedagogy derived from this conjecture hence involves presenting model texts and analyzing the features inherent in them. However, this product approach to teaching writing has been heavily criticized for its over-emphasis on grammatical accuracy and its assumption that there is only one single way to accomplish the writing task, which is to imitate as closely as possible the model texts of proficient writers (Hillocks 1986). Learners' spontaneous and creative expressions of ideas were often suppressed, if not completely banned, resulting in a loss of intrinsic motivation, which is defined as engaging in an activity for its own sake and for enjoyment, in the absence of incentives such as point systems (Schunk, Pintrich and Meece 2008). The detrimental effect was observed to be more prominent among younger second language learners (Rogers and Graham 2008). Some studies in EFL contexts involving adolescents also revealed their teachers' concern that this approach provides little, if any, insights on catering to learner diversity (Graham and Perin 2007).

Realizing the need to reform the traditional instructional approaches to writing, recent years have seen the gradual emergence of a process-writing approach, which is built on the premise that writing is a "*thinking process in its own right*" (White and Arndt 1991, pp. 17). Some crucial features of this pedagogy that distinguish itself from the "product" approach include the need for constant drafting and revising, the emphasis on idea generations well before any writing tasks are carried out and the "publishing" phase, in which the final written product is displayed and evaluated by a purposeful target audience (Harmer 2004). Graham and Sandmel (2011) added that in a lesson adopting the process-writing approach, students were encouraged to develop a sense of ownership towards their writings, and teachers needed to provide a supportive and non-threatening environment for them to freely express their ideas. Not surprisingly, this approach would require significantly longer planning and teaching time than merely giving students a topic to write about based on some model texts.

Ever since the process approach gained its widespread popularity during the 1990s, there has been a bulk of empirical studies geared to examining its effectiveness across various language-learning contexts and with different cohorts of learners. Several meta-analyses have been conducted to summarize their findings, which revealed slight but significant improvements of the overall quality of student writings after the process approach is adopted (e.g. Goldring, Russell and Cook 2003; Graham and Perin 2007; Rogers and Graham 2008). Of particular relevance to the present study is a recent meta-analysis conducted by Graham and Sandmel (2011), which reviewed 29 experimental and quasi-experimental studies on process writing among young learners in Grade 1 to 12. Like the other meta-analyses, a modest gain in the overall quality of writing was observed, with 24 studies showing a statistically greater-than-zero treatment effect and a statistically significant effect size of 0.34. However, the effect size was reduced to non-significant when the researchers focused only on five studies that mainly explored struggling or at-risk students. Another striking finding is their failure to reveal any significant boosting effects in student motivations, which was measured in six of the studies reviewed. While admitting that this was contrary to their expectations, Graham and Sandmel did point out that a few methodological limitations, like the difficulty of measuring motivation and isolating spurious variables in school settings may be the cause for such null effects. They also argued in their concluding remarks that process writing should be combined with other instructional approaches to yield the greatest possible effects, such as skill-based instruction on planning and revising, yet they did not touch upon other alternatives such as the use of e-learning tools. More research is therefore needed to address this issue.

1.2 Research on e-learning tools in writing

The advancement of modern technology in the digital era has brought about a new form of language learning, known as e-learning or computer-mediated communication (CMC) by researchers. This innovative form of learning is believed to bring about a number of benefits to learners compared to the traditional paper-and-pencil mode. Lai (2017), for example, claimed that the various benefits of autonomous language learning, such as greater perceived meaningfulness and personal relevance (Benson 2001), can be achieved through the use of technology in language lessons, and this would contribute to sustained motivations of learners during the learning process (Teng 2018).

A number of e-learning tools have emerged in recent years with the aim to assist different aspects of language learning. With respect to writing, one of the most popular tools is known as Wiki, an application which allows real-time editing of a writing document by a group of people. Storch (2013) reviewed more than fifteen recent studies involving mostly adult L2 learners using a Wiki to complete writing tasks. These studies varied in the form of research designs, duration, group size and tools used to collect data, and a few of them did mimic all the stages of the process writing approach. Chao and Lo (2011), for example, asked EFL students in Taiwan to complete a Wiki task (writing a story together) by going through five distinct stages of process writing, namely collaborative planning, individual drafting, peer revision, editing, and finally publishing. A similar design was used by Lund (2008) to explore EFL high-school learners in Norway. The findings of L2 e-learning writing research were mixed, but could be clustered into three major dimensions, namely learners' motivation, group dynamics during the writing task, and the quality of the final written product.

Learners' motivation was one of the most commonly researched variables among all the studies reviewed. Regardless of the methods used to tap their motivation, the studies unanimously revealed a highly positive attitude when the e-learning approach was adopted. Part of this can be attributable to the novelty effect of using technology (Storch 2013), but there were other reasons as well. Miyazoe and Anderson (2010), for example, asked EFL Japanese students to use different online e-learning tools such as wikis, blogs, and discussion forums to carry out writing tasks and tapped into their beliefs using surveys. These students, who were themselves weak in English, cited wikis as highly motivating, as they possess the function of real-time editing by peers and teachers, hence providing the assistance students need to complete the tasks. That said, a small number of studies did report some frustrations caused by technical aspects that were experienced by adult learners (e.g. Lee 2010).

Group dynamics like contributions, engagement, and interactions between group members were also frequently explored but produced mixed results. There were some studies which showed that students in collaborative writing groups actively expanded or refined the writings of their peers, though they were confined to content aspects (e.g. Mak and Coniam 2008; Elola and Oskoz

2010). However, some other studies revealed negative effects, as group members were either incapable of revising or editing the writing of their peers (e.g. Arnold et al. 2009) or were unwilling to contribute at all (e.g. Kessler et al. 2012; Kost 2011; Lee 2010). Kessler and Bikowski (2010) also discovered the "social loafing" phenomenon, in which students in large groups (i.e. 5 to 6) believed that other members should be responsible for the writing tasks, hence feeling less obliged to write on their own. Storch (2013) attributed this phenomenon to the failure of developing a sense of "text co-ownership" between peers, which takes time to develop. Mak and Coniam's (2008) longitudinal study with ESL students in Hong Kong somehow confirmed this argument. Like other studies, these researchers found that learners paid minimal effort to editing their peers' work at first, but their willingness to contribute gradually increased after working together for two months, and they were able to produce longer texts with higher accuracy in groups than individually.

With regard to the interaction patterns, very few studies actually analyzed the S-S and T-S interactions during the collaborative writing process, which might provide very crucial information on why certain tasks worked and others failed. Li and Zhu's (2011) study on Chinese EFL students using wikis was perhaps the only one which examined this issue in greater depth. Based on Storch's (2009) model of dyadic interaction, these researchers discovered three patterns of S-S interactions, namely mutually supportive, authoritative/responsive and dominant/withdrawn. Not surprisingly, students who interact using the first two patterns found the collaborative writing tasks more interesting, enjoyable and beneficial to their language learning, as compared to the third one. Despite the interesting findings, Li and Zhu did not further investigate why these interaction patterns were formed.

The final and most salient aspect is the quality of the writings produced at different stages, both in terms of content and language used. The findings in this aspect were again very divergent. There are studies which discovered fewer number of grammatical errors spotted and richer contents when e-learning is adopted in group writing tasks (e.g., Mak and Coniam 2008; Kost 2011; Lee 2010), while some others found little or no effects at all (e.g., Elola and Oskoz 2010; Kessler 2009). A closer scrutiny of these studies revealed that group dynamics, as aforementioned, or affective factors, such as the emotional states of the learners, may be able to account for such differential results, though these arguments have yet to be verified in future studies. Storch (2013) concluded by stating that adequate training for students, not only on technical aspects, but also in metacognitive aspects like how to verbalize their thoughts and give appropriate feedback to their peers, are indispensable in order to maximize the effectiveness of these e-learning tools in L2 collaborative writing.

1.3 The present study

The present study is primarily motivated to address several unresolved issues in the literature. First, the failure to yield significant boosting effects on student motivation in previous process-writing studies (e.g. Graham and Sandmel 2011) reflects the inadequacy of using the "process" approach alone to teach writing, as pointed out by Graham and Sandmel in their conclusion, yet there was little guidance to frontline educators on how it can and should be combined with other approaches to maximize its effectiveness, not only on improving the writing quality but also on enhancing the motivations of young learners. Second, while numerous empirical studies have thoroughly demonstrated the advantages of e-learning writing tools such as Wiki to L2 mature language learners, surprisingly little is known on whether and how these tools can benefit younger learners. How teachers and students in the primary classroom interact during the collaborative writing process is also completely unexplored. It is still unknown as to whether these young learners can verbalize their thoughts and use meta-language to give feedback to their peers on the ideas that they generated as well as on the overall quality of the writing. Equally important is to tap into the beliefs of their teachers for using e-learning in writing lessons, an area that many previous e-learning studies have not touched upon. A hybrid approach of process writing in small groups, coupled with e-learning writing tools for primary school pupils can therefore shed some light on filling these research gaps. Adding a control group using traditional paper-and-pencil learning mode to carry out process writing can also help strengthen any claims regarding the effectiveness of the e-learning tools in the present study.

In light of the above arguments, the research questions to be addressed in the present study are listed as follows:
1. Does using e-learning tools to carry out process writing tasks boost primary pupils' motivations, when compared to the traditional paper-and-pencil mode?
2. Does using e-learning tools to carry out process writing tasks result in higher quality of writings, when compared to the traditional paper-and-pencil mode?
3. What are the interaction patterns of primary pupils during the e-learning collaborative writing task?
4. What are the teachers' perceptions of using e-learning tools to accomplish process writing tasks?

2 Method

2.1 Participants

Four local English teachers and 130 students (68 boys and 62 girls) from a 24-class primary school in Hong Kong participated in the research. The students in this primary school are of normal intelligence and disciplined, yet they mainly come from low socio-economic backgrounds. In the present study, Primary 5 pupils aged between 10 and 11 from four mixed-ability classes were chosen. As the school does not adopt ability streaming, the academic performance of the four classes is similar. With regard to their EFL background, as all of them were born and educated in Hong Kong, they should have started learning English since they entered the local kindergartens. However, most of their parents know little about English and rarely ask their children to join extra-curricular activities conducted in English, hence they receive limited exposure or formal instruction in the language outside school. In terms of writing ability, as they are generally not proficient writers, they have to rely heavily on the vocabulary and grammar structures in textbooks to construct sentences. This cohort was selected as they had some prior experiences of using e-learning tools such as Kahoot and Quizlet in English lessons when they were in Primary 4, so they should be able to operate mobile devices with relative ease. Parents were informed through a school notice written in Chinese about the aim and details of the research, as well as the researcher's contact information. They also needed to indicate on the notice whether to let researchers collect their children's data for research purposes. Only two parents disagreed to do so and their students' data was not used for analysis in the present study.

All four teachers teaching these students are degree holders with teacher-training diplomas in English, and possess at least five years of frontline teaching experiences in the subject. The Native English Teacher, the English Panel Chair, and the principal did not teach the Primary 5 classes, but they were involved in the research to a certain extent by joining the co-planning meetings prior to the lessons, observing the first two and last two writing lessons of two classes (one with e-learning tools and one without) in real time, and completing lesson observation forms designed by the school, as well as taking part in the focused-group interview after the lessons. The researcher, who works in a local university and serves as an English consultant of the school, also chaired the co-planning meetings and focused-group interview, as well as joined the lesson observations with the English Panel Chair in school.

2.2 Research design

The Primary 5 students were all taught to complete the same writing task in their textbooks. The task requires them to write a letter to a pen friend to tell him about what happened during their Sports Day, which was held around a week before the first writing lesson. A total of eight writing lessons, which spanned over a four-week teaching cycle (i.e. two writing lessons per week), were planned according to the framework of a process-writing approach. Students had to complete the writing task in pairs, so the patterns of interactions during the writing process could be unveiled (RQ3). Besides, as these students are not proficient writers, paired writing would make the task less challenging, whilst also providing the scaffolding needed for them to complete individual writing assignments at home later. The teachers adopted mixed ability grouping approach, in which a more-able student was asked to work with a less-able one.

The first two lessons focused on generating ideas. Teachers first showed them photos of Sports Day and taught them vocabulary about different sports events and medals. Students were also given a notice of Sports Day so they could recall background information such as the date, time, and venue. After receiving the necessary input from the teachers, they were asked to brainstorm their initial ideas either on the computer or on a worksheet. The focus was on idea generation and any grammatical and spelling mistakes that do not impede understanding of the content were not corrected until the editing stage. In the next two lessons, the teachers went through all the ideas generated by students and aggregated them into meaningful categories, such as background information, description of the sports events, the results, the feelings of athletes, and the prize presentation ceremony. Based on the ideas generated, students then wrote their first draft in sentences and paragraphs. Upon completion of the first draft, the teachers read their drafts then provided written comments on content (e.g. whether ideas are sufficient and well-elaborated) and organization aspects (e.g. whether cohesive devices were used). Lessons 5 and 6 focused on self and peer editing, and revision of the first draft. Students were given back their first drafts with teacher comments included. Then, they proofread the writings of each other and highlighted the grammatical (e.g. subject-verb agreement and use of tense) and spelling mistakes they observed. Based on the comments from teachers and peers, students revised their writings and produced a final draft in the last two lessons. They also needed to put their writings in the format of an email, by writing email addresses, a subject, a greeting, and a closing. The teachers then chose a few students to read their drafts to the whole class and provided verbal feedback on the quality of their writings, on aspects such as richness of content, clarity of ideas, accuracy of language use, and organization.

Students were asked to contribute their own ideas to their classmates as well. The final drafts were scored by teachers after the 8th lesson. Table 1 shows a summary of the focus and activities of the eight writing lessons.

Table 1: Summary of the writing lessons.

Lessons	Focus	Activities
1–2	Idea Generation	Students generate ideas related to Sports Day, such as background information, details of events, and the results
3–4	Writing First Draft	Students put the ideas into sentences and paragraphs to produce the first draft, which is submitted to their teachers for initial comments on content and organization
5–6	Peer Editing and Revising	Teacher returns the first draft to students, students study the writings of their peers and point out their grammar and spelling mistakes. Students read the feedback from their teachers and peers and revise the first draft accordingly.
7–8	Further Revising and Publishing	Students continue to revise the first draft and produce a final draft in the format of an email. Teacher invites a few students to read their completed writings and provides verbal comments to students. After the 8th lesson, teacher awards scores to their final drafts.

A quasi-experimental design was adopted to explore the effectiveness of the e-learning tools in the present study. Two classes served as intervention groups. Students were each given an iPad with two e-learning tools installed, namely Padlet and Google Docs, throughout the entire writing process. Padlet is an online whiteboard used for idea generations, while Google Docs serves as an alternative to Wiki, which allows simultaneous group writings, peer editing, and revising to be carried out online in real-time. As both teachers and students did not have experiences in using the above tools, they all received a one-hour training session by a computer technician in the school to familiarize themselves with the e-learning tools before the teaching cycle began. The other two classes served as a control. The teachers in these two classes followed the same lesson plan, same teaching steps and same teaching materials, except that students completed the writing task on worksheets.

To ensure that the writing ability of the four classes of students were similar to each other in the beginning of the study, the researcher asked the school to provide writing scores of their tests prior to the study. The scores of these students were subjected to a one-way ANOVA, and the difference was not significant *(p=0.35)*.

2.3 Data source and analysis

There were three sources of data arising from this research, namely focus group interviews, classroom observations, and student writings.

Two focused-group interviews were conducted separately with the four Primary 5 English teachers as well as the three observers (i.e. the Native English Teacher, the English Panel Chair, and the principal) after the entire teaching cycle ended. The interview protocol comprises ten open-ended questions in English, which tap teachers' beliefs on a number of aspects related to the research questions (see Appendix 1). Though the interview was conducted in groups, each teacher or observer was encouraged to express his/her individual opinion during the interview, so as to provide a comprehensive picture of different lessons. The interview data of these teachers and observers was transcribed by a student helper and coded on dimensions relevant to the research questions, namely "Student Motivation," "Quality of Student Writings," "Interactions between Students" and "Teacher Perception of E-learning".

Lesson observation data was also gathered for analysis. All eight lessons were videotaped and the Communicative Orientation to Language Teaching (COLT) Scheme developed by Spada and Frohlich (1995) was used for coding the critical moments in the lessons. The COLT scheme is widely adopted by L2 classroom researchers due to its comprehensiveness in capturing critical classroom episodes in content, language, and organization aspects (Nunan and Bailey 2009). The scheme comprises two parts. In Part A, teaching mode, content and lesson organizations are described, while communicative features like the use of target languages are documented in Part B. Only two dimensions in Part A of the coding schemes were adopted in the present study, namely "Participant Organization", which documented whether the ongoing activity was teacher-led or students working by themselves, and "Content," which documented what the teacher was focusing on during his/her speech. To obtain additional information about classroom interactions during pair-work tasks, the researcher also chose two pairs of students who sat next to the researcher's video camera (as their interactions can be clearly seen and heard) and adopted the Seating Chart Observation Records (SCORE) approach (Gall and Acheson 2011) which requires the researcher to draw a seating chart and count the number of turns taken between students and teachers, as well as among students during the lessons. A meaningful T-S interaction is coded whenever a teacher calls on a student and gives any instruction to him/her, or a student raises a question to the teacher. A meaningful S-S interaction is coded if any student starts talking to any student and that student responds, whether in L1 or in English. The interaction is coded even if the spoken content is irrelevant to the writing task. The researcher draws an arrow to denote the person who initiates the conversation. Though not as comprehensive as a structured spoken discourse analysis, this can serve as a useful indicator for capturing the quantity of S-S and T-S interactions during lessons.

To ensure high reliability of the data generated in the coding procedures, the researcher asked one of her colleagues, who was a research assistant with training in qualitative analysis, to code the interview transcriptions and video recording using the above approaches, which was then compared with the researcher's own coding. A total of two 1-hour interview transcriptions and thirty-two 35-minute lessons were coded, which took about 40 hours in total. The inter-coder reliability, calculated by the percentage agreement on coding between the two raters, was found to be reasonably high, with a rate of 0.82 for interviews and 0.85 for lesson observations. Any substantial differences were discussed and clarified before analysis was conducted.

Students' final writings were also analyzed quantitatively in terms of their language and content score. Teachers awarded a score of 0 to 4 for language and 0 to 6 for content for each student, based on the rubrics set by the textbook publisher and refined by the teachers (see Appendix 2). To eliminate any potential biases in the scoring and to ensure a similar standard of marking among teachers, six sample scripts from each class were randomly chosen using students' class numbers for review by the English Panel Chair. The marks were adjusted if deemed necessary.

Unlike other studies on adult learners, questionnaires were not administered to tap the beliefs or motivations of the learners in the present study, due to their low face validity among primary pupils. Table 2 shows a summary of the data gathered in the present study, and their corresponding research questions.

3 Results

3.1 RQ 1 and 2: Effectiveness of e-learning tools (motivation and quality of student writings)

The classroom observation field data, which was organized and coded using the COLT scheme, revealed aspects related to how the lessons were carried out. As expected, the classroom activities among all four classes did not differ much, as all of them adopted the same lesson plans, except using different modes (i.e. mobile devices vs paper-and-pencil). Of particular interest is the quantity and quality of teacher talk, as well as student reactions observed in

Table 2: Summary of the data gathered in the present study.

Data Source	Ways of collection and analysis	Matching RQs
Teacher interview	Seven teachers were interviewed. They were the Principal, the Native English Teacher, the English Panel Chair and four local teachers who teach Primary 5 classes. The interview protocol comprises 10 questions (Appendix 1). The interview data was transcribed and excerpts related to the RQs were reported.	#1, #3, #4
Lesson observations	Sixteen writing lessons (eight for e-learning group, eight for paper-and-pencil group) were videotaped. Qualitative analysis was carried out using the COLT scheme and SCORE approach to code the data and identify critical moments in the lessons.	#2, #3
Student writings	Teachers mark the writings and award scores on content and language, based on the rubrics in textbooks (Appendix 2). The scores were analyzed using t-tests.	#2

the lessons, which could provide some clues on whether students were engaged in the lesson. Using the dimensions of "Participant Organization" in Part A of the COLT scheme, the lesson was coded as whole-class, group-work, or individual-work activity. As the lessons were designed to involve writing in pairs, there was no time allocated for individual work across all classes. Table 3 shows the proportion of time devoted to whole-class activities or group-work in the e-learning and paper-and-pencil classes respectively.

Table 3: Proportion of time devoted to whole-class vs group-work activity.

Mode	Whole Class	Group Work
E-learning	40%	60%
Paper-and-pencil	48%	52%

In the e-learning classes, the teachers spent on average 40% of the time on whole-class activities, while the remaining 60% of the time was devoted to students' pair-work writing with e-learning tools. As students in the paper-and-pencil classes did not need to understand the technical details of operating the e-learning tools, one should expect that students in these two classes would be given more time to finish the writing task with their peers. However, this was not the case. These two teachers only devoted 52% of the time on this, which was far less than the e-learning classes (60%). A teacher in the e-learning classes gave the following explanation for the differences:

> I think students should be given more time to explore the e-learning tools themselves and interact with their peers, hence I didn't really talk a lot. Of course, I needed to give them the input and make sure that they understand the instructions beforehand.

To allow a more in-depth look into what teachers were actually doing or talking about during the whole-class activities, the researcher used the "Content" dimension in Part A of the COLT scheme to further classify the whole-class activity into three categories, namely management (e.g. giving directions to students, maintaining classroom discipline), task focus (e.g. teaching grammar, vocabulary and genre of the text, discussing ideas generated by students) and other topics irrelevant to management or the writing task (e.g. greetings, dealing with logistics). The proportion of time spent on these three areas is shown in Table 4 below:

Table 4: Proportion of time devoted to management, focus on language and other topics.

Mode	Management	Task Focus	Other Topics
E-learning	18%	70%	12%
Paper-and-pencil	26%	68%	6%

Teachers in both the e-learning and paper-and-pencil classes spent approximately 70% of the whole-class time on guiding students how to carry out the process writing task. However, a surprising finding was that in the paper-and-pencil classes, 26% of the time was devoted to management, as compared to only 18% in the e-learning classes. Videotapes of lesson observations as well as interview data from teachers further revealed that the management time in the e-learning classes was mainly on technical aspects of using the e-learning tools, whereas in the paper-and-pencil classes teachers mainly devoted management time to discipline students on their misbehaviors.

With regard to student reactions, the researcher discovered that students in the e-learning classes were generally eager to answer the teachers' questions during the teacher-talk stage, as observed by the large number of hands raised. Whereas in the other two classes, when asking the same question, the teachers often needed to wait some time before they could elicit answers from students. Interview data also echoed some of the findings from observations. Teachers in the e-learning group, as well as the colleagues observing the lessons, were overwhelmingly positive when talking about the students' responses.

> "They were extremely excited when they knew they could use iPads, as this was something they have never done before. Even the naughtiest students were found to be on-task and trying to explore the tools. They really look forward to using it in the beginning of the lessons, so they are well-behaved." said one of the teachers who taught the e-learning class.

In addition to the general excitement of getting to operate a mobile device (i.e. iPads) during the lessons, the English panel chair also mentioned aspects related to the actual functions of the e-learning tools.

> They love to see their writings being displayed on the computer screen, even though they are full of mistakes. Also, they can edit their own writings and those of their peers instantly without having to take out a correction pen. This is something you cannot do with paper and pencil, and the kids seem to find this very interesting.

For the traditional paper-and-pencil group, when being asked about students' overall performance during the lessons, the teachers seemed to focus on the difficulty of the task, and did not mention a lot about student motivation:

> The students are able to generate some ideas about the background information of Sports Day, but the peer editing and revising task proved to be a bit difficult for them. They didn't know how to correct their peer's writings and for those who did, only spelling mistakes were corrected.

The Native English Teacher, who observed the lessons of both groups, commented on off-task behaviors during the pair-work:

> A few students apparently lost track of what they had to do in the paper-and-pencil class and started chatting in Chinese. We didn't see a lot of these behaviors in the e-learning class, as students were very focused on manipulating their iPads.

Regarding the overall quality of students' final writings, the writing scores of the two groups of students (i.e. e-learning group and paper-and-pencil group) were averaged and subjected to a two-sample t-test. For the scores on language, the difference in the mean scores were found to be significant ($t=2.060$, $p<0.05$), yet the two groups did not differ significantly on the content score awarded by the teachers ($t=0.955$, $p>0.05$), nor the total number of words ($t=0.288$, $p>0.05$). Interview data provided additional information on these differences. The English Panel Chair, who reviewed sample writings from all classes and observed their lessons, said:

> Students in the e-learning classes spent a lot of time proofreading their own mistakes, often in spelling and sometimes in tenses, but they didn't write a lot. Those in the paper-and-pencil classes made a lot more careless mistakes, which I believe could be avoided if they proofread, but they just didn't.

Taken together, students in the e-learning classes appear to have been more engaged than those in the control classes, as evidenced by lesson observation data showing the relatively low proportion of teacher-talk on management and positive student reactions, as well as interview data from teachers. With regard to their quality of writings, the language score of students in e-learning classes was higher than the paper-and-pencil group, but significant difference was not found for content aspects.

3.2 RQ3: Interaction patterns in collaborative writing with e-learning tools

To obtain information about interaction patterns between teachers and students, the researcher chose two groups of students and recorded the instances of S-S and T-S interactions during the pair-work activity, as defined and coded using both the COLT scheme and SCORE approach. In the e-learning classes, there were a total of 42 meaningful instances of S-S interactions during the 8-lesson span, whilst only 25 such instances were recorded in the paper-and-pencil group. The number of T-S interactions, which was often initiated by the students themselves during pair-work task, was also found to differ a lot between the two groups (14 times in the e-learning group with 12 times initiated by the student vs 6 times in the paper-and-pencil group with 5 times initiated by the student). The researcher was unable to further classify the S-S interaction patterns into the three categories in Li and Zhu's (2011) study, namely mutually supportive, authoritative / responsive and dominant / withdrawn pattern, as these students rarely chatted on topics that were deemed relevant to the writing task. However, interviews with teachers revealed a bit about the quality of S-S interactions during the pair-work task in the e-learning group and the paper-and-pencil group. In the e-learning group, for example, there seemed to be a lot of talk in students' L1 on technical questions and translating words. This is how one of the teachers in the e-learning class put it:

> Students in the e-learning classes were talking a lot about what they had to do with the tools [in Chinese]. After they got settled the technical stuff, the students seemed to work rather independently. They also frequently asked the teacher about words that they didn't know.

Students in the paper-and-pencil classes did not seem to talk about the writing task either, as their teachers pointed out that their utterances were either in Chinese about unrelated issues or related to "translation of words."

In summary, even though the lesson observation data for interaction patterns revealed a higher number of S-S and T-S interactions for e-learning classes, the dialogues were either uttered in L1 or focusing on issues that were unrelated to the writing task, as revealed from the interview data. Students in both treatment and control classes were not seen to be using meta-language to discuss how to improve their writings.

3.3 RQ4: Teacher beliefs in e-learning tools

The four Primary 5 teachers, the Native English Teacher, the English Panel Chair as well as the principal were asked about their views of the e-learning tools used during the lessons. The results revealed their skeptical attitudes. For example, when asked if she would want to try this approach again, one Primary 5 teacher lamented about time constraints:

> *I have to admit that this is certainly a brand-new thing, but this has taken me more than 10 lessons to go through just a piece of writing with my students. To me, this is really time-consuming. I end up having to borrow lessons from other teachers to catch up with the progress. I am not going to use this approach again unless there is plenty of time for me to do so.*

Her arguments were echoed by the English Panel Chair and three participating teachers, who agreed that both teachers and the pupils need to spend a lot of time to familiarize themselves with the e-learning tools. The English Panel Chair added that any technical problems unresolved would put the lesson to a complete halt:

> *Often times when you or your students have problems with the iPads or the app, you have to wait for a long time for the technician to come and get it fixed. The lesson cannot continue and students will start to grumble and disciplinary problems will then arise. It takes away precious lesson time and causes frustrations.*

The principal, though more positive in her wordings, still remained cautious and emphasized that the school needs to devise a detailed implementation plan on when and how to use e-learning during lessons. She also pointed out that some veteran teachers were not ready to have their way of teaching changed:

> *If you ask a teacher who is going to retire in the next couple of years to use e-learning, she is going to say, 'forget about it', as she is so used to her chalk-and-talk mode that she does not need to plan or evaluate anything about her lessons. She can just step inside the classroom*

and teach. Using e-learning would mean turning her back to a novice teacher and starting everything all over again. Do you think she will do that?

Taken together, the major obstacles of implementing e-learning appeared to lie within the mindset of teachers themselves.

4 Discussion

Overall, the rich amount of data gleaned from interviews, lesson observations as well as student writings all purported to indicate the comparative advantages of using e-learning tools in process writing over that of the paper-and pencil mode. The significant increase in engagement among students in the e-learning classes is consistent with the notion that e-learning tools foster autonomous language learning, which in turn leads to sustained engagement in the task (Lai 2017). Students, when given the mobile devices and the e-learning tools, are more willing to put effort into their writing because of the perceived freedom that could not happen with worksheets. Teachers, in turn, also seem to be aware of their "change of roles" and provided students more time to complete the task instead of talking a lot. All these have contributed to the development of students' autonomy in class. It appears then that the present study, though exploratory and small-scale in nature, provides some initial clues to address Graham and Sandmel's (2011) concern that a hybrid approach of teaching writing is needed to supplement what process writing alone cannot achieve, and e-learning tools might be the solution to this.

With regard to the quality of the writings, the present study has shown a slight but significant difference in grammatical accuracy in the final writings of the e-learning classes. While it is premature to draw any casual relationships from this study alone, a possible explanation could be that students generally find it easier to identify and correct their own mistakes when they are typed on a mobile device, than when written on a piece of paper, as the e-learning tool that we used (i.e. Google Docs) was equipped with automatic spell-check and grammar-check functions, which could highlight some obvious students' mistakes in spelling and grammar. That said, students still need to rely on their own language skills, to correct the highlighted mistakes. As for students in the paper-and-pencil classes, their messy handwriting might also make it hard for these mistakes to be identified and corrected. However, there were not any significant differences for content aspects, as the effect might have been offset by the fact that students in the e-learning classes needed more time to familiarize themselves with the tools, hence giving them less time to actually write a lot of details. These claims will have to be further verified in future studies.

The interaction patterns observed during pair work revealed that though students in the e-learning classes chatted more often with each other and to their teachers, they did not seem to benefit a lot from working collaboratively with each other, as evidenced by the poor quality of interactions. Their discourses did not focus on improving the quality of each other's passage, nor were they related to brainstorming ideas or providing feedback to the writings. This seems to bolster Storch's (2013) argument that without explicit training for students on how to verbalize their thoughts during collaborative writing, such as expressing their initial ideas, providing feedback and negotiating with their partners on what to include and what to be taken away at the final stages, students would not benefit from writing in groups. Due to recent trends in promoting cooperative learning in schools, there seems to be a laymen assumption among frontline educators that all kinds of group work involving mixed-ability grouping are necessarily better than individual work, as these kinds of social experiences provide the scaffolding for additional language development that cannot be otherwise achieved when working alone (Vygotsky 1981). However, any scaffolding is necessarily mediated by language use. If students lack the language needed to interact with their peers in English, they would resort to the use of L1, chat on irrelevant topics or stop communicating at all, as observed in the present study. This would offset the potential benefits of collaborative writing and may even lead to disciplinary problems. Teachers should therefore provide sample dialogues in English to facilitate these dyadic interactions and constantly monitor whether these dialogues are being used during collaborative writing. For example, when giving feedback during the stage of idea generation, students can be taught to say the following expression, "Your idea is pretty good, but you may also talk about . . . ", while an example on correcting mistakes would be "You made a spelling / grammar mistake here. The correct spelling / word should be . . . ".

The concern on time constraints and teacher readiness raised by frontline educators comes as no surprise and reflects a more prominent issue at stake, which is well beyond the scope of the present study. In fact, any innovative pedagogical approaches would likely not be welcomed by teachers in Hong Kong, as has been shown elsewhere in some field studies which explore the usefulness of Task-based Language Teaching (TBLT) in local secondary schools (e.g. Carless and Harfitt 2013). In these studies, teachers were often blamed for their reluctance to leave their comfort zones and keep pace with the latest trends in education to try out innovative strategies. This, at least in part, is attributable to an examination-oriented education system which place strong emphasis on test scores rather than the learning process of students. Teachers are merely concerned about how to complete the progress of teaching, and to make sure that their students know how to pass the tests. Not until the high-stake tests are abolished and teachers' mentality is altered, any efforts in implementing innovative e-learning approaches would be futile, due to strong oppositions from teachers.

5 Limitations and future directions

The present study is the first attempt to explore the effectiveness of e-learning coupled with process writing approaches in a primary school setting, but has left a number of questions unanswered, which awaits future research to address them.

First, the amount of classroom research regarding the effectiveness of e-learning tools on young learners is extremely scarce to date, hence any conclusions drawn from the present study is likely to be preliminary. Whether similar results can be obtained with younger primary pupils or secondary school students are unknown. The present study should therefore be replicated in other contexts and with different age cohorts, so that a developmental trajectory of children's digital literacy development can be sketched and innovative pedagogies on process writing targeted at specific age groups can be developed to aid frontline educators.

Second, the present study did not explicitly measure or control factors related to teachers, such as years of experience, instructional strategies and instructional style, which might account for the variance of student outcomes. Though the present study attempted to minimize these effects by using experienced teachers and devising lesson plans for them to follow, there were still variations in how they actually delivered the lessons. Future studies should therefore either analyze in depth the classroom discourse during lessons, or use surveys to tap into teachers' instructional styles and beliefs, so that the influence of teacher-level variables can be unveiled.

The influence of sociocultural factors is another area that researchers cannot overlook, as it could exert enormous influence on teachers' beliefs and hence the success of the implementations of e-learning tools. Comparative studies involving pupils under different educational systems would allow this issue to be explored in greater depth.

With regard to the methodology used, researchers should consider adopting a longitudinal or action-research approach to examine issues about e-learning in classrooms. This can help shed light on questions which cannot be answered in one-shot experimental studies, such as whether students are able to adapt to the new mode of learning over time, hence accomplishing the tasks at ease and with higher quality, and whether teachers' worries would decrease over time as they have witnessed students' improvements. There was also a possibility that the e-learning tools triggered a novelty effect by temporarily boosting motivation and writing scores, as observed in the present study, but such effect might attenuate over time as students' excitement about using the tools decreases. These arguments should be verified in future endeavors, as they have huge policy implications on whether e-learning tools should be widely adopted in primary classrooms.

6 Conclusion

In this digital era, no one can stop the wave of technological advancements, which is constantly restructuring how students learn and how teachers teach in classrooms. Educational researchers therefore have the indispensable role to illuminate the minds of teachers and equip them with the skills needed to cope with these changes. More field studies on the effectiveness of various e-learning tools, as well as students' and teachers' readiness in using them, are urgently needed in this regard.

References

Arnold, Nike, Ducate Lara & Kost Claudia, R. 2009. Collaborative writing in wikis: Insights from a culture project in a German class. In Lara Lomicka and Gillian Lord (Eds.) *The next generation: Social networking and online collaboration in foreign language learning (pp. 115–144).* San Marcos, TX: CALICO.

Benson, Phil. 2001. *Teaching and Researching Autonomy in Language Learning.* London: Longman.

Carless, David & Harfitt Gary J. 2013. Innovation in secondary education: a case of curriculum reform in Hong Kong, In Ken. Hyland and Lillian Wong, (eds.) (2013). *Innovation and Change in English Language Education.* London: Routledge.

Chao, Joni, & Lo Hao-Chang. 2011. Students' perceptions of wiki-based collaborative writing for learners of English as a foreign language. *Interactive Learning Environments* 19(4). 395–411.

Elola, Idoia & Oskoz Ana. 2010. Collaborative writing: Fostering foreign language and writing conventions development. *Language Learning and Technology*, 14(3),51–71.

Gall, M. D. & Keith Acheson. 2011. *Clinical supervision and teacher development: Preservice and inservice applications, 6th Ed.* Hoboken, NJ: John Wiley and Sons.

Goldring, Amie, Russell Michael & Cook, Abigail. 2003. The effects of computers on student writing: A meta-analysis of studies from 1992–2002. *Journal of Technology, Learning, and Assessment,* 2(1),1–51.

Graham, Steve & Perin, Dolores. 2007. A meta-analysis of writing instruction for adolescent students. *Journal of Educational Psychology*, 99(3),445–476.
Graham, Steve & Sandmel Karin. 2011 The Process Writing Approach: a meta-analysis, *The Journal of Educational Research*, 104(6),396–407.
Harmer, Jeremy. 2004. *How to teach writing*. London: Longman.
Hillocks, George. 1986. *Research on written composition: New directions for teaching*. Urbana, IL: National Council of Teachers of English.
Kessler, Greg. 2009. Student-initiated attention to form in wiki-based collaborative writing. *Language Learning and Technology*, 13(1),79–95.
Kessler, Greg & Bikowski Dawn. 2010. Developing collaborative autonomous learning abilities in computer-mediated language learning: attention to meaning among students in wiki space. *Computer Assisted Language Learning*, 23(1),41–58.
Kessler, Greg, Bikowski Dawn & Boggs Jordan. 2012. Collaborative writing among second language learners in academic web-based projects. *Language Learning and Technology*, 16(1),91–109.
Kost, Claudia. 2011. Investigating writing strategies and revision behavior in collaborative writing projects. *CALICO Journal*, 28(3),606–620.
Lai, Chun. 2017. *Autonomous language learning with technology : Beyond the classroom*. Bloomsbury: PLC.
Li, Mimi & Zhu Wei. 2011. Patterns of computer-mediated interaction in small writing groups using wikis. *Computer Assisted Language Learning*, 24(1), 1–22.
Lee, Icy. 2010. Exploring wiki-mediated collaborative writing: A case study in an elementary Spanish course. *CALICO Journal*, 27(2),260–276.
Lund, Andreas. 2008. Wikis: a collective approach to language production. *ReCALL* 20(1),35–54.
Mak, Barley & Coniam David. 2008. Using wikis to enhance and develop writing skills among secondary school students in Hong Kong. *System*, 36(3),437–455.
Miyazoe, Terumi & Anderson, Terry. 2010. Learning outcomes and students' perceptions of online writing: Simultaneous implementation of a forum, blog, and wiki in an EFL blended learning setting. System, 38(2), 185–199.
Nunan, David & Bailey Kathleen. M. 2009. *Exploring second language classroom research: a comprehensive guide*. Boston: Heinle: Cengage Learning.
Rogers, Leslie & Graham Steve. 2008. A meta-analysis of single subject design writing intervention research. *Journal of Educational Psychology*, 100(4),879–906.
Schunk, Dale, Pintrich Paul & Meece Judith. 2008. Motivation in education: theory, research, and applications (3rd ed.). Upper Saddle River, N.J.: Pearson/Merrill Prentice Hall.
Spada, Nina & Frohlich Maria 1995. *Communicative orientation of language teaching observation scheme: Coding, conventions and applications*. Sydney: NCELTR Macquarie University.
Storch, Neomy. 2009. *The nature of pair interaction. Learners' interaction in an ESL class: its nature and impact on grammatical development*. Saabrucken, Germany: VDM Verlag.
Storch, Neomy. 2013. *Collaborative writing in L2 classrooms*. Multilingual Matters: Toronto.
Teng, M. Feng. 2018. *Autonomy, agency, and identity in teaching and learning English as a foreign language*. Singapore: Springer.
Vygotsky, Lev. 1981. The genesis of higher mental functions. In James V. Wertsch (ed.) *The concept of activity in Soviet Psychology* (pp. 144–188). Armonk, NY: M.E. Sharpe.
White, Ronald & Arndt Valerie. 1991. *Process Writing*. New York: Longman.

Appendix 1

Interview Protocol (For Teachers and Principal)
1. Do you think the lessons successfully achieve the objectives in the lesson plan? Why or why not?
2. What do you think about students' overall engagement and participation during the lesson?
3. What do you think about students' interactions during the pair-work activity?
4. What do you think about the quality of student writings produced after the lessons?
5. What do you think about the effectiveness of the process writing approach to teach writing?
6. What do you think about the effectiveness of the e-learning tools / worksheets used to supplement process-writing?
For participating teachers:
7a: What difficulties did you / your students encounter during the lessons?
8a. How did you deal with them?
For observers:
7b: What difficulties did you observe during the lesson?
8b: What did the teacher do to deal with them?
9. What do you think about using e-learning tools in writing lessons?
10. Will you adopt this mode of learning in your future lessons? Why or why not?

Appendix 2

Writing marking scheme with rubrics

Writing marking scheme

Score	Content
	Rubrics
6	– Provide a lot of interesting ideas with many supporting details. – The description is very clear and coherent.
5	– Provide interesting ideas with some supporting details. – The description is clear and coherent.

3-4	– Provide sufficient and relevant ideas with some supporting details. – The description is generally clear.
2	– Provide some relevant ideas but lack of supporting details. – The description is not clear.
1	– Attempt to write a paragraph by giving very limited information/ ideas only. – Provide unclear information/ ideas that may confuse the reader.
0	– Provide totally irrelevant ideas or practically make no attempt at all.

Language	
Score	Rubrics
4	– Use a wide range of vocabulary, sentence patterns and cohesive devices with few / no grammatical mistakes.
3	– Use a small range of vocabulary, sentence patterns and cohesive devices with few grammatical mistakes.
2	– Use a small range of vocabulary, and sentence patterns with some grammatical mistakes.
1	– Use a small range of vocabulary and verb forms with many grammatical and spelling mistakes.
0	– Provide totally irrelevant ideas or practically make no attempt at all.

Amy Kong
A dual case study of perceptions of strategy-based training and peer review stances among Hong Kong secondary students: An activity theory perspective

Abstract: While there is ample literature on how peer review can be implemented effectively by training, research that documents students' perceptions of training and its influence on peer review stances is relatively limited, especially among second language secondary students in Hong Kong. Adopting activity theory, the present study explored secondary students' perceptions of the effectiveness of training on the use of meta-cognitive, cognitive, and mediating strategies for peer review and how such training might mediate the extent to which they executed the activity. Two case studies of paired students implementing peer review in an after-school English writing course were conducted. They were native Cantonese-speaking, secondary-one students in Hong Kong. Multiple sources of data were collected, including recordings of dyadic peer review sessions, stimulated recalls, and interviews. Qualitative analyses of the transcripts indicate that students acknowledged the importance of training as it offered a clearer direction of how to exercise peer review. Students revised the texts collaboratively as writers and reviewers by using various strategies introduced in training. A contradictory case was also reported in which a reviewer displayed an authoritarian stance. This study sheds light on how to optimize the effect of training by introducing diverse strategies to secondary students for peer review.

Keywords: peer review, activity theory, training, strategies

1 Introduction

Peer review, during which students read drafts written by their classmates and give feedback to improve their writing, has engendered a growing body of research over the past decades. Studies of peer review entail effectiveness of peer review (e.g., Blain 2001; Braine 2003; Chaudron 1984; Hedgcock and

Amy Kong, The Hang Seng University of Hong Kong

https://doi.org/10.1515/9781501512643-003

Lefkowitz 1992; Lee 1997; Paulas 1999; Tsui 2000; Zhu 2001), students' perception of peer review (e.g., Amores 1997; Hirose 2012; Jacobs, Curtis, Braine, and Huang 1998; Sengupta 1998; Zhang 1995), and peer interaction (e.g., De Guerrero and Villamil 1994, 2000; Kong and Bui 2019; Villamil and De Guerrero 1996). Among these studies, the impact of training on the effectiveness of peer review has also been the focus (e.g., Berg 1999; Min 2006; Rahimi 2013; Stanley 1992; Zhu 1995). However, research that examined how secondary school students display peer review stances after training is of paucity. Adopting activity theory, the current study explored secondary students' perceptions of the effectiveness of training on the use of strategies for peer review and how training might mediate the extent to which they executed the activity.

2 Literature review

To ensure the optimal effect of peer review, some scholars (e.g., Hansen and Liu 2005; Edwards and Liu 2018; Stanley 1992) accentuate the importance of training, during which metacognitive and cognitive strategies as well as mediating strategies should be introduced before students conduct peer review. Metacognitive strategies are higher level executive skills (Brown, Bransford, Ferrara, and Campione 1983) that encompass selective attention for special areas of a learning activity, advanced planning and organization, monitoring during the process, and evaluation upon completion. On the other hand, cognitive strategies manipulate the information during a learning activity directly to enhance learning. There is hardly a distinct separation of cognitive strategies and metacognitive strategies. Livingston (1997) ascertains that cognitive strategy instruction is an approach to developing students' thinking skills to enhance learning and metacognition instruction should provide students with these cognitive strategies. Macaro (2006) further identifies the importance of metacognition in any strategy use by incorporating goal(s) in the deployment of a strategy. It is, therefore, important to highlight the goal of peer review during training, which is to improve the writing task through collaboration and negotiation (Hansen and Liu 2005). For the reviewers, peer review involves evaluating the writing tasks in relation to intelligent questions at a macro and micro level (Graesser, Pearson, and Magliano 1995), which is a cognitive-demanding process. In this regard, teaching students how to ask questions appropriately could be the focus of the training. This can be achieved through providing a purposeful feedback form that selects the key criteria covering both the global aspects and the language features of the specific writing task

(Hansen and Liu 2005), so that students' attention will be directed to the key areas to be assessed to ease their cognitive load. To the writers, the training should pitch the attitude of open-mindedness when they negotiate with the reviewers going through the criteria for assessment and clarify their intentions to provide higher quality of work.

In addition to metacognitive and cognitive strategies, students should be instructed to deploy a myriad of mediating strategies that lead to an increase in clarification and negotiation of meaning, thereby boosting the level of cooperation. Gurrereo and Villamil (1996) conducted a study and unveiled various scaffolds that facilitate negotiation during peer review, including advising, eliciting, reacting, asking for clarifications, and instructing. Edwards and Liu (2018) also categorized effective comments into three types, namely, evaluation, suggestions, and asking for clarifications. They further acknowledged that clarifications can intensify interaction because they generate a chance for the peers to discuss their perspectives in detail so that the author can know more clearly why and how to revise the text. They also allow the author to retain ownership of the text instead of treating the author as a passive recipient of instruction, which may eventually increase the writer's openness to accept their peer's comments.

Studies have been carried out which examined the impact of training on the effectiveness of peer review. Stanley (1992) guided her students to undergo an extended coaching procedure, which included analyzing evaluation sessions, exploring rules for effective communication, and studying the genre of student writing. She reported that compared with the uncoached students, students who received coaching demonstrated a greater level of engagement in peer review interaction and gave clearer guidelines for the revision of drafts. Berg (1999) observed that the revised drafts of the trained students showed greater improvement in the global level than those of the untrained students, regardless of proficiency level. Similarly, Zhu (1995), Min (2006), and Rahimi (2013) recorded more responses in the trained peer review groups and an enhanced standard of revisions compared with before training.

Despite a manifestation of the effectiveness of training, none of these studies were set in the secondary context, where, in the past decades (e.g., Benson 2007; Lee 1997), peer review has been advocated as a way to promote learners' autonomy. Moreover, except Hoijeij and Baroudi (2018), who explored perceptions of peer review training of Arabic native speakers at a foundation intermediate English class in university, almost no studies in the past addressed how students' perceptions of training may influence their peer review stances, that is, how students position themselves and orient towards their peers during peer review (Zhu and Mitchell 2012). Exploring the role of training in peer review stances is important since it offers a holistic perspective on student participation in peer review as a result of training.

To explore how students' perceptions of training impact peer review stances, this study adopts activity theory, which is based on the Vygotskyan theoretical framework about learning (Lantolf 2000; Lantolf and Appel 1994; Lantolf and Thorne 2006; Pavlenko and Lantolf, 2000). Activity theory understands human activities as complex and socially situated phenomena, and posits that activity and consciousness are dynamically interrelated (Leont'ev 1978). In other words, "learning and doing are inseparable" (Jonassen and Rohrer-Murphy, 1999: 65). The current study takes the lens of activity theory because peer review is a social and collaborative activity; one cannot provide a convincing answer to the questions of when and how to conduct peer review in order to maximize its effectiveness without considering the process of the activity itself. One approach to activity theory was developed by Engestrom (1987, 1999), who has created a modern incarnation of activity theory (see Figure 1) that effectively maps the complexities of a social practice in a wide array of settings. Within such a collective system, the actions of individuals are based on four mediators: the artefacts, the community, the rules, and the division of labour.

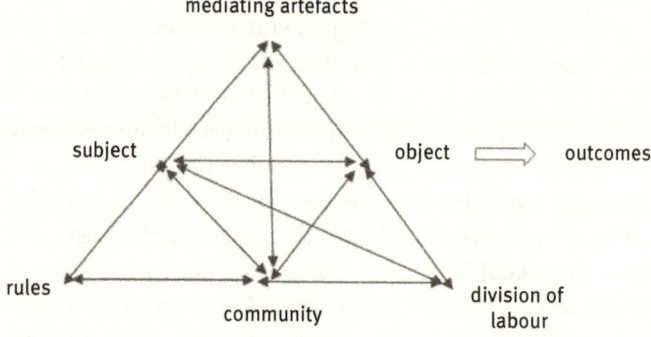

Figure 1: Activity theory diagram (Engestrom, 1987).

Engestrom's (1987) system is a powerful socio-cultural lens through which we can analyze peer review by focusing on the interaction of human activities and the human mind within its relevant context. The subject is the actors engaged in peer review. The object is the orientation of the activity that arises from the motive; for example, in peer review, when learners share the common goal of improving the writing task through collaboration, they negotiate and edit the writing together, which motivates the activity. The mediating artefacts can be any tools, languages,

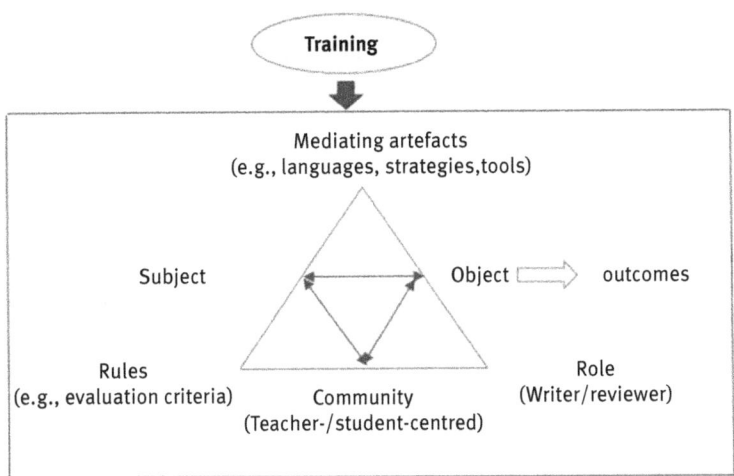

Figure 2: Impact of training on the peer review activity system.

or strategies used in the peer review activity. Community is the participants (i.e., the writers and the reviewers) who share the same object that shapes and leads direction to the act. Rules guide how the activity occurs. Division of labour involves the regulational norms of the activity. Examples of these could be the reviewer's and writer's roles. All these elements are inter-related, which will affect the actions and operations during the activity, leading to different outcomes. The present study aims to explore students' perceptions of strategy-based training and how these perceptions affect their peer review stances for two pairs of students undergoing peer review. The way they executed peer review will be examined in terms of the four meditators (artefacts, roles, rules, and community) situated in the peer review activity system (See Figure 2). The documentation of any instances contradictory to the expected outcomes of training, if any, could also unearth the inadequacies of training when it is applied in a social participation context.

3 Method

With a view to exploring how learners conduct peer review with respect to their perceptions of training, a case study design was adopted to collect in-depth and systematic data about second language (L2) writers' peer review stances. According to Yin (2009), a case study offers an insight into the questions of how and why a phenomenon occurs within a real-life context. Moreover, case studies are also powerful when the aim is to explore "the extraordinary diversity of L2 writers and writing contexts from an expanded sociocultural perspective" (Casanave, 2003: 88).

3.1 Participants

Twenty secondary-one (equivalent to the first year of junior high school) students voluntarily participated in the current study. They came from two secondary schools of which the banding is number one and the medium of instruction is English (EMI) in Hong Kong. Students studying in a band-one EMI school are usually considered more competent English learners than those studying in lower-banding schools. Among these twenty participants, two pairs of students from the same school (Olive vs. Andy; Hannah vs. Wing) were randomly selected as two case studies in the current paper to examine their perceptions of the strategy-based training and their peer review stances. Pre-interviews were conducted with each participant to explore their prior peer review experiences. According to the interviews, both Olive and Andy underwent peer review irregularly in primary schools in English writing classrooms; however, students were not allowed to interact during the process, nor were they trained in how to conduct peer review. What they were instructed to do was to give ticks on forms. On the other hand, Hannah and Wing did not have any peer review experiences before.

3.2 The study design

The participants were invited to take 12 sessions of an after-school writing course, which was taught by the researcher. Each session lasted for around 60 to 90 minutes. Throughout the course, the researcher introduced students to five pieces of narrative writing with respect to the context, metalanguage, and structural elements of each writing.

Before the writing course, the researcher interviewed participants about their past peer review experiences and perceptions of peer review, using a semi-structured format. Compared with unstructured and structured interviews, semi-structured interviews can give researchers more organized and focused access to other people's opinions regarding the research topics whereas at the same time giving interviewees a certain degree of power and control over the course of interviews (Nunan, 1992).

The second lesson marked the introduction of the first writing topic, after which students had to finish the writing task at home. In the next lesson, the students were paired up, and were given 30 minutes to conduct peer review. Before peer review, a peer evaluation form was distributed to individual students for reference. The researcher went through the structural elements and language features on the form to ensure they understood the meaning of the items on the form. The teacher also reminded them of the goal of the activity and the use of cognitive strategies, mediating strategies, and appropriate expressions during the activity.

The interactions of the first, third-, and the last peer review sessions were audio-recorded and transcribed to explore what sorts of strategies were adopted during peer interaction. To unveil students' underlying reasons for their orientations, students were invited to take part in a stimulated recall session individually one day after each peer review session, during which the student was shown some episodes of the previous peer review session, and prompted to explain why they displayed certain behaviour and what their feelings were towards some peer review instances. Stimulated recall is one effective way to "prompt participants to recall thoughts they had while performing a task or participating in an event" (Gass and Mackey 2000: 17). Bloom (1954) justified the reliability of stimulated recalls by showing that 95% of recalls were accurate if participants were prompted within 48 hours after an activity. With the adoption of stimulated recalls one day after peer review, different social factors and even individual differences that affect peer review could be understood more thoroughly.

After the whole course, participants were semi-structure-interviewed by the researcher about their perceptions of training and peer review. All the interviews and stimulated recall sessions were conducted in Cantonese, their mother-tongue, to facilitate their recalling process.

It should be noted that the students' and their parents' consent had been granted before they took part in the course. They were fully informed that the students' interactions, stimulated recalls, and interviews would be recorded and used for data analysis and that all the data would be kept confidential.

3.3 The training

With reference to the metacognitive and cognitive strategies suggested by Edwards and Liu (2018) and mediating strategies proposed by Gurrereo and Villamil (1996), the training sessions were designed. Using a sample text, the researcher gave a training session to the participants before the first formal peer review session (see Appendix I). The training catering for the writing task was repeated each time before students conducted peer review for reinforcement (see Appendix II). The objectives of the training were three-fold.

First, in terms of meta-cognitive strategies, participants were emphatically reminded that the goal of peer review was to improve the writing task collaboratively. They should alternatively be taking up the roles as a reviewer or a writer. Affection to the peer's writing and openness to the peer's comments should be retained during the process.

Second, regarding cognitive strategies, students were given the feedback form that lists all the criteria to be assessed for both the content and the language of the writing. To ensure the effectiveness of peer review, students were asked to go through the writing three times. First, they should read through the text and give comments on the content pursuant to the structural elements listed on the form. Then, they could read it once again in detail to indicate the mistakes related to the selected language items on the evaluation form. Finally, they could skim the work for the third time to grasp an overall impression of its organization and style. They were also encouraged to write down comments with reference to the criteria listed on the form. Such selective focus helped ease their cognitive load.

Last, students were presented with some mediating strategies which could be employed during peer interaction. Examples of these include advising, eliciting, asking for clarifications, reacting (giving evaluations), and instructing. In addition, the training introduced appropriate language expressions to students by providing them with a checklist showing them useful phrases or sentences to be used in peer review. Students were reminded to give constructive comments (e.g., *You should talk about why you like your schoolmates*) instead of vague ones (e.g., *your writing needs improvement*) to ensure their peer knows specifically which parts need improving. The structural elements and the language features of each writing task were also introduced to students before peer review so that they could comment with appropriate metalanguage expressions. Students were asked to use English during interaction; however, they could adopt code-mixing – using both Cantonese (first language, L1) and English (L2) – in case they encountered predicaments in expressing themselves in English.

3.4 Data analysis

The audio-taped pair-talk sessions were transcribed and coded into different segments called episodes, which was defined as a segment in the pair talk during which learners focused explicitly on the essays. Each episode was further coded to sort out what scaffolding strategies the learners had adopted during peer review. 30% of the data was checked by other research assistants to ensure the inter-reliability of the coding process. The stimulated recalls and the interviews were also transcribed and analyzed to triangulate the data obtained from the transcripts of their interactions.

4 Findings

The data collected from the stimulated recalls and the pre-/post-interviews were triangulated with the transcribed audio-taped peer review sessions to explore how students' perceptions of training influence their peer review stances in terms of the four mediators including artefacts, roles, rules, and community.

4.1 Perceptions of training and peer review stances within the artefact-mediated activity

4.1.1 The use of mediating strategies

In both the stimulated recall sessions and the post-interviews, all students acknowledged the importance of learning an array of mediating mechanisms during training. In fact, strategies such as giving evaluation, asking for clarification, and advising were frequently employed by students across the three peer review sessions. Below show some examples of their utterances:

> *Advising*
> I think you can write more about your school teachers.
> There is something wrong with the adjective. Maybe you can use another one.
> *Asking for clarifications*
> Could you explain why you love your school?
> What do you mean by being late?
> *Eliciting*
> Why do you use the '-ing' here? What tense do you think you should use?

However, whereas reviewers sometimes employed various scaffolds, leading to the collaborative nature of peer review, Olive tended to display a more authoritative stance by frequently evaluating the writing of her partner, Andy. For example:

> *Reacting (Giving evaluation)*
> The description of your school teachers is excellent.
> The description of your school facilities is not enough.

In the stimulated recalls, when asked about her reasons for incessant adoption of reacting during peer review, Olive ascertained that asking for clarifications, as instructed by the training, was an effective strategy; however, sometimes due to convenience, she preferred expressing all the necessary comments that emerged in her mind before she forgot. However, her preference shaped her peer review stance as highly authoritative, and such authority sometimes silenced Andy (please see the section on "the role-mediated activity" for details).

4.1.2 The use of appropriate language expressions

In the post-interview, students claimed that the training as well as the evaluation forms had provided them with language expressions for effective English communication.

In the current study, one pair of students, Hannah and Wing, used the L2 to interact with their peers in most episodes. In the stimulated recalls, when asked about the reason for their code choice, both claimed another main goal of peer review was to improve their English communication skills, and so they wanted to grasp every chance to speak in English.

> *Hannah: I love talking in English. It's a good chance to improve my English-speaking skills.*
>
> *Wing: English is important in society. When I grow up, I also need to use it to communicate with others, so I want to grasp every chance to practice talking in English.*

When they were asked whether training had helped them to convey their messages in English, both of them agreed that the English expressions taught during the training session helped them to make oral comments in English more effectively.

There were instances when students did not know how to express themselves in English. On those occasions, they used their L1, Cantonese, to express themselves. Andy and Olive was a pair that frequently adopted code-mixing. For example:

> *Andy: (English) so you can write more clearly about the school . . . the class . . .*
>
> *Olive: (English) what do you mean?*
>
> *Andy: (Cantonese) How to say in English 8:05 a.m.?*

In the stimulated recall, Andy posited that he should speak English in the English writing course. However, he was not used to speaking English. To facilitate communication, he sometimes chose to adopt code-mixing.

> Andy: I am not used to talking in English, but because it's an English class, I tried to talk in English. I think it is difficult to talk in English. If I didn't know some of the words, I shifted to Cantonese. I think it's a good idea to allow us to adopt code-mixing.

Both Olive and Andy said in the final interview that even though training taught them some useful English expressions that could facilitate their interactions, they still encountered some words that were hard to express in English. On those occasions, they shifted from English to Cantonese. Their code-choice supported the findings of de Guerrero and Villamil (2000), in which their participants also used their L1 as the lingua franca during peer review. In the stimulated recall sessions, both of them said that by using the L1, they could express their emotion better. This suggested that use of the L1 is still a better tool to express students' emotion and intensify interaction.

4.2 Perceptions of training and peer review stances within the rule-mediated activity

4.2.1 Focus on all aspects of the writing

The students followed the training guidelines quite closely. All the students gave comments on both the language and the content and followed the suggestion – reading the text three times. The interviews showed that this orientation was the result of training.

> Olive: Primary teachers did not instruct us in a way that was as detailed as your training. I think I am more professional now as I commented both on the content and the language. I think both of them are important. I think it was more useful to give feedback concerning all aspects.
>
> Wing: I followed what I was told in the training. I read the writing twice. First, I read through the content. Then I looked into the grammatical mistakes. After that, I talked to my partners about my comments. And finally, I ticked the form.

4.2.2 Deep changes and concrete advice

In the present study, all students claimed they followed the guidelines instructed in the training and were able to provide constructive and detailed comments. For example, during the peer review of the genre "My Homepage", they all indicated which particular sub-sessions (e.g., Me, My family, My hobbies, My school,

My friends) their peer had to elaborate on. For the peer review of "A News Reports" and "A Story", they also gave comments on the preciseness of the body paragraph. Below are some examples of their constructive comments.

> Olive (English): You should have described how serious the incident was . . . .
>
> Hannah (Cantonese): He was dead because of the failure of treatment or he was just dead on the spot?
>
> Wing (English): [I think] in the first paragraph, you said that "I had some problems when I woke up". Before this sentence, "Amy and I planned to go to Disneyland", I think you can write more. For example, you should have described the fact that you had talked on the phone with Amy.
>
> Andy (Cantonese): Just one big problem . . . the ending is just here . . . just one sentence. It's not meaningful enough . . .

4.3 Perceptions of training and peer review stances within the role-mediated activity

In the post-interviews, all students acknowledged the training helped to shape their role as an appreciative reviewer who gave constructive advice, as well as an open-minded writer who was humble to accept the peer's suggestions.

4.3.1 Role as a reviewer

The training emphasized the collaborative nature of peer review, during which students took turn to be the reviewer and negotiate with the writer to improve the writing task. All of them loved the ideas of discussing the writing with their classmates because this could help them understand more about how the writer thought. For example:

> Hannah: I love talking to my peer now because it is more impressive and detailed to know what she thought about when she wrote. It would be useless if I were asked to tick the form only.

Because of such acknowledgement, most of them treated their role seriously by circling the mistakes in the text, followed by explanation. They also gave their peer comments by offering some suggestions or by asking him/her why he/she wrote so. What is more, students behaved in a respectful way and showed affection in most of the peer review sessions, as they were advised in the training. In addition to suggestions for improvement, students actually offered compliments to their peer to boost his/her confidence as a writer. For example:

> Wing (English): I think your language is pretty good, but you should use the simple present tense more carefully.
>
> Hannah (English): I think overall, it's pretty good, but you can use more adjectives to describe why she loves her friend.

Also, the reviewers showed respect to the authorship. Before they wanted to make some changes of the ideas of the writing, they usually asked the writer for clarifications first. If the author was able to provide a sound reason, the reviewers also respected the peer's choice and stopped condemning their peer's work. For example,

> Andy (English): So you can write [some] more clearly about the school . . . the class . . .
>
> Olive (English): What do you mean?
>
> Andy (Cantonese): Originally the school starts at 8:05 a.m., and ends at 3:45 p.m. but you write at . . .
>
> Olive (English): But I write here . . . it's the starting time of the first real lesson, excluding the class teacher's session . . .
>
> Andy (English): I see . . .

Nonetheless, despite the intense and collaborative nature, interactions were sometimes authoritarian, as seen in Olive, who gave too much evaluation without allowing her partner to respond. For example, in the episode below, Olive made a general evaluation of Andy's news report and gave him suggestions directly by the end of the peer review session. Her assertive tone, continuous commentary, and authoritarian manner silenced Andy.

> Olive (English, in assertive tone): I think your headline is pretty good, but your tense needs improvement. For example, this one should be in the past tense, not the present tense. I think you need to improve your prepositions as well, but I think it's not the most important; the most important is the body paragraph. There isn't enough fact. For example, you should talk more about the accident.
>
> Andy (Cantonese): I don't know . . .

When asked in the stimulated recalls about the reason for her over-frequent employment of reacting (giving evaluation) and advising, Olive explained she did so in case she forgot what she wanted to say to Andy. She welcomed Andy's justifications; unfortunately, he did not, and she assumed he accepted her comments.

4.3.2 Role as a writer

When taking up the role as a writer, students claimed they followed what was instructed by the training – to be open-minded to their peer's comments. They listened to their peer's suggestions. When asked in the final interviews whether they made revisions according to their peer's feedback, their answers were all positive. Moreover, most writers provided explanations humbly when they were questioned by the peer. In the following episode, Wing was unsure why Hannah said she was late when she woke up. Hannah then referred to the previous sentence which indicates the reason "because the alarm clock did not go off". This clarified the reviewer's uncertainty.

> Wing: . . . when I woke up, why were you late? (Asking for clarifications)
>
> Hannah: because my alarm did not go off. (Offering justifications)

On the other hand, due to the authoritative stance of Olive, Andy kept silent in peer review. As revealed in the second stimulated recall, Andy admitted that he was being a little shy when talking to the opposite sex. He stated that he felt quite shocked when he knew he was paired up with a girl. In the post-interview, Andy said that he would have been more comfortable if he had been paired-up with a boy, and expressed his reluctance to pair up with the opposite sex in the future. The training of the current study did not highlight the gender factor during peer interaction, but it seems that it also has a role to play in peer review.

4.4 Perceptions of training and peer review stances within the community-mediated activity

The pre-study training highlighted the importance of the goal of peer review, that is, to allow students to work collaboratively and interactively with each other to better the writing tasks. In other words, it tended to shift the traditional teacher-based L2 writing classroom, in which the teacher is the only one to give students feedback, to the student-centred class, in which students are also responsible for their own writing.

All students gave credit to this goal as they agreed it could help to improve their writing task by listening to one more reader's perspective. Most students welcomed the opportunities to learn from their peer, and valued their peer's comments. They said in the final interviews that it was more useful and objective to include one more type of feedback in addition to the teacher's feedback.

> Wing: I think it was fairer! In the past, we only received comments from the teacher; now I can have one more perspective from my classmate.

Moreover, from the interview data, all students valued the training since it had encouraged them to speak to each other, leading to a collaborative, student-centred environment. To a certain extent, this has promoted learning autonomy and shifted the traditional L2 writing classroom from teacher-based to student-based.

> Andy: I did have few experiences of peer review in primary school. But the teacher did not ask us to talk. Everyone was silent in class. We just circled each other's mistakes. I think it is more useful and less boring when we are taught how to speak to each other in class.

> Olive: I had similar experiences before and we were allowed to speak to each other. However, we just seldom spoke up. There was no training on how to interact with the other student. I think your training was useful.

5 Discussion

The study has provided a detailed picture of how training influenced peer review instances in terms of the four mediators: artefacts, roles, rules, and community within the peer review activity system. Students acknowledged that with the help of the training, they adopted an array of mediating artefacts and appropriate language expressions tailor-made for each writing task during peer review. The training also affected students' rules of conducting peer review that covered both the meaning and surface aspects of the texts. As instructed by the training, most students were divided into the roles of an open-minded and humble writer as well as an appreciative and helpful reviewer when they worked together collaboratively during the activity. This created a student-centred classroom, in which more autonomy was given to the students to decide their own revisions instead of being passively controlled by the teacher, which is an important theme in recent work on teacher development (Benson 2007).

Previous studies on effect of training on peer review (e.g., Berg 1999; Min 2006; Stanley 1992; Zhu 1995) were mainly conducted from the quantitative perspective in the tertiary education setting in which quality of revisions and comments were compared between trained students and untrained students. The current study has advanced knowledge about peer review in the secondary school context by identifying the influence of training on peer review from the activity theory perspective.

In fact, the literature of peer review in L2 writing documenting research that adopted the activity system was fairly scant in the past, but has become more common over the last decade. For example, Myung-Hye (2012) adopted Engestrom's activity theory to explore how roles and tasks are distributed among EFL students who engage in peer response and reported that a division of labor did exist between two EFL students in Korea. In addition, guided by activity theory, Yu and Lee (2015) conducted a case study on two Chinese university students and uncovered that students' motives could directly affect stances and patterns of interaction during peer review. Zhu and Mitchell (2012) also examined ESL students' peer review stances from an activity theory perspective by linking their orientations to peer review to their motives for participating in the activity. However, these studies were not conducted in the secondary school context, where learners' autonomy has been emphasized in recent years.

Drawing on activity theory, the present study has explored how participants strategically mediated the peer review processes with diverse resources within the peer review activity system. Moreover, the central question of the present study is whether training imposes any desirable impact on different mediators. As shown in the post-interviews, most students revealed that the training had offered remarkable assistance with a clear goal, detailed evaluation forms, as well as effective strategies and appropriate expressions for them to ask right questions and give right comments. These strategies increased interaction and collaboration during peer review (Edwards and Liu, 2018). The present findings have also offered some additional support to previous studies concerning the mediating strategies adopted during peer review. For instance, previous studies by Kong and Bui (2019) as well as Villamil and De Guerrero (1994, 1996) and De Guerrero and Villamil (2000) have revealed that peers tended to use their L1 as the lingua franca to facilitate the communication processes during peer review. Such an adoption of L1 was also shown in the present study.

In addition, the training instructed students on how to conduct peer review more effectively by looking at the content first, followed by the language. All students in the present study stated, in the stimulated recalls, that they followed the rules as recommended in the training and such a way of carrying out peer review was useful and effective. Also, the recap of the structural elements and the linguistic features of each particular genre before peer review also provided students with clearer signposts of what to comment on and how to comment. With the aid of the evaluation forms, they were constantly reminded when reviewing their peer's writing to focus on both the content and the language of the text.

The training session also helped to develop reviewers' sense of open-mindedness and respect to the writer's work. They showed appreciation most of the time, as revealed by their overall positive comments by the end of the review *I think your writing is great*. Intensive collaboration, which was derived by a great variety of scaffolding mechanisms introduced during training, was also witnessed during the peer review sessions in the current study. These scaffolding mechanisms not only involved giving advice, but also asking for clarifications and providing justifications, which in turn increased the extensiveness of interactions, and increased a sense of collaboration during peer review (Edwards and Liu 2018; Kong and Bui 2019). When students gave advice to their peers, their peers open-mindedly accepted it. Students in the present study took it in turn to be the writer and the reviewer during each peer review session. In most cases, students showed collaboration with each other, open-mindedness to the reviewer's comments, and respect to the writer's work. Their attitude of being respectful and open-minded during interaction and awareness of collaboration were the results of training.

While the study demonstrates how training assists students in utilizing the mediating resources during peer review more effectively, it also engenders a contradiction. For example, as revealed by the stimulated recalls and the post-interview with Andy, he was reserved to the idea of talking to the opposite sex during peer review. From his case, it seems that apart from training, the gender issue may be another important factor that affects peer review stances. The central question of the present study is the effect of training on the peer review activity system. Therefore, it is beyond the scope of this article to discuss the impact of the individual and social factors on peer review. However, it is believed that throughout the learning process, L2 learners are actually participating in a learning activity in which individual's performance and changes should be understood as a complex social being, by which individual variables and social factors should also be taken into account (Lewis, Enciso, and Moje 2007).

6 Conclusion

The present study has offered a detailed, descriptive account of the impact of training on the four mediators within the peer review activity system. It is believed that secondary school teachers could employ appropriate training to achieve the optimal outcomes of peer review in L2 writing classrooms, that is, students collaborating with each other to improve the writing tasks, thus shifting the classroom from teacher-centred to be collaborative and student-centred in nature. However, in addition to training, teachers should also take into account the gender factor when implementing peer review.

It should be noted that the whole course of the present study was conducted in an after-school enhancement setting and it only lasted for 12 sessions. Therefore, a longer ethnographic study should be conducted in the future to explore the feasibility of conducting peer review in the formal school setting. Moreover, the current study design can serve as reference for future research in which students' sample writing before and after peer review training could be collected, compared, and analyzed to explore the effect of peer review training on students' writing development.

References

Amores, Maria J. 1997. A new perspective on peer-editing. *Foreign Language Annals* 30 (4), 513–522.

Benson, Phil. 2007. Autonomy in language teaching and learning. *Language Teaching* 40 (1), 21–40.

Berg, E. Catherine. 1999. The effects of trained peer response on ESL students' revision types and writing quality. *Journal of Second Language Writing* 8 (3), 215–241.

Blain, Sylvie. 2001. Study of verbal peer feedback on the improvement of the quality of writing and the transfer of knowledge in francophone students in grade 4 living in a minority situation in Canada. *Language Culture and Curriculum* 14 (2), 156–170.

Bloom, Benjamin. 1954. The thought processes of students in discussion. In S. French (Ed.), Accent on teaching: Experiments in general education (1st ed., pp. 23–46). New York, NY: Harper & Brothers.

Braine, George. 2003. From a teacher-centered to a student-centered approach: A study of peer feedback in Hong Kong writing classes. *Journal of Asian Pacific Communication* 13 (2), 269–288.

Brown, Ann L., John D. Bransford, Roberta A. Ferrara & Joseph C. Campione. 1983. Learning, remembering, and understanding. Technical Report No. 224. Retrieved from https://files.eric.ed.gov/fulltext/ED217401.pdf

Carson, Joan G. & Gayle L. Nelson. 1996. Chinese students' perceptions of ESL peer response group interaction. *Journal of Second Language Writing* 5, 1–19.

Casanave, Christine Pearson. 2003. Looking ahead to more sociopolitically-oriented case study research in L2 writing scholarship: But should it be called "post-process"?. *Journal of Second Language Writing* 12 (1), 85–102.

Chaudron, Chaudron. 1984. The effects of feedback on students' composition revisions. *RELC Journal* 15, 1–16.

De Guerrero, Maria C. M. & Olga S. Villamil. 1994. Social-cognitive dimensions of interaction in L2 peer revision. *Modern Language Journal* 78 (4), 484–496.

De Guerrero, Maria. C. M. & Olga S. Villamil. 2000. Activating the ZPD: Mutual scaffolding in L2 peer revision. *Modern Language Journal* 84 (1), 51–68.

Engestrom, Yrjö. 1987. *Learning by expanding: An activity theoretical approach to developmental research*. Helsinki, Finland: Orienta-Kousultit Oy.

Engestrom, Yrjö. 1999. Activity theory and individual social transformation. In Yrjö Engestrom, Reijo Miettinen & Raija-Leena Punamaki (eds). *Perspectives on activity theory.* Cambridge: Cambridge University Press.

Edwards, Jette Hansen & June Liu. 2018. *Peer response in second language writing classrooms* (2nd ed). Chicago Distribution Center: University of Michigan Press.

Graesser, Arthur C., Person, N.K., & Magliano, J.P. 1995. Collaborative dialog patterns in naturalistic one-on-one tutoring. Applied Cognitive Psychology, 9, 359–387.

Gass, Susan M & Mackey, Alison. 2000. Stimulated recall methodology in second language research. London: Routledge.

Hansen, Jette & June Liu. 2005. Guiding principles for effective peer response. *ELT Journal* 59 (1), 31–38.

Hedgcock, John & Natalie Lefkowitz. 1992. Collaborative oral/aural revision in foreign language writing instruction. *Journal of Second Language Writing* 1 (3), 255–276.

Hirose, Keiko. 2012. Comparing written-only and written-plus-spoken peer feedback in a Japanese EFL university context. *Asian Journal of English Language Teaching 22*, 1–23.

Hojeij, Zeina & Sandra Baroudi. 2018. Student perceptions on peer feedback training using a blended method: A UAE case. *Issues in Educational Research* 28 (3), 655.

Jacobs, George M., Andy Curtis, George Braine & Huang Su-Yueh. 1998. Feedback on student writing. *Journal of Second Language Writing* 7 (3), 185–212.

Johnson, Roger T. & David W. Johnson. 1986. Action research: Cooperative learning in the science classroom. *Science and Children* 24 (2), 31–32.

Jonassen, David H & Rohrer-Murphy, Lucia. 1999. Activity theory as a framework for designing constructivist learning environments. *ETR&D 47 (1)*, 61–79.

Kong, Amy & Gavin Bui. 2019. Reader stances and writer responses in L2 peer review among secondary school students. *The Asian EFL Journal* 23 (5), 139–186.

Lantolf, James P. 2000. *Sociocultural theory and second language learning.* New York: OUP.

Lantolf, James P. & Gabriela Appel (eds.). 1994. *Vygotskyan approaches to second language acquisition.* Norwood, NJ: Ablex.

Lantolf, James P. & Steven L. Thorne. 2006. *Sociocultural theory and the genesis of second language development.* NY: Oxford University Press.

Lee, Icy. 1997. Peer reviews in a Hong Kong tertiary classroom. *TESL Canada Journal* 15 (1), 58–69.

Leont'ev, Alekseĭ Nikolaevich. 1978. *Activity, consciousness, and personality.* Englewood Cliffs, NJ: Prentice Hall.

Leont'ev, Alekseĭ Nikolaevich. 1981. The problem of activity in psychology. In James V. Wertsch (ed.), *The concept of activity in Soviet psychology.* Armonk, N.Y: Sharpe.

Lewis, Cynthia, Patricia Enciso & Elizabeth Birr Moje. 2007. *Reframing sociocultural research on literacy: Identity, agency, and power.* Mahwah, NJ: Lawrence Erlbaum Associates.

Livingston, Jennifer A. 1997. Metacognition: An overview. State University of New York at Buffalo (Electronic version).

Livingston, Jennifer A. 2003. Metacognition: An overview (ERIC Document Reproduction Service No. ED474273). Retrieved from https://files.eric.ed.gov/fulltext/ED474273.pdf

Lockhart, Charles & Peggy Ng. 1995. Analyzing talk in ESL peer response groups: Stances, functions, and content. *Language Learning* 45 (4), 605–651.

Macaro, Ernesto. 2006. Strategies for language learning and for language use: Revising the theoretical framework. *The Modern Language Journal* 90 (3), 320–337.

Min, Hui-Tzu. 2006. The effects of trained peer review on EFL students' revision types and writing quality. *Journal of Second Language Writing* 15 (2), 118–141.

Mendonca, Cassia O. & Karen E. Johnson. 1994. Peer review negotiations: Revision activities in ESL writing instruction. *TESOL Quarterly* 28 (4), 745–769.

Huh, Myung Hye. 2012. How EFL students take a position in peer feedback activities: An activity theory perspective. *English Language and Literature* 58 (6), 1085–1101.

Nelson, Gayle L. & John M. Murphy. 1993. Peer response groups: Do L2 writers use peer comments in revising their drafts? *TESOL Quarterly* 27 (1), 135–141.

Nunan, David. (1992). *Research methods in language learning*. Cambridge: Cambridge University Press.

Paulus, Trena M. (1999). The effect of peer and teacher feedback on student writing. *Journal of Second Language Writing* 8 (3), 265–289.

Pavlenko, Aneta. & James P. Lantolf. 2000. Second Language learning as participation and the construction of selves. In James P. Lantolf (ed.), *Sociocultural theory and language learning* (pp. 155–177). Oxford: Oxford University Press.

Rahimi, Mohammad. 2013. Is training student reviewers worth its while? A study of how training influences the quality of students' feedback and writing. *Language Teaching Research* 17 (1), 97–89.

Sengupta, Sima. 1998. Peer Evaluation: 'I am not the teacher'. *ELT Journal*, 52, 19–28.

Stanley, Jane. 1992. Coaching student writers to be effective peer evaluators. *Second Language Writing* 1 (3), 217–233.

Tsui, Amy & Maria Ng. 2000. Do secondary L2 writers benefit from peer comments? *Journal of Second Language Writing* 9 (2), 147–170.

Villamil, Olga S. & Maria C.M. De Guerrero. 1996. Peer revision in the L2 classroom: Sociocognitive activities, mediating strategies, and aspects of social behaviour. *Journal of Second Language Writing* 5 (1), 51–75.

Yin, Robert K. 2009. *Case study research: Design and methods (applied social research methods)*. London and Singapore: Sage.

Yu, Shulin & Icy Lee. 2015. Understanding EFL students' participation in group peer feedback of L2 writing: A case study from an activity theory perspective. *Language Teaching Research* 19 (5), 572–593.

Zhang, Shuqiang. 1995. Reexamining the affective advantage of peer feedback in the ESL writing class. *Journal of Second Language Writing* 4 (3), 209–222.

Zhu, Wei. 1995. Effects of training for peer response on students' comments and interaction. *Written Communication* 1 (4), 492–528.

Zhu, Wei. 2001. Interaction and feedback in mixed peer response groups. Journal of second language writing 10 (4), 251–276.

Zhu, Wei & Deborah A. Mitchell. 2012. Participation in Peer Response as Activity: An Examination of Peer Response Stances from an Activity Theory Perspective. *TESOL Quarterly* 46 (2), 362–386.

Appendix I A Formal Training Session for Peer Review

1. What Is Peer Review?
- You should read each other's writing and give comments on it. In other words, you need to work together to make the writing better!

2. Why Peer Review?
- To appreciate and learn from each other's writing.
- To train your critical thinking–what is a good writing? How to make it better?

3. Procedures of Peer Review
- First, read the text once. Based on the evaluation form, comment on its content. For example, if you think the writer does not talk about the school facilities, you can put a tick in the box of "Needs Improvement".
- Second, read the text once again. Circle or underline the mistakes about the language items listed on the evaluation form.
- Last, read the text very quickly to feel its overall organization and style.

4. How to Behave during Peer Review?
- Reviewers: Show interest and respect towards the peer's writing.
- Writers: Show your openness to your peer's comments. Answer their questions. Clarify your thoughts. You are working with each other to improve the writing!
- **Don't work alone**. Please keep eye contact with each other – You are talking to each other.

5. How to TALK during Peer Review?
- **Content:** Give your peer hints before telling the suggestions directly. For example, in the writing "My Secondary School", if you think the writer does not talk about the school facilities, you can put a tick in the box of "Needs Improvement" first. Then, before you directly tell your peer the suggestions, you can ask the writer: ***What is missing in this paragraph?***
- **Language:** You may circle/underline the mistakes (e.g., inappropriate use of tenses or vocabulary) and ask your peer to correct them one by one first. If he/she has difficulties, give him/her some hints and help them to correct the mistakes.

6. Comment Types and Useful Sentences in Peer Review
- **Asking for clarifications: (Strongly Recommended!)**
  Why do you love your school?
  What do you mean by XXX?
  Why do you use the simple past tense here?
- **Guiding your peers indirectly (Strongly Recommended!)**
  The use of tense here . . . do you know what's wrong with it?
  Can you think of another adjective you should use here?
- **Giving suggestions to your peers:**
  I think you can write one more about your school teachers.
  There is something wrong with the adjective here. Maybe you can use another adjective like . . .
- **Evaluating your peer's work:**
  The description of your school facilities is excellent.
  The description of your essay is not clear enough.
  I like your use of adjectives that describe personalities a lot.
  I don't like your choice of words.
- **Teaching your peer directly:**
  Please use the simple past tense here because the event has passed.
  The word should be spelt as 'X-X-X-X'

7. Other Useful Sentences for Peer Review

I am not sure what you mean here. Could you explain?
Can you come up with some better words?
You have worked so hard on this paper. But I think you can describe more about . . . .
Can you tell me why you say . . . ? (e.g., why you like you schoolmates?)

8. Vague Expressions You Should Avoid!!

Your writing is quite good (How good is it?)
Your writing is bad! (This is discouraging, and why is it bad?)
Your text needs improvement. (Please tell your peer what he/she should improve.)
You should write more in your text. (What should your peer write more?)

Appendix II Sample Evaluation Form on "My Homepage"

– Content and Structure

	Excellent ☺☺☺☺	Pretty Good ☺☺	Average ☺	Needs Improvement ☹
1. There is an attractive heading.				
2. There are relevant sub-headings.				
3. There is an interesting description of 'Myself' – e.g. name, age, physical appearance and personality.				
4. The section on 'My Family' is clearly described.				
5. There is a clear description of 'My Favourite Hobbies'.				
6. The description of the section on 'My School is' is interesting.				
7. The section on 'My Best Friend' is clearly described.				

Other comments:
– Language Use

	Excellent ☺☺☺	Pretty Good ☺☺	Average ☺	Needs Improvement ☹
1. The simple present tense is used correctly.				
Any bad examples:				
2. Suitable expressions or adjectives describing appearance are used.				
Any good examples: Any bad examples:				
3. Adjectives describing personality are used appropriately.				

Any good examples:
Any bad examples:

4. Grammar is mostly correct.

5. Words are of a wide range and generally accurate and appropriate.

6. Punctuation and spelling are correct.

Other comments:
- **Genre**

	Excellent ☺☺☺	Pretty Good ☺☺	Average ☺	Needs Improvement ☹
The general tone and style of the homepage show that the writer is aware of the purpose, context and audience of the genre.				

Other comments:

Wilson Cheong Hin Hong

Improving English as a foreign language learners' writing using a minimal grammar approach of teaching dependent clauses: A case study of Macao secondary school students

Abstract: Traditional English as a Foreign Language (EFL) grammar books categorize subordinating clauses into relative clauses, noun clauses, and adverbial clauses (e.g. Harris 2013). Likewise, secondary school teachers in Macao typically put emphasis on differentiating the functions and forms of each type of clause. This teaching method is often too complicated for students to apply the knowledge in actual writing. As a result, many sentential errors due to first language (L1) transfer repeatedly emerge in students' writing. The current study proposes to abandon this traditional categorization. Teachers are advised to put emphasis on the similarities instead of the differences of the clauses in order to simplify teaching. To evaluate the effectiveness of the proposed method of teaching, a three-month case study was carried out to investigate the writing errors made by two pairs of lower-intermediate EFL learners in Macao. In a one-and-a-half-hour weekly session, one pair of learners were individually taught about dependent clause features whereas the other pair by categorization. The learners produced a weekly 250-word essay amid the training. Analysis of learners' writings suggests the *clause-element* learners made better and steadier progress than the *categorization* learners. However, there was no sign that participants used more complex structures in later essays. Implications regarding grammar and writing pedagogy are discussed.

Keywords: writing instruction, EFL writing, subordinate clauses, clause markers, writing errors

1 Introduction

Turn over an English grammar textbook or go onto a grammar teaching website and chances are you will find chapters or discussion on relative clauses, noun

Wilson Cheong Hin Hong, Macao Institute for Tourism Studies

https://doi.org/10.1515/9781501512643-004

clauses, and/or adverbial clauses. This classification may not correspond to the one proposed by linguists (Liu 2014), but English teachers and grammar book writers largely agree with this categorization of English clauses (e.g. Harris 2013; Murphy 2012). In the case of Macao, apart from the very rare instances of schools developing their own teaching materials, the overwhelming majority of secondary schools use Hong Kong grammar textbooks (Xin 2010), which are typically structured according to grammar topics and subtopics. To give a few examples from some widely used grammar books, *Grammar Express (with answers)* contains units on "relative clauses with subject relative pronouns" and "relative clauses with object relative pronouns" (Fuchs and Bonner 2007: vii), *Focus on Grammar 5* has topics on "noun clauses: subjects, objects, and complements" and "adverb clauses" (Schoenberg and Maurer 2011: iii), and *Certificate English Usage* includes units of "noun clauses", "relative clauses" and a list of adverbial clauses broken down into "ways of expressing . . . purpose" and "ways of expressing . . . cause and effect", etc. (Harris 2013: vi). Understandably, English teaching syllabi follow what has been laid down in textbooks as structural and descriptive grammar (Ellis 2006), and the classification is supposedly there to help students better grasp the structures of complex English sentences. However, the effectiveness of such categorization is little investigated. The predominant adoption of this convention by textbook writers may result in teachers overemphasizing the distinction between the various types of clauses, despite its unknown effect on language learning. Some schools in Macao go as far as requiring students to identify the types of clauses and their respective functions according to the abovementioned classification, as illustrated in an example test section shown in Figure 1.

As can be seen in the exercise, each type of clause can be further broken down into various subtypes, amounting to as many as 20 subtypes of clauses! The amount of time and effort that young learners need to devote on metalinguistic training to acquaint themselves with such a task is beyond my imagination. Clearly, there are a number of problems with such highly-structured method of teaching:

1. The terminology could be difficult for students to understand. Words such as *complement, adverbial,* and *apposition* are all novel linguistic concepts to learners. Some of the terms may not even correspond to students' first language.
2. The terminology themselves and the classification may not always be accurate, and may not be consistent across textbooks (Collins and Lee 2005).
3. Students may have rarely come across certain types of clauses. Explicit grammar instruction would not be effective if students have not come to a stage of familiarity with the target language items (Gray 2004).

4. The syntactic and instructional complexity can easily cause confusion for learners.
5. There is no clear connection between form-learning and actual linguistic production (Ellis 2006).

In view of these problems, the current study proposes to do just the opposite – dropping all the distinctions and minimizing instructional complexity by reducing

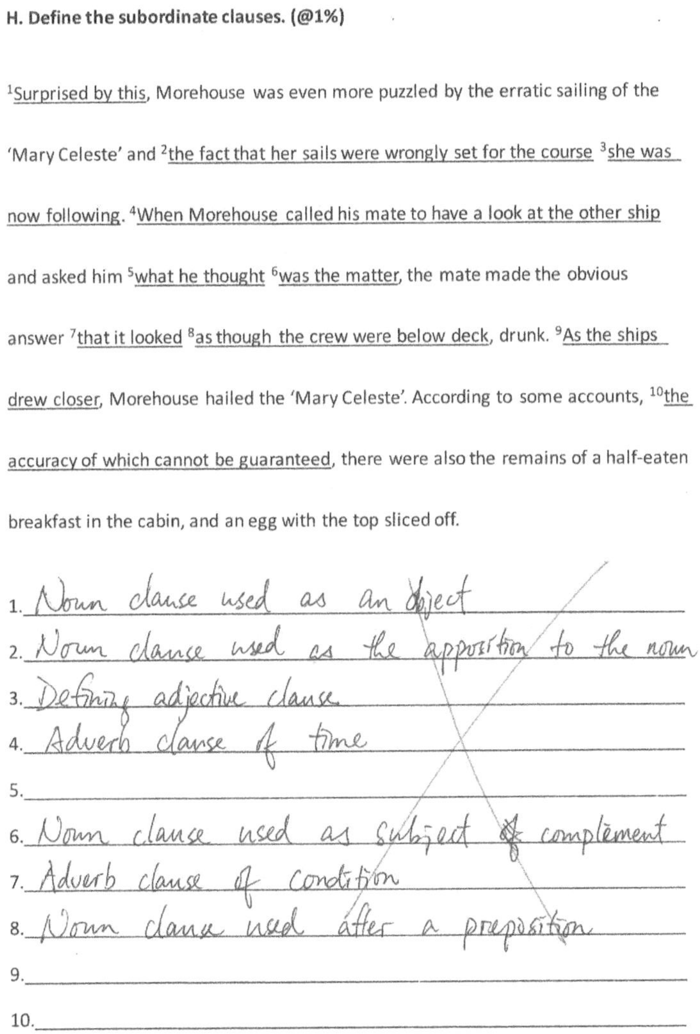

H. Define the subordinate clauses. (@1%)

[1]Surprised by this, Morehouse was even more puzzled by the erratic sailing of the 'Mary Celeste' and [2]the fact that her sails were wrongly set for the course [3]she was now following. [4]When Morehouse called his mate to have a look at the other ship and asked him [5]what he thought [6]was the matter, the mate made the obvious answer [7]that it looked [8]as though the crew were below deck, drunk. [9]As the ships drew closer, Morehouse hailed the 'Mary Celeste'. According to some accounts, [10]the accuracy of which cannot be guaranteed, there were also the remains of a half-eaten breakfast in the cabin, and an egg with the top sliced off.

1. Noun clause used as an object
2. Noun clause used as the apposition to the noun
3. Defining adjective clause.
4. Adverb clause of time
5.
6. Noun clause used as subject & complement
7. Adverb clause of condition
8. Noun clause used after a preposition.
9.
10.

Figure 1: An assessment section on dependent clauses from a junior secondary school in Macao.

clauses teaching into one single concept of "clause elements". Students save time and effort without a need to familiarize themselves with terminologies and distinguish one clause type from another. As a result, the teaching can be more easily applied in students' actual writing.

Further, research on English clauses instruction have largely focused on relative clauses (e.g. Chan, Yang, Chang, and Kidd 2018; Kirjavainen, Kidd, and Lieven 2017), with far less investigation on the teaching of noun clauses and adverbial clauses. There is not a single study to the author's knowledge that examines the three types of structures altogether. Thus, the study can provide a new method of EFL complex sentence instruction and possibly a new perspective of research investigation. This study attempts to answer three questions:

1. Can learners write complex sentences correctly without learning the distinctive features and functions of different types of dependent clauses?
2. Does teaching of different types of clauses encourage production of a wider variety of clauses?
3. Is minimizing instructional complexity more effective than classifying the types of dependent clauses (or vice versa) in facilitating written production?

2 Literature review

2.1 Dependent clauses and clause elements

The concepts of complex sentences and dependent clauses are apparently common-sensical and well-agreed on by researchers and teachers alike. But in reality, they are not. In many Hong Kong grammar coursebooks, a dependent/subordinate clause only refers to a finite clause, which contains a finite verb (i.e. verb with tenses) (e.g. Harris 2013; Schoenberg and Maurer 2011). A non-finite clause, on the other hand, is referred to as a "phrase", as in, for example, "participial phrases" (e.g. *Standing next to an old man*, Jacky waited). The same classification is observed in research articles (e.g. Hunt 1965; Polio 1997). Some other researchers included both finite and non-finite clauses when discussing dependent clauses (Bardovi-Harlig and Bofman 1989; Storch 2005), as illustrated in the following italic segments:

1. Oddmund came in, *locking the door behind him*.
2. *After he came in*, he locked the door. (Payne 2010: 328)

To be consistent with most grammar coursebooks and in consideration of the objective to simplify grammar instruction, the current study only considers *finite*

clauses that are structurally or semantically incomplete as dependent clauses, which traditionally consist of relative, adverbial, and noun (i.e. nominal) clauses. On the other hand, a sentence segment that contains a non-finite verb is referred to as a *phrase*. Hence in a dependent clause, the first observable clause element is a finite verb. Another clause element is a *clause marker*, marking the beginning of a dependent clause, sometimes manifested as a complementizer (e.g. that), relativizer (e.g. who) or conjunction (e.g. because) (Radford 2009). However, not all dependent clauses in English begin with an explicit clause marker. For instance, structures involving epistemic verbs may opt to use a null (i.e. tacit) complementizer, as in:
3. John knows (*that*) Mary was not telling the truth.

Or when a relativizer is the object of a relative clause:
4. That was the lady (*whom*) we met in the party last Saturday.

Note that these clause markers are optional, and by default, English dependent clauses have to begin with a clause marker (Radford 2009). On the contrary, there are no lexical clause markers in the Chinese language (Xu and Langendoen 1985). Consequently, Cantonese-speaking students who are of lower EFL proficiency typically omit the English clause markers in their writing. Since the current study targets beginner EFL writers, participants were not informed of the optional clause markers but were instead told to employ a clause marker whenever they wanted to write a sentence that involves a second finite verb. Detailed intervention procedures will be discussed in a later section.

2.2 Instructional complexity and learning efficiency

In his seminal article on principles of EFL teaching, Krashen (1982) proposed that grammatical instruction should be conducted in the most easily-understandable fashion as complex rules are basically not learnable. He asserted that "teaching complex facts about the second language is not language teaching, but rather is 'language appreciation' or linguistics" (1982: 120). He argued that rules should be simple and memorable, and will only be helpful when students have sufficient input of the respective grammar item. One example of learnable punctuation rule that he provided is to "capitalize the first letter of every sentence" (1982: 98). The rule is apparently oversimplified, but could nonetheless be helpful to Chinese students, who typically make comma splice mistakes in writing (Chuang and Nesi 2006).

Building on Krashen's acquisition theory, Robinson (1996) conducted a quasi-experiment with 104 non-native EFL learners to test the learning efficacy under eight conditions of grammar instruction: simple and complex rules acquired through implicit, incidental, rule-search, and instructed means. The rationales behind the experiments were that simple rules could be learned effectively through explicit grammar teaching while complex rules are better acquired implicitly (Reber 1989). Subjects were pretested, trained, and tested using grammaticality judgement tests. It was found that for simple rules, direct instruction resulted in significantly higher accuracy in judging both grammatical and ungrammatical sentences, while implicit learning resulted in the lowest accuracy in both. More interestingly, for complex rules, participants did very well in spotting the grammatical sentences but very poorly in ungrammatical sentences, a sign taken as success in rule-learning instead of actual acquisition (White 1991); last but not least, the subjects did moderately better in both conditions under implicit learning. Robinson concluded that explicit instruction of complex rules may not translate into L2 acquisition, but neither can a structure be effectively acquired without any formal teaching. Subsequent studies on related issues were carried out but with a shifted focus on implicit and explicit learning and their interface (e.g. Robinson 2010), which is beyond the scope of investigation in the current paper.

However, there is also evidence suggesting that grammar instruction of more complicated grammar structures results in better learning efficacy (Housen, Peirrard, and Vandaele 2005). In Housen et al.'s study, 69 L1-Dutch L2-French learners were split into two classes, one receiving instruction on a simple structure while another on complex metalinguistic rules. Instructional efficacy was measured using a pretest and posttest design. Results showed that both groups benefited from the explicit teaching, but the complex-structure class made better progress than the simple-structure group. However, the latter finding should be viewed with extreme caution, as Housen and his team also noted, because the series of pretests indicated that the complex-structure class comprises of mostly proficient English users while the simple-structure class was far less proficient. The apparent differences in learning outcome might be due to different levels of mastery of a second language. That is, advanced users are better able to understand metalinguistic rules and can more easily apply newly acquired structures in oral and written production, while lower-level learners face more challenges during the acquisition.

2.3 Mistakes in Cantonese-speakers' writing

Chan (2010) put forth a taxonomy of written errors of Cantonese EFL learners by examining 696 pieces of free writing written by 387 students in Hong Kong. Error analysis (EA) and transfer analysis (TA), the latter of which identifies errors with reference to leaners' L1 and the former does not, were adopted to spot anomalous English usage in the compositions. Of particular interest to the current study are errors related to sentence structures, including:

1. misuse of conjunction (e.g. *Although we can't have our own life there, but now we are happy*),
2. in-prepositional phrases (e.g. *In many years ago, my father . . .*),
3. independent clauses as objects or subjects (e.g. *You don't need to worry about the problem will struck you*),
4. verb form selection (e.g. *Every day he driving his car*),
5. misuse of relative clauses (e.g. *She will cook the food what I like to eat*),
6. reduced relative clauses (e.g. *I have a large family which including grandmother*),
7. omission of relative pronouns (e.g. *You are the first come to Hong Kong*),
8. serial verb constructions (e.g. *My mother took a stick beat me*),
9. punctuation problems (e.g. *I saw her face, I will know that she was very angry*), and
10. omission of copulas (e.g. *They will very happy*). (Chan 2010: 302–308)

Most of the abovementioned errors are caused by L1 interference while others are due to inadequate mastery of the target language. These errors (referred to as *sentential errors* in later sections) accounted for over 25% of all errors across different levels of learners, and generally appeared more frequently in lower-level learners than in more advanced learners' writing (see Table 1). Note that the lower-intermediate learners did not necessarily make the most number of mistakes in all error types. Other unmentioned errors, such as misused affixes, appeared more frequently among upper-intermediate and advanced learners. Generally speaking, though, lower-intermediate learners committed more sentential errors (52.5% among all errors), upper-intermediate learners more non-sentential errors, and advanced learners fared better in most categories.

Apart from their frequent occurrence, sentential errors are typically considered having more error gravity than other mistakes (Vann, Meyer, and Lorenz 1984). Error gravity refers to how tolerable a mistake is in terms of its effect on overall comprehensibility of a text. Word choice aside, errors in relative clauses, verb forms, and order of words are among the most intolerable mistakes (p. 431), potentially causing the greatest strain in reading.

Table 1: Written errors made by Cantonese EFL learners (Chan 2010: p. 310).

Sentential error type	#Tokens	%Total errors in corpus	%Total errors in each type			L1 transfer
			Lower intermediate	Upper intermediate	Advanced	
misuse of conjunction	42	0.84	31	59.5	9.5	Yes
in-prepositional phrases	49	0.98	73.5	24.5	2	Yes
independent clauses as objects or subjects	54	1.08	53.7	31.5	14.8	Yes
verb form selection	144	2.88	36.8	47.2	16	No
misuse of relative clauses, reduced relative clauses, omission of relative pronouns	158	3.16	18.4	53.2	28.5	Yes
serial verb constructions	190	3.8	78.4	18.4	3.2	Yes
punctuation problems	204	4.08	56.9	35.2	7.8	No
omission of copulas	426	8.52	71.6	23.7	4.7	Yes

Table 2: How identifying clause elements helps students determine sentence correctness.

	Complex sentence	#clause marker	#finite verb	Grammatical?
Original sentence	Both cases **are** about a person **used** a knife to stab others.	0	2	No
Correction version 1	Both cases are about a person **who** used a knife to stab others.	1	2	Yes
Correction version 2	Both cases are about a person **using** a knife to stab others.	0	1	Yes

2.4 How teaching clause elements can improve EFL sentence structures

A close examination of the sentential errors committed by lower-intermediate level EFL learners reveals that nearly all mistakes are due to the absence,

Table 3: A comparison of instructional procedures between the two groups of participants.

Segments	Elements	Minimal grammar group (C & W)	Categorization group (H & S)
Revision (10 mins)	Previous teaching	The learner talked about what she learned in the previous lesson followed by the teacher's feedback.	
Teaching (50 mins)	Approach	Lecturing and written exercises	
	Topics	Clause types Main clause Dependent clause Clause elements Finite verbs Dependent clause markers Commas and periods	Clause types Relative clauses defining non-defining Noun clauses subjects objects complements Adverbial clauses cause and effect purpose contrast
	Practice	Designed by the author Error correction exercises Sentence writing Sentence translation	Ready-made textbook/internet materials Gap-fill exercises Sentence combining Multiple choice questions Error correction
Essay checking (20 mins)	Treatments	Clause errors discussed in terms of absence/ redundancy/misuse of clause elements Elicitation and discussion of other errors (e.g. prepositions, articles, collocations)	Clause errors discussed in terms of the forms of different clause types Elicitation and discussion of other errors (e.g. prepositions, articles, collocations)
Final remarks (10 mins)	New writing topic	The learner was told to write a 250-word opinion essay before the next class. The topic was explained and if time allowed, the learner would brainstorm some ideas in class.	

overuse or misuse of clause elements. Hence, Chan's (2010) proposed common errors can be classified in another way:

1. Clause marker problems
   – Misuse of conjunction
      e.g. *Although we can't have our own life there, but now we are happy.* (Double dependent clauses)

- Independent clauses as objects or subjects
  e.g. *You don't need to worry about the problem will struck you. (Missing *that*)
- Misuse of relative clauses
  e.g. *Obesity is a disease that someone who is very fat in an unhealthy way. (Redundant *who*)
- Omission of relative pronouns
  e.g. *The earthquake happened in Japan some years ago was a catastrophe. (Missing *that*)
- Punctuation problems
  e.g. *I have a sister, she doesn't like me. (*but* missing/double matrix clauses)
2. Finite verb problems
   - Verb form selection
     e.g. *Every day he driving his car. (Misused non-finite verb)
   - Reduced relative clauses
     e.g. *I have a large family which including grandmother. (Misused non-finite verb)
   - Serial verb constructions e.g. *My mother took a stick beat me. (Double finite verbs)
   - Omission of copula e.g. *They will very happy. (Missing finite verb)

In sum, students should be taught that **one (and only one) clause marker and two finite verbs should *coexist* whenever there is a second clause in a sentence.** Thus, these errors can be fixed by simply supplying sufficient appropriate clause elements to form complex sentence structures. For instance, if students see that there are two finite verbs in a sentence, they should supply one clause marker; likewise, if they see that a clause marker is used but there is one finite verb and one non-finite verb used in a sentence, they should "upgrade" the non-finite verb to a finite verb. Alternatively, students can correct a sentence by taking away both clause elements to reduce the clause into a phrase. For example, if a supposed dependent clause begins with a clause marker but follows with a non-finite verb, the clause marker can be taken away to reduce the clause into a phrasal structure; or if a clause marker is absent, the second finite verb could be "downgraded" into a non-finite one. There are multiple possible combinations when structuring complex sentences, and teachers should spend time allowing students to experiment with all these combinations through error-correction exercises and sentence-writing exercises.

3 Design of the quasi-experiment

3.1 Subjects

The current study employs a qualitative approach of analysing a total of 29 essays collected over a period of three months. Four female participants (C, W, H, and S) who studied in the same class of a local secondary school volunteered to take part. Research consent was obtained but subjects were not aware of the different experimental conditions. These students reported that they had heard of relative clauses (hereafter RC) and noun clauses (hereafter NC), but not adverbial clauses (hereafter AC). However, they were not able to verbalise what they are, how a clause is different from a phrase, nor were they able to identify or distinguish different types of clauses. In short, the participants had limited metalinguistic knowledge about clauses or sentential terminology.

An Oxford Quick Placement Test was conducted prior to the experiment, and all four participants were found to be at the upper B1 quadrant (lower-intermediate) of the Common European Framework of Reference for Languages. Past studies indicated that subjects of clausal structure investigation cannot be too low in proficiency as they may not be accustomed to writing in English (Chan 2010), while they cannot be too advanced because proficient users tend to replace clausal structures with complex phrases (Lu 2011).

3.2 Intervention and data collection procedures

Apart from two holiday breaks and a test week, participants took part in a weekly one-and-a-half hour session for a total of nine weeks. The intervention lasted for exactly one school term of that particular local school so that prolonged absences due to examinations and holidays could be avoided. Considering the need to review the essays with individual participants, the participants were tutored individually by the researcher, under two different experimental conditions; participants C and W were shown example complex sentences and instructed on clause elements, consolidated by doing sentential-error correction exercises, and then they attempted writing complex sentences. Participants H and S were taught the relative clauses, noun clauses and adverbial clauses and their subtypes according to three grammar coursebooks and some internet resources. They also worked on the exercises provided in the books and websites, including sentence completion, sentence combining, multiple choice questions, and predominantly gap-filling exercises. All materials used were suitable for lower-intermediate to intermediate learners of English.

Towards the end of each of the first eight sessions, all participants were given a topic and required to write a 250-word opinion essay. They were instructed to turn in their writing for in-session checking in a subsequent lesson. Studies on written syntactic complexity indicated that opinion essays yielded more syntactic complexity in writing than other genres (Lu 2011; Way, Joiner, and Seaman 2000); untimed writings can also elicit more complex structures than timed ones (Ellis and Yuan 2004). Thus, participants were asked to do the writing in their free time instead of during a tutorial session. The possibility of dishonest acts were considered, and participants were warned against that. However, considering there is no grading or peer pressure, and the fact that the volunteering participants were highly motivated to improve their writing ability, such behaviours were improbable and unnecessary. Nonetheless, dishonest acts could be easily spotted during the checking, and there was no such case identified.

Each student was therefore expected to write eight pieces of writing (no writing was submitted in the first lesson). Unfortunately, due to personal reasons, participant S of the categorization group decided to quit the tutorial in the sixth lesson. Hence, only five essays were collected from her. Still, her participation was included in the study due to limited experimental subjects.

3.3 Data validity and analysis

Although participants mentioned that they have "heard of" relative clauses and noun clauses, subsequent interactions between the researcher and the participants demonstrated that they could hardly recall any linguistic knowledge gained from earlier school instruction. Thus, the effects of prior linguistic knowledge should be minimal.

To reduce the effect of experimental bias, several measures had been taken. First, each participant was tutored individually so that they received equal attention and interaction time. The sequence of the lesson and the duration of each segment were strictly followed to ensure a consistent teaching condition apart from the teaching content, which is harder to control as there is no readily available materials for the *minimal grammar group*. However, the teaching segment of the *categorization group* stringently followed the explanation of textbooks and used the exercises provided.

The 29 essays were coded by the author and a research assistant individually using NVivo 11. A number of coding categories were first laid down:
1. Sentential error types
   a) missing, misused, or double clause markers (e.g. *There are a lot of crime of rape ⋏ were happen in a city.)
   b) punctuation mistakes, including sentence fragmentation and run-on sentences (e.g. *If everyone keeps on opening the air-conditioner.)
   c) missing, misused or double finite verbs (e.g. *In this case, how do we protect these women is legalise the abortion.)

2. Clause types
   a) relative clause (e.g. *There are a great number of travelers come to Macau.)
   b) noun clause (e.g. * . . . I think make a lot of friends is a meaningful things.)
   c) adverbial clause (e.g. *Although someone said we can't kill a life but we should think about the mother first.)

Initial inter-coder reliability showed 80.3% of consistency. Upon comparing the nodes, it was found the majority of disagreements were related to confusion of clause-marker issues with punctuation mistakes. The coders subsequently agreed that punctuations should be considered a priority when coding errors. Hence, in the second round of coding, a 95.8% consistency was recorded. All codes were revisited by the author one month after the second coding. Three changes were then made regarding the error types.

4 Findings

4.1 The minimal grammar pair (C & W)

4.1.1 Participant C

In the minimal grammar pair, C's major mistakes were using a non-finite verb in matrix or dependent clauses (e.g. *I didn't mean the other not to be friend anymore) and missing clause markers (e.g. *There are a great number of travelers ⋏ come to Macau) (see Figure 2). These mistakes were greatly reduced in the 3rd writing. Run-on sentences persisted until the 5th writing. Overall, clausal errors were reduced in the last three writing pieces. However, the intervention did not seem to encourage more usage of dependent clause structures (see Figure 3). Note that since the essays come in slightly different lengths, to standardize the values, the number of sentential errors and clauses were calculated per every hundred words.

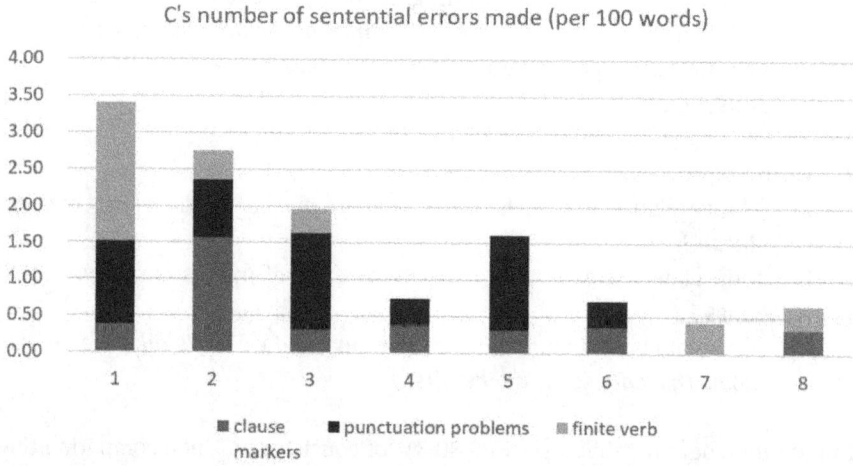

Figure 2: Number of sentential errors made by C.

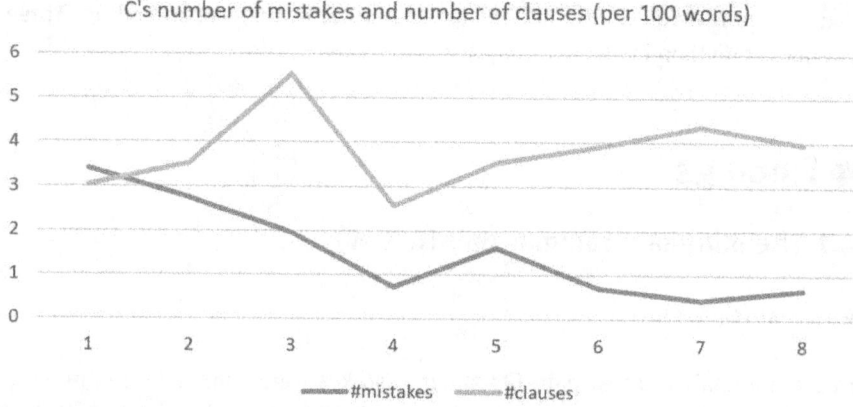

Figure 3: Comparing C's number of sentential errors with the number of dependent clauses.

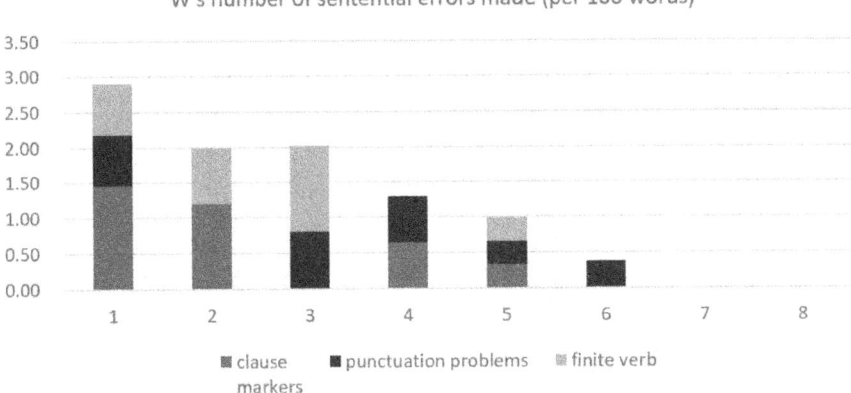

Figure 4: Number of sentential errors made by W.

4.1.2 Participant W

Rather similarly, the major mistakes of W were absences of a clause marker (e.g. *There are a lot of crime of rape ∧ were happen in a city*.) and missing a finite verb in dependent clauses (e.g. **You no need to worry about eating.*) (see Figure 4). Fragmented or run-on sentences were not a big problem for W. There were basically no sentential mistakes recorded in the 7th and 8th writing. One verb-missing problem was noted in the 6th essay (**That ∧ the reason why we need to keep fit.*), but it did not show pattern with her other mistakes. Similar to C, there was no obvious increase (nor decrease) in the use of dependent clauses, but the error rate reduced steadily (see Figure 5).

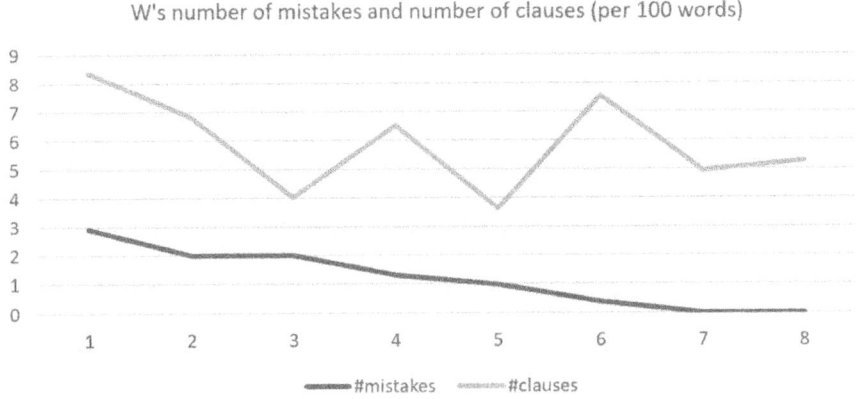

Figure 5: Comparing W's number of sentential errors with the number of dependent clauses.

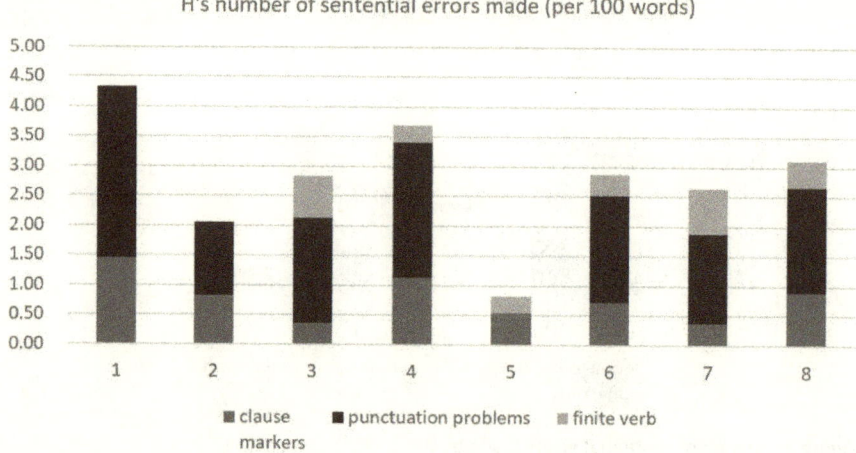

Figure 6: Number of sentential errors made by H.

4.2 The categorization pair (H & S)

4.2.1 Participant H

The categorization pair, on the other hand, did not observe such an improvement pattern (see Figure 6). For H, absence of clause markers (e.g. * ∧ *We make a friend in the Internet must be careful.*) and overuse of clause markers (e.g. **For the elders and for the young, so please help to think of those population.*) were observed. Run-on sentences were predominant (e.g. **She changed in my study ways, I learned more things in her.*), which persisted until the final piece of writing. Basically, the more run-on sentences H committed, the less complex sentences she used (see Figure 7). Overall, H committed more sentential errors than all other participants.

4.2.2 Participant S

Participant S also exhibited a great number of run-on sentence mistakes (e.g. **You may hear this from family, adult or TV program, in fact, there are too many bad men around us.*), and similar to H, there was no clear sign of such errors reducing in later essays (see Figure 8). Improvement was observed with the use of clause markers since the 2nd essay. However, absence of finite verbs in the matrix clause (e.g. **we will shopping or watching TV.*) and dependent clause

Improving English as a foreign language learners' — 83

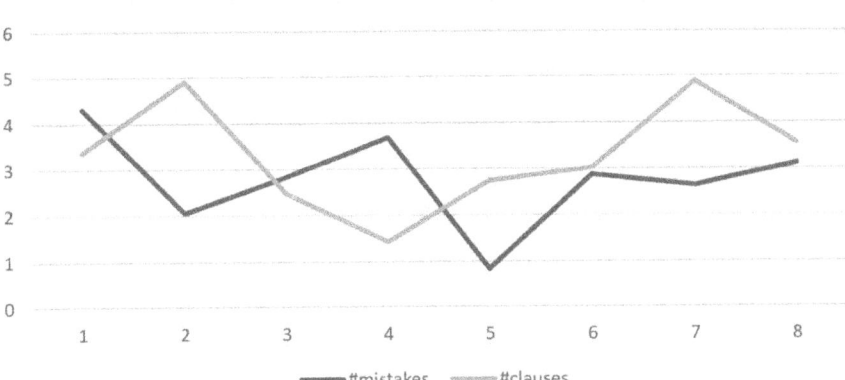

Figure 7: Comparing H's number of sentential errors with the number of dependent clauses.

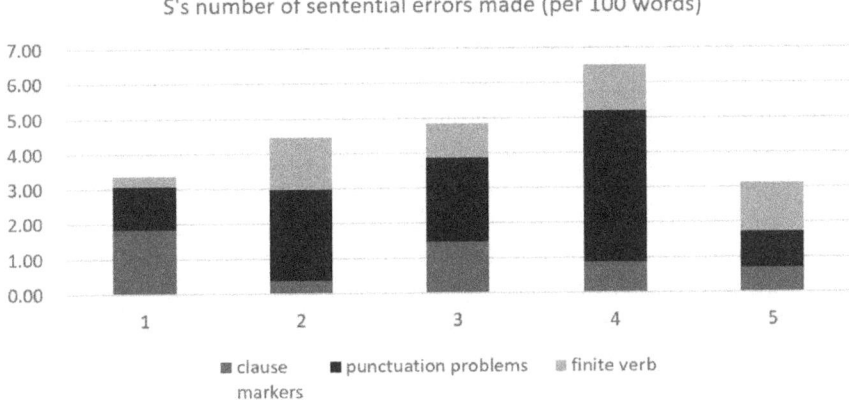

Figure 8: Number of sentential errors made by S.

(e.g. *If many people ˄ in the city, the car or bus quanlity will increase too.*) persisted till the final (i.e. 5th) essay. Also, less use of dependent clauses (see Figure 9) came along with more run-on sentences, as observed in the 2nd and 4th essays.

The most number of ACs and the least number of RCs were recorded. The four participants consistently used the most number of ACs and the least number of RCs. However, the error rate goes exactly the other way round, with RC the most problematic whereas AC the least. These patterns were observed in each participant without exception (see Table 4). Error-wise, clause marker mistakes appeared almost equally among the three clause types. Although punctuation problems were the most frequently occurring error, only a relatively small

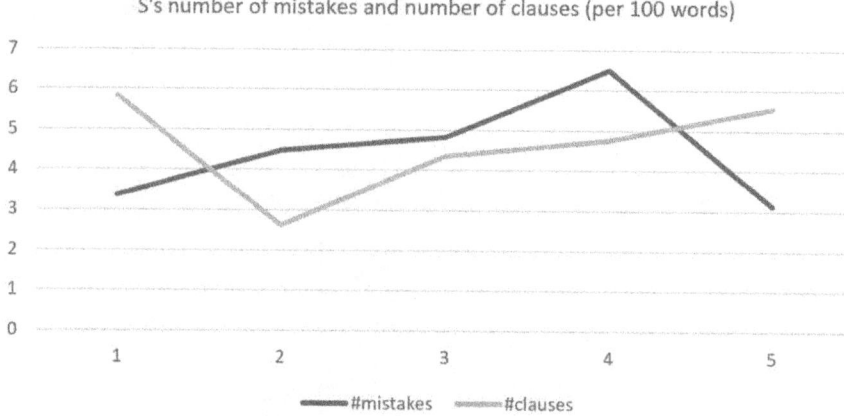

Figure 9: Comparing S's number of sentential errors with the number of dependent clauses.

Table 4: Number of dependent clauses written and error rates.

Participant	Clause type	#clauses	% errors	Sample sentences
C	Adverbial	46	6.5%	*You can know what your friends are doing at first time such as you are beside them.
	Nominal	25	12%	*Let's see what other benefits that it would take.
	Relative	14	14.3%	*There are a great number of travelers come to Macau.
W	Adverbial	61	3.3%	*Although someone said we can't kill a life but we should think about the mother first.
	Nominal	47	8.5%	*I think a good place to live means a city can make us convinient to go anywhere.
	Relative	21	23.8%	*It is because there are no woman will use the heart or love to look after a baby.
H	Adverbial	48	10.4%	*If the company keeping producing these bottled water and the customers will keep on buying them . . .
	Nominal	15	26.7%	* . . . I think make a lot of friends is a meaningful things.
	Relative	12	58.3%	* . . . there are many electrical devices are produced.

Table 4 (continued)

Participant	Clause type	#clauses	% errors	Sample sentences
S	Adverbial	29	24.1%	*When my family at home, we will shopping or watching TV . . .
	Nominal	27	25.9%	*. . . that mean give the knowledge to their future to change their live.
	Relative	8	37.5%	*Nowadays, Macau is a small village become a busy city . . .

percentage were related to ACs with the rest not being registered in complex clause structures. Likewise, finite-verb errors were mostly related to ACs, but were occasionally observed in NCs and RCs (see Table 5).

Table 5: Types, number and percentages of errors.

Error type		# errors	% ACerrors	%NC errors	%RC errors	Sample sentences
Clause marker	Missing					*. . . there is nothing ∧ is totally good for us. (C)
	misused	54	37%	29.6%	33.3%	*It would have more opportunity . . . to announce something what you hope others know. (C)
	Doubled					*Although we are always been advised some truth but human curious make us forget . . . (S)
Punctuation	run-on	87	18%	1.1%	5.7%	*I think to study music except increase our endurance and confidence, it can also make us relax ourselves. (W)
	fragmented					*If everyone keeps on opening the air-conditioner. (H)
Finite verb	Missing					*. . . the boss raise their selary when their business done well. (C)
	misused	39	28.2%	7.6%	7.6%	*In this case, how do we protect these women is legalise the abortion. (W)
	Doubled					*. . . our parents will be feel despair with us is a must. (H)

5 Discussion of findings

All four participants attempted to write complex sentences since the first session but all started out being highly inaccurate. Subsequent writings showed neither instructional methods in the experiment yielded more use of complex sentences/dependent clauses. Students only used clauses that they were very familiar with, but not the ones taught in the sessions. For instance, following the design of the grammar books, non-defining relative clauses and the possessive relative pronoun *whose* were extensively taught and drilled, but H and S did not use any of the structures. Likewise, adverbial clause markers such as *in order that, for fear that* were trained in gap-fill and sentence-combining exercises, but they were never seen in students' writing. What seems to affect students' use of complex sentences is their own strategies; apart from using adverbial clauses, H and S used commas (,) to denote some sort of relationship between two sentences (e.g. **The environment is also very bad, mosquito fly together*). Despite the teacher's effort to continually point out the run-on sentence mistakes, students still failed to prevent a lot of run-on sentence errors when they wrote. This echoes Truscott's (1996) proposition that corrective feedback per se is helpful in a limited way. However, I suspect the main reason for the ineffectiveness was H and S did not grasp a memorable and concise rule of punctuation (Krashen 1982). That is, they should refer to the finite verb and clause marker when deciding if a segment is a sentence or a clause. Contrarily, C and W were able to verbalize a rule such as "one finite verb, no clause marker, so it's a complete sentence"; hence, C and W barely committed any punctuation errors in subsequent writings. Overall results suggest a possibility that instruction on finite verbs and clause markers is more effective in helping learners to produce legal complex sentences than the teaching of AC, NC and RC clause types and subtypes.

Although most punctuation errors were recorded, only a small proportion of them resulted from attempts to write complex sentences, and the mistakes were all fragmented sentences (e.g. **So that we have not to waste any chance we have.*). The majority of complex sentence errors recorded were clause marker problems, with missing clause markers most prevalent (e.g. ** . . . there is nothing ∧ is totally good for us.*). This can be explained in terms of participants' L1. Thus, it is suggested that teachers explain this structural difference between Chinese and English complex sentences before following the detailed explanations of English clause structures offered in textbooks, because the explanations may not be relevant to students' understanding of how complex sentences are formed. Further, the shallow discussion of a wide variety of clause markers in coursebooks are perhaps minimally conducive to learners' writing because 1. lower-intermediate EFL learners would only employ a limited number of clause markers (e.g. *but, when, because, if, which, that*) in writing because they have not received enough input of other markers (e.g. *in case, despite, where*) (Krashen 1982) apart from the few examples provided in textbooks. 2. Cantonese EFL learners seldom use a wrong clause marker in a dependent clause. In the data, only three cases of misused clause marker were noted (e.g. * . . . *announce something what you hope others know.*). Thus, it is suggested that teachers only use the textbook explanations to raise students' awareness of existing markers but do not strictly follow the extensive drilling of them. Some of the exercises provided in textbooks should be reserved for a later stage of learners.

Apparently, these all boil down to the design of coursebooks, which the author deems not too helpful to both teachers and Cantonese speaking students. For instance, in the current data RCs are the least used in writing but the most error-riddled. Although textbooks tend to contain a number of chapters on RC (e.g. Eastwood 2008; Murphy 2012), their focus is typically on choosing the correct RC marker instead of developing students' understanding of when and why an RC marker is needed in a sentence. On the other hand, NCs employed more often in student writing but most grammar coursebooks reviewed rarely discussed them. At first glance, the data might misguide readers into thinking NCs are less problematic than RCs. However, a closer look will reveal that only NCs that involve epistemic verbs are typically grammatical (e.g. *Some people think students should focus on their study.*) because the clause marker *that* is optional. As it is non-existent in Chinese, the majority of NCs used as subjects, objects, or complements were illegally structured. In other words, NCs can be equally, if not more, problematic than RCs. Last but not least, mistakes related to finite verbs are another major source of sentential errors. Specifically, absence of a matrix verb (e.g. * . . . *doctor will ∧ far away.*) and wrong use of finite or non-finite verbs (e.g. **The poor people living in urban areas.*) were prevalent. Unfortunately, verb finiteness is hardly a topic of discussion in grammar books. All in all, grammar coursebooks do not seem to address EFL students' needs or weaknesses in writing.

Teachers are therefore suggested to design materials and exercises specific to students' writing needs. A good place to begin with is to compare complex sentence structures between students' L1 and the target language. Verb finiteness and why a clause marker is necessary in a secondary clause in English are also topics worth spending time on. I do not deny that there is a need to teach students the use of a wide variety of connecting words, but this should be deferred to a later stage when students have a larger repertoire of complex sentences.

6 Conclusion

This article discusses the traditional classification of dependent clauses and how it is adopted in EFL teaching in Macao. The author argues that secondary schools in Macao do not necessarily have to follow the classification; what is much less necessary is to train lower-intermediate students to distinguish the subtypes of dependent clauses. Instead, teachers are advised to instruct the commonalities among different dependent clauses, namely, "clause markers" and "finite verbs". Reducing highly complicated topics such as dependent clauses into simple and memorable concepts should be an objective of grammar instruction (Pica 1985).

Evidence from the current study also suggests without knowledge of what a finite verb is and how it constitutes a clause, the teaching of different complex structures will not facilitate correct formation of sentences. Neither will the teaching of new structures guarantee their use in students' writing. The author suspects that learners may not want to risk making mistakes or they do not feel comfortable applying newly acquired structures, a sign taken to support Krashen's (1985) input hypothesis. That is, students have to come across a structure multiple times before they actually produce it, whereas instruction alone cannot enhance production. When students' mistakes were compared with the controlled exercises in coursebooks, a mismatch was found. The grammar coursebooks can undoubtedly raise students' awareness of certain structures, which can potentially be helpful to students' comprehension of a text or an audio recording. However, they may not be able to improve students' writing abilities. A grammar coursebook that targets EFL writing should consider learners' L1 interference, language stage, and place emphasis on structures that learners are likely to use erroneously.

As a final remark, the results obtained from the current study should not be overgeneralized due to its qualitative nature. The main objective of the study was to suggest, with experimental evidence, a minimal grammar instruction method to introduce complex sentence structures, so that students can more effectively apply their knowledge in writing. Future studies can employ a quantitative measurement across different secondary schools in Macao (e.g. English-medium, Chinese-medium, and international schools) to give a more comprehensive insight into students' written errors and how EFL teachers approach them. Furthermore, EFL writing researchers could view dependent clauses as an integrated unit of investigation when examining learner's writing or teachers' instruction.

References

Bardovi-Harlig, Kathleen. & Theodora Bofman. 1989. Attainment of syntactic and morphological accuracy by advanced language learners. *Studies in Second Language Acquisition* 11(1). 17–34.

Chan, Angel, Wenchun Yang, Franklin Chang & Evan Kidd. 2018. Four-year-old Cantonese-speaking children's online processing of relative clauses: a permutation analysis. *Journal of child language*, 45(1). 174–203.

Chan, Alice Y. W. 2010. Toward a taxonomy of written errors: Investigation into the written errors of Hong Kong Cantonese ESL learners. *TESOL Quarterly*, 44(2). 295–319.

Chuang, Fei-Yu & Hillary Nesi. 2006. An analysis of formal errors in a corpus of L2 English produced by Chinese students. *Corpora*, 1(2). 251–271.

Collins, Peter & Jackie J. F. Lee. (2005). English grammar in current Hong Kong textbooks: A critical appraisal. *TESL Reporter*, 38(2). 37–49.

DeCapua, Andrea. 2008. *Grammar for Teachers: A Guide to American English for Native and Non-Native Speakers*. US: Springer-Verlag.

Eastwood, John. 2008. *Oxford Practice Grammar Intermediate*. Hong Kong: OUP Oxford.

Eckman, Fred R., Lawrence Bell & Diane Nelson. 1988. On the Generalization of Relative Clause Instruction in the Acquisition of English as a Second Language1. *Applied Linguistics*, 9(1). 1–20.

Ellis, Rod. 2006. Current issues in the teaching of grammar: An SLA perspective. *TESOL Quarterly*, 40(1). 83–107.

Ellis, Rod & Fangyuan Yuan. 2004. The effects of planning on fluency, complexity, and accuracy in second language narrative writing. *Studies in second Language acquisition* 26(1). 59–84.

Fuchs, Marjorie, & Margaret Bonner. 2007. *Grammar Express (with answers) (For Self-Study and Classroom Use)*. Hong Kong: Pearson Longman.

Gray, Ronald. 2004. Grammar correction in ESL/EFL writing classes may not be effective. *The Internet TESL Journal*, 10 (11). http://iteslj.org/Techniques/Gray-WritingCorrection.html (accessed 12 June 2020).

Harris, C. 2013. *Certificate English Usage Fifth Edition*. Hong Kong: Aristo Education Press Ltd.

Housen, Alex, Michel Pierrard & Siska Van Daele. 2005. Structure complexity and the efficacy of explicit grammar instruction. In Alex Housen & Michel Pierrard (eds). *Investigations in instructed second language acquisition* 235–269. New York: Mouton de Gruyter.

Huang, James C. T., Audrey Y. H. Li & Yafei Li. 2009. *The syntax of Chinese*. Cambridge: Cambridge University Press.

Hunt, Kellogg W. 1965. *Grammatical structures written at three grade levels (No. 3)*. Champaign, IL: National Council of Teachers of English.

Kirjavainen, Minna, Evan Kidd & Elena Lieven. 2017. How do language-specific characteristics affect the acquisition of different relative clause types? Evidence from Finnish. *Journal of child language*, 44(1). 120–157.

Krashen, Stephen. 1982. *Principles and practice in second language acquisition*. New York: Pergamon Press Inc.

Krashen, Stephen. 1985. *The input hypothesis: Issues and implications*. CA: Laredo.

Xu, Liejiong & Terence D. Langendoen. 1985. Topic structures in Chinese. *Language*, 61(1). 1–27.

Liu, Yali. 2014. English Subordinators in Finite Clause: Definition and Classification. *International Journal of English Linguistics*, 4(4). 55.

Lu, Xiaofei. 2011. A corpus-based evaluation of syntactic complexity measures as indices of college-level ESL writers' language development. *TESOL Quarterly*, 45(1). 36–62.

Murphy, Raymond. 2012. *English Grammar in Use – Fourth Edition*. Hong Kong: Cambridge University Press.

Payne, Thomas E. & Thomas Edward Payne. 2010. *Understanding English grammar: a linguistic introduction*. London: Cambridge University Press.

Pica, Teresa. 1985. The selective impact of classroom instruction on second-language acquisition. *Applied Linguistics*, 6(3). 214–222.

Polio, Charlene G. 1997. Measures of linguistic accuracy in second language writing research. *Language learning*, 47(1). 101–143.

Radford, Andrew. 2009. *English sentence structure*. London: Cambridge University Press.

Reber, Arthur S. 1989. Implicit learning and tacit knowledge. *Journal of Experimental Psychology: General*, 118. 219–235.

Robinson, Peter. 1996. Learning simple and complex second language rules under implicit, incidental, rule-search, and instructed conditions. *Studies in Second Language Acquisition*, 18(1). 27–67.

Robinson, Peter. 2010. Implicit artificial grammar and incidental natural second language learning: How comparable are they?. *Language Learning*, 60. 245–263.

Schoenberg, Irene & Jay Maurer. 2011. *Focus on Grammar 5 (4th Edition)*. Hong Kong: Pearson.

Storch, Neomy. 2005. Collaborative writing: Product, process, and students' reflections. *Journal of second language writing*, 14(3). 153–173.

Truscott, John. 1996. The case against grammar correction in L2 writing classes. *Language learning*, 46(2). 327–369.

Vann, Roberta J. Daisy E. Meyer & Frederick O. Lorenz. 1984. Error gravity: A study of faculty opinion of ESL errors. *TESOL Quarterly*, 18(3). 427–440.

Way, Denise Paige, Elizabeth G. Joiner & Michael A. Seaman. 2000. Writing in the secondary foreign language classroom: The effects of prompts and tasks on novice learners of French. *The Modern Language Journal*, 84(2). 171–184.

White, Lydia. 1991. Adverb placement in second language acquisition: Some effects of positive and negative evidence in the classroom. *Interlanguage studies bulletin (Utrecht)*, 7(2). 133–161.

Xin, Guangwei. 2010. *Publishing in China: An Essential Guide*. Singapore: Cengage Learning Asia Ltd.

Melissa H. Yu

A pedagogical inquiry into students' writing skills development from the perspective of English as a lingua franca: Insights from secondary and tertiary English language education in Taiwan

Abstract: Albeit numerous studies have explored various subjects within the theoretical framework of English as a lingua franca (ELF), little research literature has considered mainstream four-skills (listening, speaking, reading and writing) teaching and learning in connection to ELF. In addition, most ELF literature has discussed listening and/or speaking rather than writing. These exiting studies have not answered queries about whether local curriculums and materials support writing training for international communication, whether students have such learning needs, and what the current writing training is for international communication. To answer these questions two questionnaire surveys and six interviews with teachers were conducted to explore how English language educational provisions help students develop writing skills for international communication. The results indicated that school and university curriculums, learning materials, and teaching were not necessarily communication-oriented or writing skills focused. Writing skills development was not students' only learning priority. Although a non-normative approach was applied to realise writing skills training for communication, training of this kind has remained a minor pedagogical concern. The implications for research and pedagogy are the analysis of the contextual factors that steer the orientations of English language education, multiple perspectives on planning and implementing ELF writing training, and actual teaching and learning for international communication.

Keywords: English as a lingua franca, writing skills, secondary English language education, university English language curriculum

Melissa H. Yu, University of Macau

https://doi.org/10.1515/9781501512643-005

1 Introduction

A number of studies have discussed the use of English for international communication in several professional domains. For instance, in Taiwan, the reviewed literature recognises that the English language plays the role of a lingua franca in engineering (e.g. Spence and Liu 2013), administration (Reynolds and Yu 2018), and nursing care (e.g. Bosher and Stocker 2015) industries. At the same time, the use of English for international communication poses challenges to the established English language education in the contexts in which English is taught and learned as a foreign language. For instance, the English as a lingua franca (ELF) phenomenon questions certain assumptions about TESOL (Teaching English to Speakers of Other Language) practices for communication, such as the native-speaking (NS) normative approach to teaching and learning English (Jenkins 2012). Against this backdrop, myriads of studies have been conducted with the findings carrying implications and providing suggestions for pedagogical innovations (e.g. Galloway and Rose 2014, 2018) and teacher preparation programme development (e.g. Bayyurt and Sifakis, 2015a, 2016b; Bayyurt and Kaçar 2018). The main value of these studies lies in the potential to stimulate curriculum gatekeepers and TESOL practitioners to rethink whether the ELF perspective has been integrated into the established curriculums or affects what is taught.

From the literature reviewed above, it is apparent that researchers from different fields of Applied Linguistics have made considerable contributions to the pedagogical ideas related to international communication. However, according to Jenkins's (2018:65) observation, "the English language education establishment has not so far caught up with global developments in English and continues to teach this lingua franca as if it was still primarily a traditional foreign language." Jenkins's comment was the motivation herein to understand what teachers choose to teach to help students communicate and how they do so. In other words, if we as ELF or TESOL researchers examine whether any proposed pedagogical innovation takes place or suggestion is taken, we need to acquire an understanding of whether the school or university curriculums have created a pedagogical context in which the ELF teaching and learning ideas can be developed and realised. The lack of teaching context analysis may devalue the proposed ideas of teaching English from the perspective of ELF. This can only be accomplished by collecting and analysing data on the university/school curriculum and the extent to which the said curriculum supports communicative teaching/learning. As Nunan (1990) suggests, communicative curriculum requires re-evaluation in terms of whether the curriculum addresses students' language needs and learning outcomes. So, only by scrutinising school/university curriculums can we begin to propose and encourage context-wise pedagogical innovations from an ELF perspective or suggest any ELF-related teaching ideas which consider classroom realities.

2 Literature review

While it is true to say that scholars have adopted a variable approach to considering the issues of teaching and learning English to communicate internationally, difficulties in incorporating the ELF perspective into TESOL practices may or may not be solved. For instance, one of the difficulties is whether TESOL teacher training programmes have offered the TESOL professionals training about how to plan and realise ELF-wise teaching. In fact, Matsuda (2009) identified that rather few pre-service teachers recognised the necessity to introduce the concepts of English as an international language (EIL) or World Englishes (WE) in established TESOL teacher training programmes. ELF-wise pre-service teacher training is still developing (Dewey 2012). Thus, it is likely that ELF-wise teacher training has not yet been widely implemented globally across TESOL programmes. Despite the ELF-wise TESOL programmes in Greek and Turkish contexts marking the beginning of ELF as an innovative perspective or alternative pedagogical route to prepare pre-service teachers for ELF classroom practice (e.g. Bayyurt and Sifakis, 2015a, 2015b; Bayyurt and Kaçar 2018), the development of these kinds of teacher training courses is still at the planning or early stage. Following this, the existing ELF teacher training courses may not be available to all pre-service teachers. Under this circumstance, it is likely that the majority of in-service teachers will have insufficient training to support them in developing ideas of teaching English from an ELF perspective and putting the ideas into practice.

Despite this being so, insufficient ELF teacher training may or may not equate to no ELF-oriented teaching or teachers' lack of intention to teach English language skills for international communication. With the concepts of ELF in mind, a decade ago, Taiwanese university English language teachers felt ambivalent towards teaching English as an international language (Lai 2008) and more recently, university teachers took mixed attitudes towards introducing concepts of English as an international language (EIL) to undergraduates (Luo 2017), suggesting the conceptual shifts of teachers' belief in teaching English from a traditional to an ELF perspective. Curran and Chern's (2017: 143) study confirm the mentioned conceptual shift, reporting that pre-service teachers with different academic backgrounds and intern teachers aligned with the concepts of ELF or WE, such as "different varieties of English should be respected and introduced to students." However, these studies focused more on whether English language teachers aligned with the concepts of ELF or WE and which ideas of teaching should be introduced to classroom practice from an ELF perspective. So far, very few studies have investigated in-service teachers' pedagogical decisions and whether the curriculum and learning materials supported them in achieving these decisions. As Seidlhofer (2004) discussed, integrating an ELF perspective into teaching will become difficult if there is no support from the curriculum and materials.

This highlights the value of research to identify whether in-service teachers set out to teach English for international communication, and how they relate such a pedagogical choice and ideas of teaching to students' writing skills development. To understand teachers' ideas of teaching, teachers' narratives should be highly valued because much of the theoretical/practical teaching knowledge "is often expressed in the narrative mode of anecdotes and stories" (Tsui, 2012: 17) in "a particular learning and teaching situation" (Kumaravadivelu, 2012: 22). Also, teachers' narratives about students' learning are important because "an insider (a practicing teacher, for instance) may have a better idea about the linguistic needs" (Kumaravadivelu, 2012: 40) of students. The methodological implication for this study is the need to conduct interviews to illuminate teachers' insider perspectives on how writing skills should be developed, in order to provide useful implications for planning suitable courses that directly address students' language needs. In particular, the interviews with teachers should focus on the examples of teaching writing and teachers' elaboration on the underlying teaching principles to encourage or discourage teaching and learning writing for international communication.

Another difficulty to incorporate the ELF perspective into pedagogy is Taiwanese EFL teachers' uncertainty about whether students aim to learn four skills for international communication. As Luo (2017) identified, teachers took mixed attitudes towards introducing the concepts of English as an international language to students because teachers were uncertain about whether students have such needs. The same may hold true to teaching students English for international communication. This means if Taiwanese students do not aim to learn English for communication, there will be little pedagogical significance to discuss how English language education develops students' writing for communication. In addition, students' needs in developing language skills should not be analysed solely from the teachers' perspectives. Any pedagogical ideas about enhancing students' English for international communication may need a "clear understanding of learners' perspectives" (Sung, 2015: 200). The implication for this study is to understand whether Taiwanese EFL students have communicative language learning needs and how the curriculums prepare them for writing to communicate.

To address the concerns discussed above, four research questions were formulated.
1. How do Taiwanese EFL students perceive learning English for international communication?
2. How are Taiwanese EFL students writing skills developed through English language education?
3. How do the available materials and university curriculum support Taiwanese EFL students' writing skills development?
4. How do teachers develop Taiwanese EFL students' writing skills for communication?

3 Methodology

To answer the research questions, a qualitative TESOL inquiry was carried out. The following is a discussion of research contexts, participants, research design, data analysis, and data collection.

3.1 Research contexts and participants

Six Taiwanese teachers joined this study. Among them, only one teacher taught the first year and second year English majors Oral Training and Composition I & II in University 1 (U1, henceforth); the others taught non-English majors the Freshmen English Courses at University 2 (U2, henceforth) and University 3 (U3, henceforth). All of the teachers had 5–10 years of experience in teaching different English language courses in Taiwanese EFL contexts. Teacher 1 (T1, henceforth) in U1 had ESL (English as a second language) experience in the United States.

Oral Training and Composition I (OTCI, henceforth) & II (OTCII, henceforth) in U1 were two six-credit hours speaking & L2 Writing courses for the first-year and the second-year English majors. Three hours of OTCI or OTCII were used to develop students' speaking every week, another three hours to foster students' writing skills. The Freshmen English Course was also a three-credit hours course for all freshmen whose major was not English. The Freshmen English Course gave students general English training which permitted teachers freedom to decide what to teach, including whether or not to develop students' writing skills.

One hundred and ninety undergraduates were also recruited as participants based on the researcher's access to these students' teachers. However, ten of them were international students. Therefore, this study only analysed one hundred and eighty-one Taiwanese students' secondary and tertiary English language learning so only one hundred and eighty Taiwanese students' responses to a questionnaire were analysed. Only twenty-five of the student participants were first-year and second-year English majors in U1. The majority were non-English majors studying 41 programmes from 12 faculties in U2 and U3. Appendix A provides further information about student participants' professional studies. Table 1 summarises the demographic information of the teacher and student participants.

Table 1: The demographic information of teacher and student participants.

U1	U2	U3
1 teacher	4 teachers	1 teacher
25 students	125 students	30 students
First- and second-year undergraduates	First-year undergraduates	First-year undergraduates
Students from one department	Students from thirty-one department/programmes of nine faculties	Students from ten departments/programmes of three faculties
English Majors	Non English Majors	Non English Majors
Oral Training & Composition 1 & 2	Freshman English	Freshmen English

3.2 Research design, data collection, and data analysis

Convenience sampling was employed to recruit participants through the researcher's access to the faculty members as well as teachers. Instead of sampling high school students to participate in this study, a questionnaire survey was carried out to explore undergraduates' learning experience because they had completed the compulsory English language education in Taiwan. So, the undergraduates rather than high schools students were in a better position to summarise and compare the English language learning experience at the secondary and tertiary levels.

One hundred eighty-one undergraduates responded to the questionnaire about four skills development for international communication based on their secondary and tertiary English language learning experience (see Appendix B).

The student questionnaire was made up of Section A and Section B. Questions in Section A aimed to understand student participants' linguistic and English language educational backgrounds. Some information obtained from Section A was used and presented as a part of contextual analysis in section 3.1. Other information was used to identify whether participants had completed secondary English language education in Taiwan. This information was deemed important for this study as it helped the researcher to decide whether participants' answers to questions in Section B could be used to discuss how Taiwanese secondary English language education developed students' writing skills for international communication (Research Question 1 and 2). For instance, international students' responses were not considered because their secondary English language educational experience was not related to English language education in Taiwan. In Section B, the questions were asked mainly to explore students' learning goals and their perception of which English language skills should be prioritised for international communication. Student participants' answers to questions in Section B of the Student Questionnaire were mainly used to answer research question 1 and 2.

Six teachers completed the questionnaire survey; the questionnaire centred on teaching goals, curriculum, materials, and experience in teaching writing. The Teacher Questionnaire was also made up of two sections (Section A and Section B). In Section A, questions were asked to understand teachers' linguistic and educational background, forming a part of the contextual analysis (see section 3.1). Section B consists of six questions addressing the pedagogical concerns about what materials teachers selected for teaching English language skills for international communication, what materials and principles supported teaching English for international communication, and what teaching objectives were set. Teachers' responses to these questions were analysed and drawn on to answer research questions 2, 3, and 4.

Six interviews with teachers were carried in the Chinese language. Appendix C provides the interview questions. Verbatim transcription of interviews was carried out and the transcripts were translated from Chinese to English. Appendix D outlines the transcription conventions and how pseudonyms were deployed to represent teachers and students. The interview data was used to answer research question 3 and 4.

Drawing on Richie, Spencer, and O'Connor (2003) thematic analysis framework, two questionnaires, six interviews, and the teaching activities were anslysed and coded. The steps to carry out thematic content analysis were familiarising the researcher with the transcripts through reading, using the original themes of the questionnaire, interview questions, and literature review to establish the coding framework, labelling the topics within the thematic coding framework, charting the themes by selecting and regrouping the labelled categories and subcategories, and mapping and interpreting the themes in relation to the perspectives of students in order to answer research questions 1 and 2 and those of teachers to address research questions 2, 3, and 4. Four themes emerged from the analysis of the student and teacher questionnaire data. Interview data were coded accordingly, including communicative learning, four-skills English language training, the school/university curriculums, and the goals of teaching and learning.

In this study, the results of analysing classroom observational data were used as the supporting evidence on writing-related learning activities. This methodological decision was made based on the intention of this study to understand how teachers related their ideas of teaching writing to their actual teaching.

4 Findings and discussion

4.1 Communicative learning and teaching

While approximately 90% (*n*=162) of undergraduates pointed out that the secondary English language educational provisions focused on examination preparation, about 20% (*n*=37) of students learned English for communication and 13% (*n*=23) for access to information. After completing their secondary education, about 67% (*n*=122) of the undergraduates prioritised learning English for communication; about 53% (*n*=96) and 47% (*n*=85) of them identified learning English to prepare for examinations and to access information, respectively. Other reasons for learning English were also mentioned, such as career development and studying abroad. Table 2 illustrates the percentage shifts in students' learning objectives under the secondary and tertiary English language educational systems in Taiwan.

Table 2: Students' English language learning goals at secondary schools and universities.

Educational Level	Communication	Examination	Access to information
Secondary	21%	90%	13%
Tertiary	67%	53%	47%

As Table 2 illustrates, the shifts in percentage confirmed the communication-oriented learning at universities although about 34% of students (*n*=61) still aimed to learn English for examination and access to information. Among the 122 undergraduates who identified that English for communication was their learning goal, 68% ($n=83$) wanted to learn English for communication together with other purposes, while less than 25% ($n=30$) wanted to learn English solely for communication. The finding shows that the majority of students aimed at communication-oriented English language learning, not communication-only English language acquisition. In other words, learning English for communication was the learning purpose for most undergraduates but not necessarily their only learning purpose. If students' purposes of learning English were multidirectional, students may not give full attention to ELF-wise learning even though the ELF-wise language training was available. So, when ELF-wise learning was not students' learning target or priority, the pedagogical paradigmatic shifts from traditional EFL towards ELF may become rather slow, as Jenkins (2012, 2018) observed or less focused as the finding revealed.

The results also showed that secondary English language learning was examination-focused and English language learning became more communication-oriented at universities than at the secondary schools. So, university students' communicative language learning needs yielded more space for ELF-wise learning at tertiary than secondary levels. However, for most students, learning English at universities was not only for communication but also for other purposes. In this situation, ELF-learning may only constitute a small part of their learning. Therefore, the value of introducing ELF-wise teaching and learning may be minimised, depending on students' learning goals and priorities. This finding supported Nunan's (1990) and Sung's (2015) argument for the importance to understand students' learning needs, such as "what they want to learn and how they want to learn it" (Nunan, 1990: 18) and "learners' perspectives" (Sung, 2015:200) on ELF-wise pedagogy prior developing any communication-related courses.

The analysis of the teacher questionnaires indicated that five out of six teachers aimed to teach students English for communication. T1's teaching was purely communication-focused. For instance, she said, "I hope they can use English to think and to communicate comfortably in their future workplaces or study." In contrast, T2 indicated that "the ultimate goal of my teaching is to cultivate their interests in English." Most of the teachers mentioned that they taught students English for communication as well as for other purposes, such as for students' further study and job requirements. So, English language teaching in universities was communication-related although teachers also taught English for other purposes. The finding that most teachers set out to teach students English for international communication contradicted the results of Lai's (2008) study, pointing to university teachers' hesitation about teaching English for international communication. The finding that teachers took positive attitudes towards teaching English for international communication echoes that of Curran and Chern's (2017) study on pre-/in-service teachers' attitudes towards the concept of ELF.

As indicated, students' English language acquisition became more communication-related at the tertiary level compared to the secondary level. However, in universities, students learned English for communication together with other purposes. Put simply, when students began studying at universities, they did not necessarily learn English for examinations at the expense of communication. In addition, the results suggest that English language teaching at universities supported students to learn English language skills for communication because most teachers aimed to teach students English for communication. The university learning circumstances encouraged ELF-wise pedagogy.

4.2 Four-skills English language training

When students were asked which language skills teaching that they have experienced, the results showed that the top three teaching priorities in secondary English language education were prescribed grammar, vocabulary, and English language usage and expressions in textbooks. Only 33% ($n=59$) of the respondents indicated that the four basic skills were often taught to them; reading skills, not the other three skills, were prioritised. When undergraduates were asked about their needs in learning English to be communicative in universities, about 56% ($n=101$) indicated that they needed to improve their speaking skills and 31% ($n=56$) said their listening skills. Only about 4% ($n=7$) identified that writing skills development was essential for them to be communicative.

These students' secondary English language education experience shows that schools provided students with rather little educational support to develop writing skills. Since students claimed their secondary English language learning was not communication-oriented, it is reasonable to say the students received inadequate English language education to develop writing skills to communicate internationally. The results also indicated that most of students (96%) did not prioritise learning writing for communication. In this case, even though Taiwanese EFL students aim to learn English for communication at universities, most students' learning focus was not writing for international communication. The above results showed the loose link between students' English language learning experience and priorities and developing writing skills for international communication at secondary as well as tertiary levels. A similar finding was identified in the analysis of the teacher questionnaire survey.

When teachers identified the most fundamental teaching principle(s) to strengthen students' communicative competence, they mentioned how students' communicative competence can be enhanced through developing certain language skills. Table 3 illustrates six teachers' teaching principles to support their points.

Table 3: Teachers' main teaching principle(s) to develop students' communicative competence.

T1	Provide them with an authentic context for **speaking**. The topics discussed should be related to their lives or current engagements. That way, they can become more actively engaged in the context.
T2	To encourage students to **speak**, not to be afraid of making mistakes
T3	Help students know what to **speak** and how to **speak**, how to communicate beyond the scope of prescribed grammar, and how to express their ideas.
T4	**Listening and speaking**
T5	**Listening** comprehension, more chances to **speak**
T6	Pair/group work; **Listening** strategies, communicative strategies

As can be seen, the six teachers tended to associate enhancing speaking and/or listening skills with developing communicative competence. In this case, there was a lack of linkage between writing skills development and the main teaching theories to support communicative competence development, although the weak link as such did not equate to insufficient or no writing training.

Overall, very few students received four-skills training when they studied English at secondary schools and the skill-based training at that time was not writing focused either. When students began to study at universities, students prioritised learning speaking and listening skills rather than writing skills for international communication. University teachers also prioritised teaching speaking or listening, not writing skills. In addition, although teachers' and students' goals of teaching and learning created good opportunities to develop an ELF-oriented curriculum/syllabus, several teaching and learning priorities for communicative pedagogy yielded limited space for writing skills training to be developed and realised. So, both teachers' and students' responses to skills-based education presented an imbalanced and narrow perspective on communicative language skills and training, focusing on certain skills only. In other words, the scope through which scholars conceptualise language skills development for international communication, such as Street and Leung's (2012) discussion about literacy skills development from the ELF perspective, appears wider than that through which teacher and student participants in this study conceptualised language skills development for international communication.

4.3 University curriculum and learning materials

During the interviews, teachers pointed out that the university curriculum of U1 and U3 encouraged communication-oriented teaching in contrast with that of U2 (see Table 4). Regarding learning materials, U1 rather than T1 chose a writing-focused textbook for students (see Table 4). T2 and T4 from U2 selected the textbook *Reading Explorer* 3 in compliance with the reading-based university curriculum. By this, T4 said, "The main reason for choosing this (She pointed at the textbook, *Reading Explorer 3*, on the desk) was because the university (i.e., U2) asked teachers to focus on reading skills development.." Instead of choosing a reading-focused textbook, T3 and T5 from U2 chose a four-skills textbook, *American Headway 3*. Regarding this pedagogical choice, T3 expressed, "I want students to practice speaking". According to the communication-based university English language curriculum, T6 from U3 chose "*Smart Choice* 2" to develop students' listening and speaking skills and indicated, "If I want to teach them (i.e., students) reading and writing skills, I will not choose this (textbook)."

Table 4: Textbooks and curriculum.

University	Curriculum Focus	Textbooks	Skills
U1	Communication	Steps to Writing with Additional Readings (Wyrick, 2008).	Writing
U2	Academic Reading Skills	T2 & T4 chose Reading Explorer 3 (Douglas, 2010) T3 & T5 selected American Headway 3 (Soars & Soars, 2019)	Reading Four skills
U3	Communication	T6 selected Smart Choice 2 (Wilson, 2008)	Four skills

It seems that U1 and U3 created teaching contexts which were suitable for teaching English skills for international communication to be developed and realised. Although three out of four teachers in U2 emphasised that they aimed to teach students English for international communication, only two of them chose textbooks which supported their teaching of writing and supported students to learn writing skills. Since the curriculum and textbooks used in U2 focused on students' academic reading rather than writing and communicative skills development, U2's curriculum and learning provided less support for teachers to teach students writing skills for international communication. In a similar vein, students in U2 may have obtained little support from this curriculum to develop writing and communication skills.

When teachers responded to the criteria on which they based their textbook choices, they identified the topics of learning materials as mattering more than the four skills or other language training. For instance, T6 explained that his main principle in choosing textbooks was whether they presented "updated, interesting, and motivating topics and content [that] can generate further discussion." T5 indicated that "students' levels [of English], authenticity [of learning materials], and topics" were criteria for selecting textbooks. Only T3 and T6 considered the four skills when choosing textbooks. During the interviews, teachers claimed available textbooks for English language skills development were writing-focused (T1), reading-focused textbooks (T2 & T4), and four skills textbooks (T3, T5, & T6) (see Table 3). These results show that T1's textbook focused on developing writing skills only and most teachers chose textbooks which were neither writing-focused nor writing-related, suggesting inadequate support from the available textbooks selected by the teachers to develop students' writing skills.

The literature review identified that little research has explored how curriculum or materials supported teachers to carry out ELF-related pedagogy. So far, students' learning priorities, university curriculum, and the selected materials did not necessarily encourage teaching writing skills for international communication. As Yu (2018) has argued, integrating an ELF perspective into teaching was not unconditional. This finding, as Seidlhofer (2004) has previously observed, suggests that if there is little support from curriculum and materials for an ELF-wise pedagogy, putting ELF-related ideas of teaching into practice becomes challenging.

4.4 Teachers perspective on writing skills development

Table 5 presents the evidence on whether teachers taught students writing and how they related writing training to communication.

Table 5 illustrates that not all teachers aimed to develop students' writing skills. T2, T5, and T6 decided not to teach students writing. Their decisions were made based on their assumptions that learning writing increases the

Table 5: Writing skills development: Pedagogical choice & teaching principle.

Teacher	Teachers' Comments on Teaching Writing
T1	"... my research interest is writing, one important theory of teaching writing is 'teacher **diswriting**'(*sic*). [That is] students can become good writers **without teachers' intervention** through **continuous practice,** and practice writing. Eventually, students become writers. So I apply this to oral training. This is also true to oral training that students practise **on their own.** Also, it is a trend for TESOL: not to constantly correct students' mistakes."
T2	"If I want to teach them [students] more, such as grammar or [I hope that] their **writing skills** will be strengthened, etc., my concern is whether these will make learning English less interesting to them anymore? If they [students] become less interested in English, they will stop learning."
T3	"... I taught students how to write a summary based on a paragraph [of reading]. I guided them through the process of how to summarise a paragraph and let students **follow the demonstrated ways to write a summary step by step.** We practiced this **twice. For the final exam,** students were asked to read four paragraphs of reading and summarise what they read. Actually, two of the four paragraphs of reading have been used to teach students how to write a summary and students have practiced writing summaries in my class. Still, they still did not write good summaries **for the final exam.**"
T4	T4 elaborated her rationale for giving students writing training, indicating that "I taught students writing **because they expressed their needs in learning writing in the course evaluation questionnaire.** . . . Since I was going to teach them how to make persuasive speeches, **I integrated writing skills development into this teaching unit.** (.) So, I taught them persuasive writing . . . Not every teacher was willing to teach writing because it took lots of time . . . However, students have had sufficient training in reading and listening during high school. . . . The students wrote sentences, which were not clear and failed to convey the intended meanings. I **presented some students' unclear sentences or paragraphs anonymously to all students, asking them to provide the alternative ways to write with clarity.**"
T5	"This year, **I decided not to teach writing.** I think (.) they [students] have had enough writing skills training. I also wanted my students to know learning English is not just about reading and writing."
T6	"If I want to teach them [students] reading and writing skills, **I will not choose this (textbook).**"

learning load and demotivates students to continue learning English. As T2's response to the questionnaire survey, the "ultimate goal" of his teaching was to make learning English interesting, not teaching writing. T5 claimed that her students have had sufficient writing training and her comment on writing skills training contradicts the findings of the student questionnaire, indicating students' have received insufficient writing skills training. T6 pointed out that writing skills were not the focus of his teaching and the textbooks that he chose did not support him to teach writing either.

The discussion below focuses on T1's, T3's, and T4's reflections on the principles and goals of teaching students writing. T1 emphasised that teachers should avoid intervening and prescribing ways of writing for students to follow. Unlike T1's way to teach writing, T3 taught writing with more intervention by letting students "follow the demonstrated ways to write a summary step by step" (see Table 5). To address students' learning needs in writing skills development, T4 let her students "discuss and outline what to write," each student composed and explored alternatives to convey meaning clearly when students' writing was found not to be clear, as T4 exemplified (Table 5). T4's student-centred approach and T1's "teacher diswriting [sic] approach" to writing skills training were like two sides of the same coin, different carvings, but with the same core nevertheless. As exemplified, T1 and T4 taught writing with less intervention and more opportunities for students to practice and explore alternatives to write, showing a non-normative approach. Their ways to teach writing were beyond the prescriptive perspective on teaching English that Seidlhofer (2011) argues against. Unlike T1 and T4, T3's ideas of teaching writing by prescribing and reinforcing certain ways to write a summary resonate with Matsuda and Matsuda's (2010) observation about the prevalence of the normative approach to teaching writing in EFL contexts.

Besides, T1 emphasised that teachers should not often correct students' spoken as well as written English. For instance, even though T1's student's writing presented linguistic deviation from NS English, such as subject-verb disagreement (see Figure 1 for an illustration), T1 focused on whether and how her students conveyed the information, not whether correct English was presented in slides. T4 indicated that she created the opportunities for her students to re-negotiate meanings when students' writing was not clear as a result of their difficulty in understanding. The meaning-focused approach to write and present slides echoes Widdowson's (2015) argument for the value of meaning-oriented communicative language use. T4's teaching activity to create learning opportunity for students to re-negotiate meaning by exploring alternatives to write resonates with Canagarjah's (2006) point made about teaching English from international perspective by facilitating students' language skills to re-negotiate meanings.

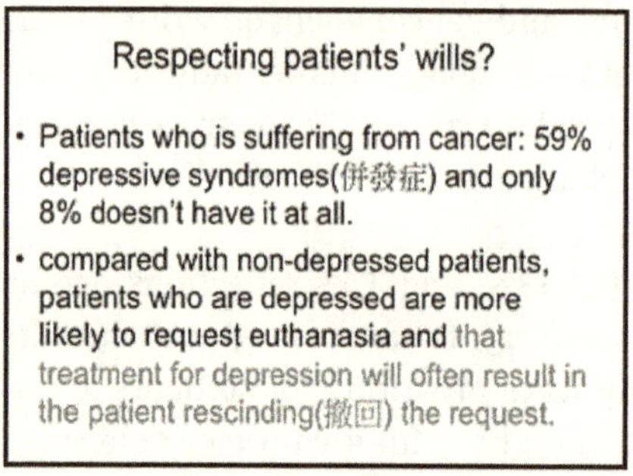

> **Respecting patients' wills?**
>
> - Patients who is suffering from cancer: 59% depressive syndromes(併發症) and only 8% doesn't have it at all.
> - compared with non-depressed patients, patients who are depressed are more likely to request euthanasia and that treatment for depression will often result in the patient rescinding(撤回) the request.

Figure 1: An example of T1's student's PowerPoint slide.

The discussion above shows that most teachers chose not to teach writing. Secondly, all the teachers did not associate communicative competence with writing skills development. Thirdly, when teachers chose or needed to teach students writing, some teachers' teaching principles and practice reflected the ELF perspective, while others' did not. As a result, within Taiwan's English language education system, the writing skills training which students had received was insufficient and not well connected to international communication.

4.5 A summary of answers to the research questions

From learners' perspective, student participants' secondary English language education did not support writing nor communicative skills development. When they began studying at the universities, they aimed to learn English for international communication, but they prioritised learning speaking and listening, not writing. Students' writing skills development was rather limited through Taiwanese secondary as well as tertiary English language education. The university curriculum and materials did not create a writing skill friendly learning context. Secondary English language teachers offered a negligible amount of writing skills training as indicated by only 6% of students reporting they received four-skills training, which focused on reading. Only 50% (n=6) of teacher participants chose to teach writing skills.

As Jenkins (2018: 65) observed, "the English language education establishment has not so far caught up with global developments in English and, continues to teach this lingua franca as if it was still primarily a traditional foreign language." Her comment truly reflects how Taiwanese secondary students learned and secondary teachers taught English language in a traditional way but it did not necessarily reflect what was actually taught and learned inside of university classrooms. For instance, T1 and T4 did not introduce the NS normative perspective during writing training or reinforce this perspective when teaching.

Although Jenkins (2012, 2018) points out that TESOL practice has not caught up with the development of the English language, the evidence obtained for this study reveals that ELF teaching and learning does not simply reflect a one-sided pedagogical decision. For instance, this case study reveals that the university curriculums, materials, teaching principles, students' learning needs and targets, and other factors determine whether there is space for writing education from an ELF perspective. The findings further suggest the complex nature of developing and realising ELF-wise teaching and learning across contexts as a result of different challenges to the pedagogical change. Nevertheless, the mentioned challenges to pedagogical changes do not mean that the educational innovations are not possible to envisage. T1's and T4's teaching illustrates good examples of such pedagogical changes.

5 Conclusion

This chapter closes with a summary of the key findings. Then, the implication of this study for teaching, learning, and researching English language skills are considered. At the same time, this chapter gives suggestions for teaching and learning English from the perspective of ELF.

Before entering universities, students' English language learning centred on examination preparation. When students began receiving tertiary education, learning English became more about, but not all about, international communication. Most students reported that they had the least experience in acquiring writing skills compared to others. They tended to assume that developing communicative competence was equated to developing speaking and listening rather than writing skills. As a result, to be communicative, students identified that their language learning needs were about developing speaking and listening skills, not writing skills. As can be seen, students' language learning experience and priorities revealed a loose link between writing skills education and international communication.

A similar finding was identified in the teachers' perspective on writing skills development. Teachers associated students' communicative competence development with their speaking and listening skills. Half of the teachers decided not to teach writing. Despite the fact that half of the teachers chose to teach writing, writing skills training only constituted a small part of their teaching and not all of their teaching reflected the ELF perspective. In this case, writing skills training was rare and developing writing skills for international communication was even rarer.

The secondary school and university curriculums did not provide students and teachers with educational contexts in which the ideas of teaching and learning English for international communication could be developed and realised. Not all the available materials and university curriculums supported writing skills development, and even when they did, not all the teachers decided to teach writing; students identified their needs to learn writing skills. As a result, teaching and learning writing skills was marginalised and developing writing skills for international communication so far has not been an essential skill for students to strive for.

Since ELF-oriented writing training was determined according to purposes of teaching and learning as well as whether the contexts were suitable for writing training to be planned and carried out, one of the most obvious implications is the importance for researchers to engage in a dialogue on the topics of English for international communication. This will enable the researchers to draw on the insights of local students and teachers and the expertise of local in-service teachers for their teaching experience and practices. The openness also enables researchers to avoid making assumptions about purposes, needs, and contexts of teaching and learning English, to avoid selecting a set of ELF concepts as input resources without assessing learning and teaching needs at local contexts, or to avoid claiming or anticipating that one-way transmission of knowledge about ELF between the selected ELF resources and input and participants' perceptual or practical changes. Through this open approach, the studies on ELF topics can not only present a shift away from pre-defined ELF knowledge but also open up new ways to think about local English language education from an ELF perspective.

Following this, another implication for future research is the need to assess students' learning needs, objectives, and contexts for learning English language skills from the perspective of ELF. Taking this case study as an example, when students studied at their secondary schools, preparing English language examinations was prioritised and then the focus of students' learning changed since they began tertiary education. If students did not need or prioritise learning English for international communication, any pedagogical interventions or ideas to enhance students' language skills will be devalued. So, students' learning needs and objectives are not a matter of routine within a context or across contexts and should not be generalised. Instead, a reassessment of students' language and learning needs should be carried out for each future research endeavor.

The third implication for future research is to triangulate multiple-sided perspectives on whether teaching and learning English is carried out for international communication. For instance, this study triangulates the perspective of teachers, students, and university curriculum on English language education and thus provides fair insights and makes relevant pedagogical suggestions on how ideas about why ELF teaching and learning can be feasible in which educational contexts. However, the existing research only presents the unilateral decision on planning and implementing ELF pedagogy. Conceptualising ELF pedagogy as such is an over-simplification. As many contextual factors affect teaching and learning English from the perspective of ELF, only triangulating multiple perspectives on teaching and learning English for international communication can provide insights into this multilateral, not unilateral, pedagogical decision-making process.

While ELF-related Teacher Training Programmes are developing, they have not yet become available to all pre-service teachers. As all in-service teachers have not received ELF-related training, it therefore becomes significant for future research to identify and illustrate the examples of in-service teachers' ELF teaching ideas, how these ideas are put into practice, and under which teaching circumstances they are suitable. The examples as such can be used as ELF-related Teacher Training resources, which benefit pre-service teachers to relate the concepts of ELF pedagogy to classroom realities. The established TESOL training programmes tend to offer pre-service teacher education the imbalanced teacher training, focusing more on theoretical input, less on practical ideas and strategies to teach language (Hüttner et al. 2012). A theory-practice balanced TESOL programmes from ELF perspective may consider offering the pre-service teachers with examples of in-service teachers' ideas of teaching language skills from ELF perspective, how they realised these ideas, under which teaching circumstances, and the results of teaching and learning. By exemplifying how in-service teachers have done and the results, the ELF teacher training courses can further give pre-service teachers opportunities to plan ELF related learning activities and resources as a part of training. By doing this, the ELF teacher training will not run into the pattern of traditional TESOL training: more theories, less practice.

Lastly, future TESOL or ELF research should consider the learners' perspective on the topics of ELF in order to generate pedagogical suggestions for developing learner-relevant courses. As Nunan (1990) and Sung (2015) suggest, students' involvement benefits the development of communicative curriculum that directly addresses students' learning needs. Also, within national educational systems, most students only have a few hours per week to learn English and if students aim to learn English for communication as well as other purposes, the time for ELF-oriented language learning will be even more limited. Thus, in agreement with the learning reality presented in this case study, it is more practical for in-service teachers to integrate an ELF perspective into the existing learning activities/courses rather than planning and implementing new ELF courses since there are myriads of contextual constraints.

References

Bosher, Susan & Stocker, Joel. 2015. Nurses' narratives on workplace English in Taiwan: Improving patient care and enhancing professionalism. *English for Specific Purposes 38*, 109–120. doi:10.1016/j.esp.2015.02.001

Bayyurt, Yasmin & Sifakis, Nicos. 2015a. Insights from ELF and WE in teacher training in Greece and Turkey. *World Englishes 34*(3), 471–484. doi:10.1111/weng.12150

Bayyurt, Yasmin & Sifakis, Nicos. 2015b. ELF-Aware In-Service Teacher Education: A Transformative Perspective. In Hugo, Bowles & Alessia, Cogo (ed.), *International Perspectives on English as Lingua Franca: Pedagogical Insights*, 117–135. London: Palgrave MacMillan.

Bayyurt, Yasmin & Kaçar, Işıl Günseli. 2018. ELF-Aware Pre-service Teacher Education to Promote Glocal Interactions: A Case Study in Turkey. In Ali Fuad Selvi & Nathanael Rudolph (ed.), *Conceptual Shifts and Contextualized Practices in Education for Glocal Interaction*, 77–104. London: Springer.

Canagarajah, Suresh. 2006. Changing Communicative Needs, Revised Assessment Objectives: Testing English as an International Language. *Language Assessment Quarterly 3*(3), 229–242. doi:10.1207/s15434311laq0303_1

Curran, Jean. E. & Chern, Chiou Lan. 2017. Pre-service English teachers' attitudes towards English as a lingua franca. *Teaching and Teacher Education 66*, 137–146. doi: 10.1016/j.tate.2017.04.007

Dewey, Martin. 2012. Towards a post-normative approach: learning the pedagogy of ELF. *Journal of English as a lingua franca 1*(1), 141–170. doi:10.1515/jelf-2012-0007

Douglas, Nancy. (2010). *Reading Explorer 3*. Heinle Cengage Learning.

Galloway, Nicola & Rose, Heath. 2014. Using listening journals to raise awareness of Global Englishes in ELT. *ELT Journal 68*(4), 386–396. doi:10.1093/elt/ccu021

Galloway, Nicola & Rose, Heath. 2018. Incorporating Global Englishes into the ELT classroom. *ELT Journal 72*(1), 3–14 .doi:10.1093/elt/ccx010

Hüttner, Julia, Mehlmauer-Larcher, Barbara, Reichl, Sussane, & Schiftner, Barbara. (2012). *Theory and Practice in EFL Teacher Education: Bridging the Gap*. Bristol: Multilingual Matters.

Jenkins, Jennifer. 2018. Not English but English-within-multilingualism. In Simon Coffey & Ursula Wingate. (ed.), *New Directions for Research in Foreign Language Education*, 65–78. London: Routledge.

Jenkins, Jennifer. 2012. English as a Lingua Franca from the classroom to the classroom. *ELT Journal, 66*(4), 486–494. doi:10.1093/elt/ccs040.

Kumaravadivelu, B. 2012. *Language Teacher Education for a Global Society: A Modular Model for Knowing, Analyzing, Recognizing, Doing, and Seeing*. London: Routledge.

Leung, Constant & Street, Brian. 2012. Linking EIL and Literacy: theory and practice. In Lubna. Alsagoof, Sandra. Lee. McKay, Guanwei. Hu & Willy. A. Renandya (ed.), *Principles and*

practices for teaching English as an International Language, 85–103. New York, NY: Routledge.
Lai, Husan Yao Tony. 2008. English as an international language? Taiwanese university teachers' dilemma and struggle . . . . *English Today 24*(3), 39–45. doi:10.1017/S0266078408000278
Luo, Wen Hsing 2017. Teacher perceptions of teaching and learning English as a lingua franca in expanding circle: A study of Taiwan. *English Today 33*(1), 2–11. doi:10.1017/S0266078416000146
Matsuda, Aya. 2009. Desirable but not necessary? The place of World Englishes and English as an International Language in Teacher Preparation Programs in Japan. In Sharifian Farzad (ed.), *English as an International Language: Perspectives and Pedagogical Issues*, 154–169. Bristol: Multilingual Matters.
Matsuda, Aya & Matsuda, Paul Kei. 2010. World Englishes and the Teaching of Writing. *TESOL Quarterly 44*(2), 369–374. doi:10.5054/tq.2010.222222
Nunan, David. 1990. Using Learner Data in Curriculum Development. *English for Specific Purposes 9*(1), 17–32. doi:10.1016/0889-4906(90)90026-9.
Reynolds, Barry Lee & Yu, Melissa Huiyen. 2018. Addressing the language needs of administrative staff in Taiwan's internationalized higher education: call for an English as a lingua franca curriculum to increase communicative competence and willingness to communicate. *Language & Education 32*(2), 147–166. doi:10.1080/09500782.2017.1405017.
Richie, Jane, Spencer, Liz, & O'Connor, William. 2003. Carrying out Qualitative Analysis. In Jane Richie & Jane. Lewis (ed.), *Qualitative research practice: a guide for social science students and researchers*, 119–262. London: Sage Publications.
Seidlhofer, Barbara. 2011. *Understanding English as a Lingua Franca*. Oxford: Oxford University Press.
Seidlhofer, Barbara. 2004. Research Perspectives on teaching English as a lingua franca. *Annual Review of Applied Linguistics 24*, 209–239. doi:10.1017/S0267190504000145
Spence, Paul, & Liu, Gi-Zen. 2013. Engineering English and the high-tech industry: A case study of an English needs analysis of process integration engineers at a semiconductor manufacturing company in Taiwan. *English for Specific Purposes 32*, 97–109. doi:10.1016/j.esp.2012.11.003.
Soars, Liz. and Soars, John. (2009). *American Headway 3*. Oxford: Oxford University Press.
Sung, Chit Cheung Matthew. 2015. Exposing learners to Global Englishes in ELT: some suggestions. *ELT Journal 69*(2), 198–201. doi:10.1093/elt/ccu064
Tsui, Amy B. M. 2012 The Dialectics of Theory and Practice in Teacher Knowledge Development. In Julia Hüttner, Barbara Mehlmauer-Larcher, Susanne Reichl, & Barbara Schiftner, (ed.), *Theory and Practice in EFL Teacher Education: Bridging the Gap*, 16–37. Bristol: Multilingual Matters.
Widdowson, Henry. 2015. ELF and the Pragmatics of Language Variation. *Journal of English as a Lingua Franca 4*(2), 359–372. doi:10.1515/jelf-2015-0027
Wilson, Ken. (2008). *Smart Choice 2*. Oxford: Oxford University Press.
Wyrick, Jean. (2008). *Steps to Writing Well with Additional Readings*. (10th ed.). Boston: Thomson Wadsworth.
Yu, Melissa Huiyen 2018. Using textbooks to teach and learn English for lingua franca communication: An insight into classroom autonomy. *The Asia-Pacific Education Researcher 27*(4), 257–266. doi:10.1007/s40299-018-0381-6

Appendix A

Student participants' majors in various faculties in universities

University	Faculty		Department/Programme	
U1	1.	Art College	1.	Department of Foreign Languages
U2	1.	Faculty of Science	1.	Department of Physics
			2.	Department of Chemistry
			3.	Department of Earth Sciences
			4.	Department of Mathematics
			5.	Department of Photonics
	2.	Faculty of Engineering	6.	Department of Mechanical Engineering
			7.	Department of Chemical Engineering
			8.	Department of Resources Engineering
			9.	Department of Material Science and Engineering
			10.	Department of Civil Engineering
			11.	Department of Engineering Science
			12.	Department of System and Naval Mechatronic
			13.	Department of Environmental Engineering
	3.	Faculty of Engineering & Computer Science	14.	Department of Electrical Engineering
			15.	Department of Computer Science and Information Engineering
	4.	Faculty of Liberal Arts	16.	Department of History
			17.	Department of Taiwanese Literature
			18.	Department of Chinese Literature
	5.	Faculty of Social Science	19.	Department of Psychology
			20.	Department of Political Science
			21.	Department of Law

(continued)

University	Faculty		Department/Programme	
	6.	Faculty of Management	22.	Department of Business Administration
			23.	Department of Accountancy
			24.	Department of Statistics
			25.	Department of Transportation and communication management Science
	7.	Faculty of Planning and Design	26.	Department of Architecture
	8.	Faculty of Bioscience and Biochemistry	27.	Department of Biology
			28.	Department of Life Sciences
	9.	Faculty of Medicine	29.	Department of Medical Laboratory Science & Biotechnology
			30.	Department of Nursing
			31.	Department of Occupational Therapy
U3	1.	Faculty of Education	1.	Department of Education
			2.	Department of Special Education
			3.	Department of Early Childhood Education
	2.	Faculty of Science	4.	Department of Applied Physics
			5.	Department of Applied Mathematics
			6.	Department of Computer Science
			7.	Thin Film Science
			8.	Bachelor Programme in Robotics
	3.	Faculty of Humanities and Social Sciences	9.	Department of Cultural and Creative Industries

Appendix B

Student and teacher questionnaires

Student questionnaire

A. Background

Please complete the following personal information.
1. My nationality is
   ☐ Taiwanese ☐ non-Taiwanese (Please specify your nationality if you are a non-Taiwanese: _____.)
2. How long have you learned English language in Taiwan?
   ☐ 5 years or less ☐ between 5 and 10 years
   ☐ more than 10 years ☐ Other: Please specify_____
3. Are you an English major?
   ☐ Yes, I am.
   ☐ No, my major is _____.
4. Have you ever attended or are you going to attend an English language programme in another country?
   ☐ Yes. Please provide the information about where and how long you have attended/are going to attend this programme.
   _____
   ☐ No.

B. Students' learning experience in English

5. The main purpose of learning English in the past was to
   ☐ pass the examination
   ☐ use English for the real world communication
   ☐ access to resources in English
   ☐ other: Please specify_____
6. Now you learn English in order to _____. (You can tick other option(s) if your answers are different from that to the last question).
   ☐ prepare for examinations
   ☐ use English for real world communication
   ☐ access resources in English
   ☐ Other: Please specify_____
7. What aspects of language are very often taught and learned in classrooms that you have experienced?
8. What aspects of English language do you think you need to acquire or need to be enhanced in Taiwan in order to use it for communicative purposes?

Teacher questionnaire

A. Teacher informant's background information
1. Please complete the following personal information. I would like to be called _____ and I am
   ☐ under 30 years old
   ☐ 30 to 40 years old
   ☐ older than 40 years old.
2. How long have you taught English language in Taiwan?
   ☐ not more than 5 years
   ☐ between 5 and 10 years
   ☐ more than ten years
   ☐ Other: Please specify.
3. Please describe your English language background as a teacher of English language in Taiwan?
   ☐ A Taiwanese teacher of English who does not use English as his/her native language
   ☐ A foreign teacher of English who uses English as his/her native language
   ☐ A foreign teacher of English who does not use English as his/her native language
   ☐ Other: Please specify
4. Have you received a masters and/or doctoral degree(s) in and English-speaking country?
   ☐ Yes, please specify country where you received your degree(s):
   _____
   ☐ No.

B. Pedagogical concerns
1. What are the criteria adopted to select the course books for teaching Oral Training 1 and 2 or the General English training for first-year undergraduates?
2. What is the most important aspect in your English language teaching practices?
3. What is your priority to select teaching materials for your students?
4. What methods and materials do you most refer to help your students develop their communicative competence?
5. What do you hope your students would be able to do with the English that you have taught them after they leave the school?
6. What are your thoughts about connecting the English you teach in the classrooms to actual English language use?

Appendix C

Interview questions

1. How did the university curriculum encourage teaching and learning English for international communication?
2. Which language skills do your teaching focus on?
3. How did you select materials to develop the four basic skills?
4. Could you give me examples of what learning activities you often use to develop students' writing skills.
5. How do you think the chosen textbooks supported you to carry out writing training?

Appendix D

Transcription convention systems for content analysis of questionnaires and interviews

1. Teacher participants are presented as follows: T1, T2, T3 . . . the first teacher, the second teacher, and the third teacher, who was interviewed about their experiences of developing students' communicative competence and writing skills.
2. **Content of interviews are in bolded text**

Conventions	Used to indicate
(.)	short pause, less than 3 seconds
[text]	the commentary of any kind (e.g. to indicate in conversation about whom the interviewee referred to when interviewee used pronouns)
. . .	the omission of student's talk
"text"	text for emphasis
bold	the content of interviews to analyse and discuss in this chapter

Maggie Ma, Mark Feng Teng
Metacognitive knowledge development of low proficiency Hong Kong English as a Foreign Language university students in a process-oriented writing course: An action research study

Abstract: This action research, from an ecological perspective, explores the metacognitive knowledge development of two low-proficiency Hong Kong English as a Foreign Language university students in a process-oriented writing course. Data were collected through focus group interviews, student writings, and teacher written feedback. The study has identified variations in the two students' engagement with different aspects of the process writing course as well as in their metacognitive knowledge development (e.g., motivation to write and metacognitive strategy knowledge related to planning and monitoring). The concept of affordances is used to explain these variations. The findings suggest pedagogical implications for further promoting weak student writers' metacognitive knowledge development.

Keywords: process writing pedagogy, metacognitive knowledge, EFL writing, affordances, low-proficiency students

1 Introduction

Process-oriented writing instruction is a technique which requires student writers to plan, evaluate, reflect, self-assess as well as peer-assess, revise, rearrange, modify, and multi-draft a text prior to producing the finished document (Seow 2002). This technique has received much attention recently in regard to teaching students who learn English as a Foreign Language (EFL) (Reynolds and Teng 2019). Process-oriented writing instruction assists students in developing metacognitive knowledge regarding their own abilities, task requirements, and cognitive strategies, and finally, enhances their self-

Maggie Ma, The Hang Seng University of Hong Kong
Mark Feng Teng, University of Macau

https://doi.org/10.1515/9781501512643-006

regulated learning to monitor and evaluate the entire composing process (Graham and Harris 2000; Teng, 2020). In Hong Kong's education system, teaching is exam-oriented and product-focused, especially in EFL writing instruction (Lam 2015). In the past three decades, process writing instruction has been increasingly implemented in EFL writing (Lo and Hyland 2007; Sengupta and Falvey 1998; Stewart and Cheung 1989). It has been reported that formative practices, such as multiple drafting, peer-directed, and self-directed feedback, as well as revision process, are often encompassed in process-writing pedagogy (O'Brien 2004). Such practices provide opportunities for students to learn various writing strategies (e.g., planning, evaluating, and revising) applicable in the whole writing process (Teng 2019a). In regard to this practice, the teacher moves away from being someone who sets students a writing topic and receives the finished product for correction, and students themselves become the agents of change by self-regulating their writing process (Teng 2019c).

Therefore, it may be expected that process-oriented writing instruction carries the potential for the development of metacognitive knowledge of writing. The development of metacognitive knowledge determines the kind of strategy or approach to be adopted by student writers (Victori 1999). However, in exam-oriented EFL teaching settings, including the one in Hong Kong, it is often challenging to develop students' metacognitive knowledge in self-directing their writing process despite having received instructions on different aspects of process writing, including teacher feedback, peer feedback, student revision, and so on (M. Lee 2015; Lo and Hyland 2007; Mak and Coniam 2008; Tsui and Ng 2000). Despite a call for developing students' self-regulated writing through process-oriented writing instruction (Lam 2015; Ruan 2005), limited research has been conducted on how it fosters student writers' metacognitive knowledge development, and in particular, its influence on low-proficiency student writers. Certain weak students require additional support in developing their strategy use (Forbes 2018; Kao and Reynolds 2017), and this may be true for the development of their metacognitive knowledge as well. In consideration of the aforementioned great need to support weak students, this action research aims to examine the metacognitive knowledge development of two Hong Kong EFL university students with a low level of writing proficiency. The findings of the present study may provide insights into how process-oriented writing instruction may assist low-proficiency students in developing metacognitive knowledge.

2 Literature review

2.1 Metacognition and writing

Metacognition is generally understood as cognition about cognition (Flavell, Miller, and Miller 2002). Metacognition has also been conceptualized as "one's knowledge and control of the domain cognition" (Brown 1982: 86). Within the broader notion of metacognition, there are two separate and distinct components: metacognitive knowledge or knowledge about cognition, and metacognitive strategies or regulation of cognition (Brown 1982; Wenden 1998). Metacognitive knowledge refers to the knowledge that learners have about their own cognition or cognition in general (Brown 1982; Wenden 1998). It may further be divided into person, task, and strategic knowledge (Flavell 1979; Wenden 1998). According to Wenden (1998), person knowledge refers to knowledge that learners have about human factors that may facilitate or inhibit learning, how the factors apply in their experience, their effectiveness as learners in general (e.g., self-efficacy beliefs), and their ability to achieve specific learning goals (e.g., achievement beliefs). Task knowledge refers to learners' knowledge about the purpose, nature, and demands of a particular task while strategic knowledge refers to knowledge about what strategies are (i.e., declarative knowledge), how to apply them (i.e., procedural knowledge), and when and why specific strategies are useful (i.e., conditional knowledge) (Schraw and Dennison 1994; Wenden 1998). Metacognitive strategies, including planning, monitoring, and evaluating, are general skills that learners use to manage, direct, regulate, and guide their learning (Brown 1982; Wenden 1998).

Both metacognitive knowledge and metacognitive strategies are important for successful writing. Writing is a complex, recursive, and strategic process, demanding the use of metacognitive knowledge and skills (Hacker, Keener, and Kircher 2009; Karlen 2017; Teng 2016). Research has shown that skillful writers use metacognitive strategies, such as planning, monitoring, evaluating, and revising, more effectively than less skillful writers (Teng 2019b; Teng and Huang 2019; Victori 1999). Underlying the use of various metacognitive strategies is metacognitive knowledge. For instance, it has been observed that good and poor EFL writers differ in their person, task, and strategic knowledge, and such knowledge plays an important role in influencing the kind of strategy or approach to be adopted by student writers (Victori 1999). It has also been demonstrated that skilled writers possess greater metacognitive strategic knowledge compared to less skilled writers (Lin, Monroe, and Troia 2007; Saddler and Graham 2007). It appears that the development in metacognitive skills and in metacognitive knowledge of writing serves as a catalyst for writing development.

2.2 The process writing approach and metacognition

The process writing approach is based on a cognitive model of writing process that regards writing as a "non-linear, exploratory and generative process" (Zamel 1983: 165). In EFL writing, the process writing approach is characterized by formative practices, including multiple drafting, teacher feedback, peer feedback, self-directed feedback, and revision (O'Brien 2004). Research has mainly focused on its implementation in contexts where writing instruction tends to be exam-oriented and product-focused (Lo and Hyland 2007; Stewart and Cheung 1989), its impact on writing proficiency (Mak and Coniam 2008), and its subprocesses such as teacher feedback and peer feedback (Lam 2013; M. Lee 2015; Tsui and Ng 2000). In particular, regarding teacher and peer feedback, certain EFL students are skeptical about their peers' ability to evaluate their writing because of the perception that their teachers are more competent professionals for providing feedback (Lam 2014). However, peer feedback is beneficial as it fosters student motivation and collaborative learning, cultivates audience awareness and a sense of ownership of the text, provides students with opportunities to practice evaluation skills, allows student writers to be more reflective of the strengths and weaknesses in their own writing, and enhances writing development (M. Lee 2015; Nguyen and Gu 2013; Tsui and Ng 2000).

The features of formative practices in process writing pedagogy include multiple drafting, peer feedback, and revision. If accompanied by strategy instruction, process writing approaches provide opportunities to practice self-regulated writing strategies associated with planning, monitoring, and evaluating (Ruan 2005). These self-regulatory strategies are involved in the regulation of cognition and enable learners to approach writing tasks in a systematic manner (MacArthur, Philippakos, and Ianetta 2014; Teng 2019c). Researchers have investigated how process writing approaches incorporating strategy instruction help foster the development of metacognitive knowledge among student writers (Lam 2015; Ruan 2005), which is a pre-requisite for the deployment of writing strategies to approach a writing task (Victori 1999) and for self-regulation in learning to write. For example, both Lam's (2015) study on Hong Kong post-secondary students and Ruan's (2005) study on Chinese EFL university students revealed that process writing pedagogy involving strategy instruction enhanced learners' person knowledge (e.g., motivation to write, greater confidence in text revision), task knowledge (e.g., better awareness of genre structure, sense of audience and purpose), and strategic knowledge (e.g., planning, evaluating, and revising).

Despite the aforementioned research, much still needs to be known about the influence of process-oriented pedagogy integrating writing strategy instruction on the development of metacognitive knowledge among student writers, particularly those with a low level of writing proficiency. According to Forbes (2018), learners' proficiency level may influence the development of their writing strategies, with a limited level of proficiency constituting a barrier for developing writing strategy use. It is likely that proficiency level may also affect weak student writers' metacognitive knowledge development. Although previous research focusing on poor EFL writers is available, such as Lam's (2015) study on the low intermediate students in the context of Hong Kong's post-secondary education and Ruan's (2005) study on Chinese students with an estimated IELTS score of 4.5 (somewhere between "limited user" and "modest user"), further research on low proficiency students is needed because these students presumably require greater support for developing their strategy use and metacognitive knowledge. Moreover, even among this group of students, there might be individual variations, rendering it necessary for teachers to understand such variations and provide support accordingly. It is, therefore, important to investigate both similarities and variations in low proficiency students' metacognitive knowledge development in response to process writing pedagogy incorporating writing strategy instruction.

This chapter adopts an ecological perspective (Van Lier 2000) to investigate metacognitive knowledge development among low-proficiency students. This perspective highlights a situative view of learning and the interaction between the learner and the environment. It emphasizes the key concept of affordances, which refers to "a particular property of the environment that is relevant . . . to an active, perceiving organism [i.e., an L2 learner] in the environment" (Van Lier 2000: 252). Within the classroom setting, affordances may be defined as "opportunities for learning which the students perceive within the learning structure" (Cotterall and Murray 2009: 42). This concept of affordances not only reflects the contextual nature of learning, but also suggests that the perceived opportunities for learning may vary from person to person. Individual learners may perceive different opportunities for action within the learning structure or view different learning opportunities in different ways (Cotterall and Murray 2009). Research has demonstrated that affordances in the form of personalization, engagement, reflection, experimentation, and support were conducive to the development of metacognitive knowledge among Japanese EFL students in the context of self-directed language learning (Cotterall and Murray 2009). Notably, learner beliefs may play a role in creating affordances in the classroom learning environment (Ma 2016).

From an ecological perspective (Van Lier 2000), this action research aims to explore how a process writing course encompassing various formative assessment practices (e.g., multiple drafting, teacher feedback, and revision) and strategy instruction influenced the metacognitive knowledge among the student participants who had a low level of writing proficiency. In particular, it focuses on the similarities and differences in the affordances perceived by the students in the learning structure in relation to the development of their metacognitive knowledge. With a focus on low-proficiency students and on their similarities and differences, the present study contributes to a fine-grained understanding of weak students' metacognitive knowledge development, generating relevant pedagogical implications.

3 The study

3.1 Research question

The present study is guided by the following research question:

> How did the process-oriented writing course in the current study shape the metacognitive knowledge of the student participants?

3.2 Context and participants

Hong Kong is characterized by an exam-oriented educational system. In its primary and secondary EFL writing classrooms, writing instruction is examination-driven, and a product-oriented approach to writing has been traditionally adopted (I. Lee and Coniam 2013). This implies that writing is outcome-based and students do not have the opportunity to experience the writing process by composing multiple drafts and revising their writing on the basis of different sources of feedback, including teacher, peer, and self-directed feedback.

This action research was conducted in an academic English writing course for first-year English major students, who were required to study both literature and linguistics, in a private university in Hong Kong. This 14-week compulsory course aimed at enabling students to write linguistics-related research papers and focused mainly on developing their research skills and academic writing skills. The two major assignments in the course were a secondary research paper (i.e., an expository essay based on secondary sources) and a primary research paper (i.e., a report on an empirical study), accounting for 30% and 40% of the course grade, respectively. The students were allowed to choose their own research topic. The students and the teacher met twice each week. Each session was conducted in English and lasted for approximately one and a half hours. There were 15 students in the class, who were all native speakers of Cantonese aged from 18 to 19 years.

The data for this chapter were part of a larger study that explored the metacognitive knowledge development of a group of Hong Kong EFL university students with differing levels of writing proficiency. The current paper focuses on two low proficiency students, Katrina and Sally (pseudonyms), because, despite the similarities (e.g., text knowledge and metacognitive knowledge concerning evaluation), they demonstrated different patterns of metacognitive knowledge development in the process writing course. In their secondary schools, the students were seldom asked to write multiple drafts in English and were exposed mainly to a teacher-centered product-based approach to English writing. They also had limited experience of peer evaluation. At the time of the study, the teacher-researcher acted as the coordinator of the course.

3.3 Method

Action research was adopted in the present study. Action research is used to bring about change or even improvements in response to a problematic situation (Burns 2010). When the teacher-researcher (i.e., first author) initially taught the academic writing course, she observed that the students lacked appropriate metacognitive knowledge to guide their writing of the two major assignments. For instance, the students were not motivated to write, lacked sufficient knowledge regarding the qualities of good research papers, and did not appear to understand the importance of planning. Therefore, she considered using action research to bring about change in her teaching situation.

Action research involves four phases: observing, planning, acting, and reflecting (Norton 2009). In the observing phase, the teacher-researcher identified a problem, as stated earlier. In the planning stage, guided by relevant research (Lam 2015; Ruan 2005; Victori 1999), the teacher-researcher planned to implement process-oriented writing that integrated strategy instruction the second time she taught the academic writing course. In this manner, the student writers' metacognitive knowledge could be developed.

In the acting stage, the teacher-researcher implemented the planned process approach to writing in her classroom. For both the secondary and primary research papers, the students were required to go through a writing cycle by producing multiple drafts and revising based on teacher and peer feedback (see Table 1). While the students needed to attend a writing conference for the secondary research paper, it was not compulsory for the primary research paper. Nevertheless, they were encouraged to discuss their first drafts with the teacher. The writing cycle was presented as a sequential process for the sake of clarity, but the teacher emphasized in class that writing was a recursive process

Table 1: Writing cycles for the secondary and primary research papers, respectively.

Secondary research paper	Primary research paper
1. Outline	1. Research proposal
2. Teacher written feedback on the outline	2. Teacher written feedback on research proposal
3. First draft	3. Peer written and oral feedback on research proposal
4. Teacher written feedback on the first draft	4. First draft
5. Peer written and oral feedback on the first draft	5. Peer written and oral feedback on the first draft
6. Student-teacher conference about the first draft	6. Student encouraged to discuss their first drafts with the teacher
7. Final draft	7. Final draft
8. Teacher written feedback on the final draft	8. Teacher written feedback on the final draft

and that the students could, for example, revise their writing in the process of drafting. To facilitate the writing process and raise the students' awareness of strategy use, the teacher explained and demonstrated various writing strategies, such as brainstorming, planning, drafting, and revising, and then the students were asked to apply these writing strategies in the writing cycle for each type of paper. Teacher and peer feedback activities in the writing cycles were also intended to aid students' evaluation and revision of their work. Notably, since it was the first time for the students to experience the process writing approach, the teacher decided to allow them to practice planning the time for their research and writing process in addition to planning how to write. The students were required to create a timeline for each research paper so that they could avoid a late submission of their work-in-progress (e.g., outline, first draft, etc.). To familiarize the students with the textual features of research papers, the teacher provided them with student samples for both the secondary and primary research papers. The teacher mentioned the type of research paper that each sample exemplified, as well as the purpose and intended audience of each type. Then the students were involved in analyzing the strengths and weaknesses of each sample paper, and they needed to conduct a discussion among themselves in order to identify the genre elements and the qualities of good writing, for each research paper. This was followed by teacher feedback in the form of explaining the similarities and differences between the student and teacher criteria, as well as the key concepts in the latter. This sample-analysis activity also served as peer review training to enhance the students' understanding of the assessment criteria.

In the reflecting stage, the teacher-researcher observed the effects of the process-oriented writing course by collecting and analyzing information from multiple sources of data, including focus group interviews, student drafts, and teacher and peer written feedback (see section 3.4). She also kept a reflective journal and reflected on the teaching practice (e.g., Was the peer feedback activity useful?) and the research process (e.g., How has the research experience aided in extending the knowledge of how to conduct research?). Although reflection is presented as the last step in the action research cycle, it was performed throughout the whole research process.

3.4 Data collection and analysis

Although only two students' data are reported in this chapter, it is important to describe the data collection methods used in the larger study in which these two students had participated. In that larger study, data were collected through focus group interviews with students, student writing (e.g., outlines and drafts), and teacher and peer written feedback. Focus group interviews were used as the major source of data to gauge possible metacognitive knowledge development among the student writers. The interview questions were informed by Victori's (1999) framework of metacognitive knowledge of writing (see the Appendix for a list of interview questions). According to Wenden (1998), interviews asking learners to retrospect upon their learning may prompt them to draw upon their stored metacognitive knowledge about learning strategies (e.g., questions related to the use of writing strategies), and the resulting accounts can be viewed as strategic knowledge. Similarly, interview questions related to learners' opinions of themselves as writers during the process of learning to write (e.g., questions related to their motivation for writing) and their opinions of the writing tasks (e.g., questions related to discourse knowledge, purpose, and audience of writing) can be utilized to gauge their person knowledge and task knowledge, respectively.

Focus group interviews involving students with varying levels of writing proficiencies were utilized to explore their metacognitive knowledge. The comparisons made regarding one another's experiences and opinions during group interactions may provide valuable insights into the research topic (Morgan 1997). Purposeful sampling was used to select the student interviewees according to different levels of writing proficiency and their willingness to participate in the research project. After the completion of the secondary research paper, two focus group interviews with a total of ten students were conducted. Each group interview contained students with a relatively high and a relatively low level of English writing proficiency. Another focus group interview was conducted with seven students having varying levels of writing proficiency after the evaluation of the primary research paper. The students' writing proficiency was determined by their performance on a pre-course writing task, and it was consistent with their writing performance in the previous writing course that they had taken. The purpose of interviewing the students after each writing task was to obtain detailed information while their memory of writing a research paper in each genre was still fresh. To prevent the students from stating socially desirable responses to the teacher-researcher, a research assistant interviewed the students. Braten and Samuelstuen's (2007) guidelines were followed to increase the validity of self-report data, and the students were provided with the instructions on the writing tasks, reminded about paying attention to the writing process, and were informed that they would be asked questions about these processes. Since the participants were English major students who were able to express their ideas in English clearly, each interview was conducted in English and lasted around one and a half hours. The students were allowed to use Cantonese to clarify their meaning, if necessary. Before the research started, the students were informed of the research purpose. Pseudonyms were used to protect their identity.

Student drafts, as well as teacher and peer written feedback, were collected to analyze the students' engagement with feedback and the extent of student revision. Student drafts included the outlines/research proposals, first drafts, and final drafts. Teacher written feedback on all the drafts and peer written feedback on first drafts were also collected. Particularly relevant to the study was teacher written feedback, as the two students highlighted its role in developing their metacognitive knowledge.

All interview data were transcribed. Since research purposes determine the level of details in transcription (Davidson 2009), the verbal component (Kowal and O'Connell 2014) excluding fillers, repetitions of words, and interjections was decided to be the focus of transcription. The transcripts were then read several times and coded according to an adapted version of Victori's (1999) coding framework. This framework was selected because it was developed specifically for analyzing the metacognitive knowledge of writing. It categorized such knowledge into person, task, and strategic knowledge. Person knowledge includes knowledge regarding one's interest in writing (motivation), one's concept as a writer and the degree of confidence in one's capacity for writing (self-concept), and the perceived problems in writing in English (writing problems). Task knowledge includes knowledge regarding the general characteristics and requirements of writing an academic text (text knowledge), the perceived purpose of writing the essay (concern for purpose), and one's concern for the reader (concern for audience). Strategic knowledge includes knowledge regarding planning ideas, organizing ideas, evaluating, and resourcing.

Based on the data in the study, Victori's (1999) framework was adapted accordingly. The category of person knowledge was narrowed down to one's concept as a writer and writing motivation, and the category of strategic knowledge was changed from knowledge regarding planning ideas, organizing ideas, evaluating, and resourcing to knowledge regarding planning, monitoring, and evaluating, which are the three components of metacognitive strategies that learners utilize to manage and regulate their learning (Nguyen and Gu 2013; Wenden 1998).

To identify the students' extent of revision according to feedback, teacher and peer written feedback was divided into feedback points, which included "symbols and marks in the margins, underlining of problems, and complete corrections, as well as more detailed comments and suggestions" (Hyland 1998: 261). The usable feedback points were further distinguished on the basis of the nature of feedback (e.g., revision-oriented feedback or praise) and its relevance (e.g., irrelevant feedback due to students' self-revision). The outlines/research proposals, first drafts, and final drafts of each student were compared to identify the usable feedback points acted upon by the student for revision. Then the percentage of usable feedback points that were acted upon to the total number of usable feedback points was calculated to determine the extent to which the students integrated teacher and peer feedback into their revision. The present study focused on the students' use of teacher feedback for revision rather than peer feedback because they did not highlight the role of the peer feedback activity in the development of metacognitive knowledge.

4 Findings

This section presents the student writers' metacognitive knowledge development in the process-oriented writing course, including person knowledge (writer identity and motivation), task knowledge (text knowledge and concern for purpose and audience), and strategic knowledge (planning, monitoring, and evaluating). Table 2 shows the similarities and differences in the students' metacognitive knowledge of writing.

Table 2: The two students' metacognitive knowledge development.

	Katrina	Sally
Person knowledge	– Self-perceived identity of a weak writer – Motivated to revise	– Self-perceived identity of a weak writer – Less motivated to revise

Table 2 (continued)

	Katrina	Sally
Task knowledge	– Gained textual knowledge (e.g., a formal tone), but needed further enhancement – Awareness of purpose but not audience	– Gained textual knowledge (e.g., essay structure), but needed further enhancement – Little awareness of purpose and audience
Strategy knowledge	– Appreciation for planning the time needed for the research and writing process – Emphasized the use of external resources such as the writing samples and the teacher for monitoring writing – Valued the opportunity of dialogical interaction with the teacher for self-reflection and revision	– Little appreciation for planning – Showed a lack of awareness regarding monitoring writing – Valued the opportunity of dialogical interaction with the teacher for self-reflection and revision

4.1 Metacognitive awareness regarding oneself as a writer

Katrina regarded herself as a weak writer. She knew that her writing was "not very good", and that she still could not "catch up with citation" despite teacher instruction on the APA citation style. She also felt that her writing was "not formal enough".

Despite the self-perceived identity of a weak writer and the associated writing problems, Katrina reported that she felt motivated to write and revise because of the multiple drafting process and teacher feedback on each draft. She considered multiple drafting "a process of learning" which could not be omitted. She highlighted teacher feedback as the driving force for the writing process, which was "reliable" and demonstrated the efforts to provide detailed customized comments for the improvement of students' writing. Such feedback motivated her to write and revise: "I really have problems, but I don't mind revising. I welcome comments." This was because teacher feedback enabled her to understand "how to learn" and "how to write". As Katrina revised both the secondary and primary research papers based on teacher feedback while Sally only did so for the secondary research paper, the extent of their revision for the secondary research paper is presented in Table 3. Katrina received 12 and 21 usable teacher feedback points for her outline and first draft, respectively. She

Table 3: The revision of the two students after teacher feedback for the secondary research paper.

	Number of feedback points received (outline)	Number and percentage of feedback points acted upon	Number of feedback points received (first draft)	Number of feedback points acted upon
Katrina	13 (12 usable feedback points)	6 (50%)	27 (21 usable feedback points)	16 (76%)
Sally	9 (9 usable feedback points)	1 (11%)	21 (19 usable feedback points)	6 (32%)

incorporated 50% and 76% of the teacher feedback into the outline and the first draft, respectively. She was so motivated by the teacher feedback that she even revised the final draft: "I found that my final draft was still very complicated, still a lot of comments, so I think this is not final draft, maybe I can do it better."

Sally also thought that she was "weak at writing". She honestly admitted that she did not know what her writing problems were because of her low proficiency: "I don't know what my problem is because I am very weak." Despite this acknowledgement, Sally stated that it was "quite difficult to keep the whole essay objective."

Contrary to Katrina, Sally did not appear to like the idea of multiple drafting. She stated the preference for writing only one draft and then correcting the minor mistakes: "I'd rather write the complete essay and then correct the minor mistakes." Sally attributed her unwillingness to write multiple drafts to the perceived large amount of teacher feedback on her outline and first draft and to its lack of specificity, as represented by the following quotes:

> "I have a very heavy workload to correct my outline. It makes me confused. My problem is too much." (outline)
> "Teacher comments are too much and it makes me feel I have to rewrite the whole essay." (first draft)
> "I can't process at that time to reorganize my whole essay." (first draft)
> "The teacher gives me a very general direction, and I am still confused at that time. I can't process what the teacher is talking about." (first draft)

These quotes indicate the perceived negative influence of teacher feedback (i.e., large amount and a lack of specificity) on Sally's cognitive processing and use of teacher feedback for revision, thus making her less motivated to write multiple drafts. Table 3 shows that compared to Katrina, Sally received slightly fewer usable teacher feedback points, 9 and 19 for the outline and first draft, respectively; however, she revised much less than Katrina, addressing only 11% and 32% of the feedback in the outline and the first draft, respectively. In fact, the teacher followed the philosophy of providing a manageable amount of specific revision-oriented feedback, as demonstrated by the following feedback points on the two students' outlines:

> "Why don't you just paraphrase or summarize the research evidence here."
> (teacher feedback on Katrina's outline)
> "It is not enough to just list the references here. You have to briefly explain how your evidence can support your topic sentence/point."
> (teacher feedback on Sally's outline)

However, while Katrina acted on the teacher feedback by paraphrasing the research evidence in her first draft, Sally did not address the feedback on a lack of explanation of the link between her claim and evidence, and the same problem continued to occur in her first draft, as highlighted by the teacher. The above contrasts between Katrina and Laura demonstrate the variation in low proficiency students' responses to feedback and their subsequent engagement with it. This is consistent with the finding of Zhang and Hyland (2018) showing individual differences in learners' engagement with feedback on writing. Such variations in engagement contributed to the different perceptions of whether the students were motivated writers or not.

4.2 Metacognitive awareness regarding the writing task

In terms of metacognitive awareness regarding academic writing, what emerged from the data was Katrina's emphasis on creating a "formal tone". For instance, she mentioned: "I learn from the essay the words like 'It is indicated that', those sentence structures. I can copy some from the sample essay." Her primary research paper contained the use of "indicate" in the active voice, as shown in "General findings indicated that male valued physical attractiveness more and prefer younger women." These data suggest that Katrina learned certain useful sentence patterns from the student samples to create a formal tone and her awareness of it, but she seemed to lack the knowledge of the various ways in which she could create this tone and tended to rely on copying from the sample texts.

Katrina seemed to be aware of the purpose of writing the secondary research paper, but she did not mention how she paid attention to audience while writing. Regarding the writing purpose of the secondary research paper, she emphasized how teacher feedback on her outline drew her attention to the purpose of the paper: "Feedback is very useful because actually I always misunderstand that I need to pick the side of the project, and then if the teacher didn't tell me, I would pick a side." A comparison between Katrina's outline and her first draft revealed that she acted on the teacher feedback to focus her first draft on "the positive and negative effects of uploading short video to the internet by the youngsters", rather than arguing for or against the issue of uploading short videos, as was the case in her outline. The data indicate that Katrina engaged with the teacher feedback, which corrected her misunderstanding, and became more aware of the purpose of the secondary research paper, which was to explain rather than to argue. She also seemed to be clear about the purpose of the primary research paper, as can be seen from the purpose statement in that paper: "The purpose of this project is to investigate how a female changes in her mate preference from adolescence to adulthood."

Sally did not explicitly talk about the writing purposes and the audience for her writing, and the salient theme concerning her knowledge about academic writing was the importance of a professional and objective writing style and the appropriate structure of research papers. For instance, she stated: "We have to write more professionally without our personal emotion. With each sentence you have to have evidence to support." This quote reflects the two aspects that Sally considered important for academic writing. Similar to Katrina, Sally also commented on the usefulness of learning from the student samples, but she highlighted the necessity of teacher explanation despite the opportunity for the students to analyze the samples first: "If I look at the whole sample essay, I can't really think of what the structure is without the teacher's explanation. But I think it is better if the teacher can explain it. Then it is good for my essay structure." This quote indicates that Sally needed more teacher scaffolding to acquire knowledge about academic writing. In addition, she did not seem to have a thorough understanding of the essay structure of the secondary research paper: "I am also confused why in the introduction we have to summarize the main points we will discuss and then we develop the three main points." This suggests that while she understood the structural elements required in a secondary research paper, she could not understand the reason behind it. In Sally's research papers, despite the occasional use of emotionally loaded words such as "totally", she appeared to be able to adopt an objective writing style in general. However, Sally's first draft exhibited an absence of an introduction and a thesis statement, and even in her final draft, a summary of the key points was missing, reflecting a lack of thorough understanding of the reason behind using that particular structure for the secondary research paper.

4.3 Metacognitive awareness of strategies

Concerning Katrina's metacognitive awareness of planning, although she did not mention the importance of planning the writing of the research papers, she did stress the significance of planning the time needed for the research and writing process. For each assignment, the students were required to work on the timeline of their research writing, so that they could submit their work-in-progress (e.g., outline/research proposal, first draft, research instrument, etc.) in accordance with the various deadlines established for these tasks. Katrina submitted her work on time for each deadline, and she commented: "I won't be the deadline fighter, so this [timeline planning] is good." This quote suggests that engaging in the activity of planning a timeline for the research and multiple-drafting process prevented Katrina from being a "deadline fighter" and raised her awareness of planning and probably monitoring the time for research and writing.

In terms of monitoring her writing, Katrina highlighted the sample paper and the teacher as two useful external resources. The teacher had emphasized in class that the students could refer to the sample paper and approach her for assistance during the writing process. Katrina's research paper exhibited certain similarities to the sample essay in terms of writing style and organization. She commented that it was a good strategy to rely on the sample paper to monitor her writing: "I rely on the sample essay." To monitor her writing, Katrina also actively sought teacher feedback on her work-in-progress. She was one among the three students who took the initiative to seek teacher advice on the first draft of the primary research paper even though the teacher-student conference was left optional for that paper. She stated: "We would like to ask more questions and approach the teacher by knowing how to write." Katrina appeared to know more about utilizing the external resources rather than herself to monitor her writing.

Regarding the evaluation of her writing, Katrina talked about how she reflected on her writing through dialogical interaction with the teacher in the teacher-student conference: "I remember the teacher gave me a lot of feedback because I like the fact that the teacher asked me some very detailed questions like 'how you define a teenager'. I think this is not a rough question. This is really like the key question of my essay." One problem with Katrina's first draft was that she did not define a teenager clearly in her research, and her conversation with the teacher prompted her to utilize secondary sources to provide a definition in the final draft. Owing to the value placed on teacher questioning and the student's engagement with teacher feedback Katrina realized the necessity of evaluating teacher feedback in relation to her own writing to determine its relevance (i.e., to include the definition of a teenager) for revision. In contrast to Katrina, although Sally talked about the planning of her writing, she did not appear to value this strategy much. She admitted that she was "not good at putting the main point of the whole essay first and then further develop it." Therefore, although she wrote the outline, she would rather avoid using it to plan her writing and adopt the practice of writing only one draft. These data suggest that Sally was not fully convinced of the usefulness of planning her writing probably because she could not do it well and believed that the old practice of writing only one draft was relatively more effective. The teacher provided an outline template asking the students to include a brief introduction containing a thesis statement; however, Sally's outline on "the influence of western feminism on women's position in Hong Kong" did not contain these two elements. Despite teacher feedback on this problem, her first draft still lacked a well-developed introduction and thesis statement. This implies that when confronted with the perceived difficulties of writing a good outline, Sally was probably influenced by her old writing belief and subsequently wrote the first draft without referring to the outline and the teacher feedback on it. Similar to Katrina, Sally also worked on the timeline of her research and writing process, but she did not appear to appreciate its usefulness for planning and monitoring the time invested for her work. Instead, she complained: "Because the teacher separated those drafts, it makes us feel non-stop deadlines." This quote indicates that just being involved in the planning activities (e.g., planning the timeline for writing) may not necessarily result in developing awareness about planning.

Sally did not explicitly talk about the monitoring strategies she had employed, which may indicate a lack of awareness regarding the monitoring of her writing. This was probably because of the infrequent use of such strategies. For instance, unlike Katrina, Sally did not mention the teacher as an external resource for monitoring. It is noteworthy that she just attended the writing conference as it was compulsory for the secondary research paper, but did not actively seek teacher feedback in the case of the primary research paper for which the writing conference was optional.

Although Sally did not actively seek teacher feedback, she appreciated the benefit of dialogical interaction with the teacher in the compulsory writing conference as compared with written feedback: "I think it [dialogical interaction] is more clear than the written comments. We can talk to the teacher, we can point out the point that we don't understand, and teachers can respond in real-time, so it is more useful." Sally valued the interaction with the teacher to enhance her understanding of teacher feedback. She also explained how such interaction stimulated her thinking: "I think it should be more face to face conversation instead of the written comments because I may read the comments and then I forget, but if I can discuss with the teacher and she leads me to think, I think it will help me to learn better." She gave one example: "Because one of my main points are not really the main point, so after the conversation, I changed the main points." These two quotes indicate that teacher feedback provided in the form of dialogical interaction with the student sharpened Sally's awareness of the need to conduct reflection, self-evaluation, and revision. In the writing conference, the teacher discussed with Sally regarding whether her third main point, concerning the influence of western feminism on Chinese culture was indeed related to her essay topic on 'the influence of western feminism on women's position in Hong Kong'. After reflection, Sally included relatively strong evidence that linked western feminism with the change in women's position in Hong Kong. The data suggest that Sally's engagement in the teacher-student writing conference and her engagement with the teacher feedback contributed to her awareness about the importance of evaluation and revision.

5 Discussion

From an ecological perspective (Van Lier 2000), this chapter has sought to explore the development of metacognitive knowledge, if any, in two low-proficiency Hong Kong EFL university student writers in a process writing course. The findings suggest both similarities and variations in their metacognitive knowledge development. In terms of similarities, the two student writers both highlighted the usefulness of student samples in enabling them to understand the features of academic writing, such as the objective writing style and appropriate structure. From an ecological perspective (Van Lier 2000), both students perceived the sample analysis activity to have learning potential. Through engaging in this activity the students developed their text knowledge. The usefulness of sample analysis activity as a classroom affordance is consistent with the finding that engaging students in analyzing and discussing writing samples or exemplars is a useful method to help them understand the genre features (MacArthur, Philippakos, and Ianetta 2014), although weak students such as Sally needed greater teacher scaffolding in this activity to acquire text knowledge. The sample analysis activity as a classroom affordance also resonates with Lam's (2015) finding that the teaching of genre knowledge within a process-oriented course can contribute to the development of text knowledge, demonstrating the importance of integrating process and genre considerations within a process-oriented course.

However, both of the students needed to further develop their text knowledge. For instance, classroom affordances related to genre instruction needed to be created for Sally so that in addition to knowing the "what" of the text, she would also understand the "why" of the structure of academic papers. In Katrina's case, classroom affordances were necessary for her to understand different text strategies to create a formal tone rather than relying on just copying sentence patterns from the sample essay. Such affordances also needed to equip students with audience awareness, because neither student had explicitly stated their concern for audience, which may be attributed to the fact that EFL students are inclined to treat their teacher as the only reader of their writing (Victori 1999). One way to address the aforementioned problems is to use classroom affordances to highlight the importance of the audience and the purpose of the text, how these elements determined textual features of the writing, and text strategies to achieve these features.

Both students also needed to understand how to integrate text knowledge with strategy use. While talking about the use of planning strategies, for example, neither student stated how they took the initiative to pay attention to the rhetorical features of the academic papers (e.g., organization, purpose, and audience). This implies that teachers need to create appropriate learning resources or activities (e.g., outline template containing questions about concerns for textual features, self-evaluation form) that enable thier students to apply text knowledge while utilizing writing strategies such as planning and revising (Teng, 2020).

The two students also demonstrated similarity in the development of metacognitive awareness concerning evaluation. Both students realized the importance of self-evaluation and revision subsequent to teacher-student dialogical interactions. It seems that the students perceived affordances in the kind of writing conference which enabled them to play an active role in seeking, interpreting, and using teacher feedback to perform the evaluation and modification of their own work–an example of sustainable feedback aiming to promote learners' self-regulation (Carless et al. 2011; Teng, 2020), which contributed to their metacognitive awareness regarding self-evaluation. EFL students in process-oriented writing classrooms are inclined to uncritically follow teacher feedback for revision (Richardson 2000), and the responsiveness of the two students to the practice of dialogical interactions and sustainable feedback indicate the potential of such interactions in enabling the weak students to reflect on and revise their work and in raising their awareness regarding self-evaluation.

Notably, although peer evaluation activities were also used in the process writing course, which according to research may raise audience awareness (Ruan 2005), motivate students to practice evaluation skills (Nguyen and Gu 2013), and enable them to be more critical of their own work (Tsui and

Ng 2000), neither student explicitly stated how this activity contributed to their metacognitive knowledge. This indicates that weak students such as Katrina and Sally may not perceive peers as affordances. For instance, Katrina relied on the teacher rather than her peer to monitor her writing. This could be attributed to the students' past experience of being exposed to product-focused and teacher-centered writing instruction, and of having conducted little peer evaluation previously. It might also be due to their perception of the teacher being a "reliable" figure for providing feedback as well as their own inability to provide "right comments" on their peers' essay. Certain EFL students tend to regard their teachers as more competent professionals for providing feedback (Lam 2014), although peers may be a potentially useful source of affordance in relation to EFL students' development of metacognitive knowledge (Cotterall and Murray 2009). Therefore, teachers in similar contexts should be aware of weak students' tendency to treat their teacher as a major source of affordance, and they should find ways to make peer evaluation a kind of affordance for the students as well.

Despite the similarities described above, the present study also identified variations in the two students' engagement with various aspects of the process writing course, and consequently, in the development of their metacognitive knowledge. Although Katrina perceived herself as a weak writer, she actively participated in the learning-to-write process by planning (and possibly monitoring) the time for the research and writing processes to avoid being a deadline fighter, learning from teacher feedback about the importance of the purpose of writing, seeking external resources (e.g., sample essays and the teacher) to monitor her writing, and actively using teacher feedback for the evaluation and revision of her writing. Her active engagement with the learning-to-write process was accompanied by her increasing awareness of being a motivated writer who acquired a sense of writing purpose as well as her awareness regarding the use of planning, monitoring, and evaluating her writing to improve the writing quality.

In contrast, although Sally complied with the teacher's requirement of writing multiple drafts in a superficial manner, she demonstrated a lower level of engagement with the learning-to-write process. For example, when confronted with the perceived difficulties related to writing an outline, she probably followed the old writing belief and wrote the first draft without referring to her outline and the teacher feedback on it. She complained about planning and managing the time for her work and did not take the initiative to seek external resources, such as the teacher, for monitoring her writing. Although she attended the compulsory teacher-student conference and also utilized a small percentage of the teacher feedback for self-evaluation and revision, she ignored the majority of the feedback and did not revise her writing as much as Katrina. Probably as a result of less active engagement with the learning-to-write process, Sally felt that she was less motivated to revise according to the teacher feedback and did not appear to demonstrate much appreciation for the planning strategies and much awareness regarding the monitoring strategies (e.g., seeking teacher's assistance), although she acknowledged that she had gained knowledge regarding academic writing and had realized the importance of self-evaluation and revision in writing.

Previous research has demonstrated that engaging students in self-regulation during a process writing course may contribute to the development of their metacognitive knowledge (Ruan 2005). The variations in the students' engagement and their metacognitive knowledge development described in this study further suggests that different degrees of student engagement may result in different degrees of development of their metacognitive awareness.

From an ecological perspective (Van Lier 2000), the different degrees of engagement of the two students in the learning-to-write process, along with the variation in their metacognitive knowledge development, could be explained by the different affordances perceived by them in the process writing course. A typical example of perceiving different affordances was the different views of the two students regarding the usefulness of teacher feedback, which led to different extents of engagement with it. The teacher followed the principle of providing a manageable amount of revision-oriented teacher feedback to both the students. While Katrina considered the teacher feedback to be detailed and stated that it catered to improving her writing ability, Sally thought that the feedback was too much and lacked specificity, which prevented her from processing and using it in her writing. Consequently, Katrina acted on a much higher percentage of the teacher feedback compared to Sally and perceived herself as a motivated writer. Similarly, it was likely that Katrina (but not Sally) viewed the teacher as an affordance for monitoring her writing of the primary research paper, which explained her initiative of approaching the teacher for feedback and her subsequent awareness of utilizing the instructor as an external resource for the monitoring process.

In addition, Sally's little appreciation for planning her writing could have been a result of her less active engagement with the planning activity of writing an outline, as can be seen from her little adherence to the outline template and disregard for the teacher feedback. This less active engagement might be related to the failure to view these two learning resources as affordances, possibly resulting from the perceived difficulties in creating an outline and her old belief of writing only one draft. L2 learners' beliefs may mediate the classroom learning environment/structure in terms of creation of affordances (Ma 2016). In the study, Sally's old writing belief might have negatively impacted her opinion of the learning opportunities offered by the outline writing activity, particularly when she encountered difficulties in producing a good outcome. Such a negative perception may cause Sally to be less willing to engage with the new approach of planning her writing, leading her to follow the old habit of writing only one draft, despite participating in the activity of writing an outline, thus resulting in her little appreciation for the planning process.

In summary, probably because of the different affordances perceived by them in response to the resources within the learning structure and of the negative impact of Sally's old writing beliefs on the creation of affordances out of the activity in which she experienced learning difficulties, the two students exhibited different levels of engagement with the learning opportunities, which resulted in different degrees of metacognitive knowledge development. Previous research has focused on the type of pedagogical interventions that may positively impact the metacognitive knowledge development among student writers as a group (Lam 2015; Ruan 2005). However, this study demonstrates that it should not be assumed that all the learners within the classroom will perceive the same affordances in the learning-to-write activities and engage equally in these activities to develop their metacognitive awareness, even if the students have been grouped into the same category, for example, "low proficiency students".

The above findings imply that teachers, as the "designers and sustainers of the learning milieu" (Boud and Molloy 2013: 710), need to pay attention to creating affordances for individual students. Firstly, teachers need to understand that merely involving students in planning, drafting, and redrafting their writing based on feedback in a process writing course may not necessarily enhance their students' metacognitive awareness. Certain learners, similar to Sally, may simply comply with teachers' requirements superficially, without really appreciating the use of self-regulatory writing strategies. Secondly, teachers need to create communication channels for students to share their perceptions of the learning potential of the resources available in the classroom (e.g., teacher feedback, outline template, etc.), so that teachers are able to understand the rationale behind their perceptions and accordingly take actions to adjust the learning resources specifically for certain students, if possible. For instance, the teacher perceived that she provided a "manageable" amount of specific feedback to Sally; however, the interview conducted in the study served as a communication channel which revealed that the student appeared to think otherwise. In this case, the teacher needs to focus only on the major issues in Sally's paper and provide scaffolding in the form of dialogical interaction, which Sally perceived as helpful in prompting her to perform self-evaluation and revision, to make such feedback serve as a source of affordances for Sally to act upon. Thirdly, since Sally's old writing beliefs impacted negatively on the creation of affordances in the planning activity in which she encountered learning difficulties, it is important for the teacher to explore ways to counter the potentially negative influence of learner beliefs, by, for example, addressing the students' learning difficulties when they experiment with "new" writing strategies during learning activities. If Sally's problems, which she encountered while creating an outline, had been solved, she would probably have exhibited more engagement in using it and would have developed an awareness regarding the importance of planning, without letting her old writing belief lead her to place little value on the planning activity and to adopt her old practice of writing only one draft.

The above findings suggest the following measures for promoting low proficiency student writers' metacognitive knowledge development the next time the writing course is offered: (1). Continuing to incorporate process and genre considerations in the process writing course by connecting the audience and purpose of texts, relevant textual features and text strategies; (2). Creating affordances (e.g., outline template containing questions about concerns for textual features) to integrate text knowledge with strategy use; (3). Helping students realize the potential of peers as affordances; (4). Creating communication channels to understand students' views of classroom learning activities as a basis for adjustment of writing activities; and (5). Providing timely scaffolding to support students' engagement with "new" learning activities to counter the potentially negative influence of their writing beliefs.

6 Conclusion

The present study explored the metacognitive knowledge development of two low-proficiency Hong Kong EFL university student writers in a course that incorporated instructions for both process writing and strategy use. The study identified variations in the two students' level of engagement with the different aspects of the process-oriented writing course, as well as in the development of their metacognitive knowledge (e.g., motivation to write, awareness of planning, and monitoring), despite their similarities (e.g., text knowledge). Such variations have been explained from an ecological perspective through the concept of affordances (Van Lier 2000). The two students seemed to perceive different affordances (learning opportunities) in the learning-to-write activities within the classroom learning structure and engaged with the activities to different extents, thereby developing different degrees of metacognitive awareness. These findings indicate that the teacher needs to pay attention to what affordances individual students may create out of the classroom learning activities, even when they are grouped into the same category such as that of "weak students". Based on the findings, the study has provided pedagogical implications regarding how teachers should take into consideration the affordances created by individual students and the possible factors affecting such a creation (e.g., learner beliefs) when they attempt to develop the students' metacognitive knowledge in a process writing course.

This study involved only two participants in a particular setting, and therefore, its findings cannot be overgeneralized. Nevertheless, its implications may be relevant to the teacher-researcher who intends to re-plan the teaching approach to better promote the metacognitive knowledge of weak students, as well as to the teachers and students in other similar settings. The present study is limited in that the double role of the teacher-researcher might have introduced a certain level of subjectivity into the study and that no introspective data providing further information regarding the students' metacognitive knowledge were collected. Future research may explore how to integrate process writing pedagogy with strategy instruction to develop metacognitive knowledge in other contexts, using multiple sources of data, including interviews, think-aloud or stimulated recall, and textual analysis.

Acknowledgement: The research described here was supported by a small research grant (Project Ref: SRGS-13-03) from the Federation for Self-financing Tertiary Education (FSTE), Hong Kong. The authors would like to thank the anonymous reviewers for their constructive comments.

References

Braten, Ivar & Marit S. Samuelstuen. 2007. Measuring strategic processing: comparing task-specific self-reports to traces. *Metacognition and Learning* 2 (1). 1–20.

Boud, David & Elizabeth Molloy. 2013. Rethinking models of feedback for learning: The challenge of design. *Assessment & Evaluation in Higher Education* 38(6) 698–712.

Brown, Ann. 1982. Learning, Remembering, and Understanding. Technical Report No. 244.

Burns, Anne. 2010. *Doing action research in English language teaching: A guide for practitioners.* New York: Routledge.

Carless, David, Diane Salter, Min Yang, & Joy Lam. 2011. Developing sustainable feedback practices. *Studies in Higher Education* 36 (4). 395–407.

Cotterall, Sara & Garold Murray. (2009). Enhancing metacognitive knowledge: Structure, affordances and self. *System* 37 (1). 34–45.

Davidson, Christina. 2009. Transcription: Imperatives for qualitative research. *International Journal of Qualitative Methods* 8 (2) 35–52.

Flavell, John. 1979. Metacognition and cognitive monitoring: A new area of cognitive developmental inquiry. *American Psychologist* 34 (10) 906–911.

Flavell, John, Patricia Miller, & Scott Miller. 2002. *Cognitive Development* 4th ed. Englewood Cliffs: Prentice-Hall.

Forbes, Karen. 2018. The role of individual differences in the development and transfer of writing strategies between foreign and first language classrooms. *Research Papers in Education* 34, 445–464.

Graham, Steve & Karen Harris. 2000. The role of self-regulation and transcription skills in writing and writing development. Educational Psychologist 35. 3–12.

Hacker, Douglas, Matt Keener & John Kircher. 2009. Writing is applied metacognition. In Douglas Hacker, John Dunlosky & Arthur Graesser (eds.), *Handbook of metacognition in education*, 154–172. New York: Routledge.

Hyland, Fiona. 1998. The Impact of Teacher Written Feedback on Individual Writers. *Journal of Second Language Writing* (7). 255–286.

Kao, Chian-Wen & Barry Lee Reynolds .2017. A study on the relationship among Taiwanese college students' EFL writing strategy use, writing ability and writing difficulty. *English Teaching & Learning* 41(4). 31–64.

Karlen, Yves. 2017. The development of a new instrument to assess metacognitive strategy knowledge about academic writing and its relation to self-regulated writing and writing performance. *Journal of Writing Research* 9 (1). 61–86.

Kowal, Sabine, & Daniel O'Connell. 2014. Transcription as a crucial step of data analysis. In Uwe Flick (ed.), *The SAGE handbook of qualitative data analysis*, 64–79. London: Sage Publications.

Lam, Ricky. 2013. Two portfolio systems: EFL students' perceptions of writing ability, text improvement, and feedback. *Assessing Writing* 18 (2).132–153.

Lam, Ricky. 2014. Promoting self-regulated learning through portfolio assessment: testimony and recommendations. *Assessment & Evaluation in Higher Education* 39(6) 699–714.

Lam, Ricky. 2015. Understanding EFL students' development of self-regulated learning in a process-oriented writing course. *TESOL Journal* 6 (3). 527–553.

Lee, Icy, & David Coniam. 2013. Introducing assessment for learning for EFL writing in an assessment of learning examination-driven system in Hong Kong. *Journal of Second Language Writing* 22 (1). 34–50.

Lee, Man-Kit. 2015. Peer feedback in second language writing: Investigating junior secondary students' perspectives on inter-feedback and intra-feedback. *System* 55. 1–10.

Lin, Shin-Ju, Brandon Monroe & Gary Troia. 2007. Development of writing knowledge in grades 2–8: A comparison of typically developing writers and their struggling peers. *Reading & Writing Quarterly* 23 (3). 207–230.

Lo, Julia, & Fiona Hyland. 2007. Enhancing students' engagement and motivation in writing: The case of primary students in Hong Kong. *Journal of Second Language Writing* 16 (4). 219–237.

Ma, Jingjing. 2016. The influence of writing beliefs on two Chinese EFL university students' use of peer feedback: An ecological perspective. *International Journal of Applied Linguistics and English Literature* 5 (3). 247–256.

MacArthur, Charles, Zoi Philippakos & Melissa Ianetta. 2014. Self-regulated strategy instruction in college developmental writing. *Journal of Educational Psychology* 107 (3). 855–867.

Mak, Barley & David Coniam. 2008. Using wikis to enhance and develop writing skills among secondary school students in Hong Kong. *System* 36 (3). 437–455.

Morgan, David. 1997. *Focus groups as qualitative research*, 2nd ed. Thousand Oaks: Sage Publications.

Nguyen, Le Thi Cam & Peter Yongqi Gu. 2013. Strategy-based instruction: A learner-focused approach to developing learner autonomy. *Language Teaching Research* 17 (1). 9–30.

Norton, Lin. 2009. *Action research in teaching and learning: A practical guide to conduct pedagogical research in universities*. New York: Routledge.

O'Brien, Teresa. 2004. Writing in a foreign language: Teaching and learning. *Language Teaching* 37. 1–28.

Reynolds, Barry Lee & Mark Feng Teng. (eds.). 2019. *English literacy instruction for Chinese speakers*. Singapore: Palgrave Macmillan.

Richardson, Susan. 2000. Students' conditioned response to teachers' response: portfolio proponents, take note!. *Assessing Writing* 7 (2). 117–141.

Ruan, Zhoulin. 2005. A metacognitive perspective on the growth of self-regulated EFL student writers. *Reading Working Papers in Linguistics* 8. 175–202.

Saddler, Bruce & Steve Graham. 2007.The relationship between writing knowledge and writing performance among more and less skilled writers. *Reading & Writing Quarterly* 23 (3). 231–247.

Schraw, Gregory & Sperling Rayne Dennison. 1994. Assessing metacognitive awareness. *Contemporary Educational Psychology* 19. 460–475.

Sengupta, Sima & Peter Falvey. 1998. The role of the teaching context in Hong Kong English teachers' perceptions of L2 writing pedagogy. *Evaluation and Research in Education* 12 (2). 72–95.

Seow, Anthony. 2002. The writing process and process writing. In Jack C. Richards & Willy A. Renandya (eds.), *The writing process and process writing. Methodology in language teaching: An anthology of current practice*, 315–320. Cambridge: Cambridge University Press.

Stewart, Mary & Marie Cheung. 1989. Introducing a process approach in the teaching of writing in Hong Kong. *Institute of Language in Education Journal* 6. 41–48.

Teng, Feng Mark. 2016. Immediate and delayed effects of embedded metacognitive instruction on Chinese EFL students' English writing and regulation of cognition. *Thinking Skills & Creativity* 22. 289–302.

Teng, Feng Mark. 2019a. Tertiary-level students' English writing performance and metacognitive awareness: A group metacognitive support perspective. *Scandinavian Journal of Educational Research*. doi: 10.1080/00313831.2019.1595712

Teng, Feng Mark. 2019b. The role of metacognitive knowledge and regulation in mediating university EFL learners' writing performance. *Innovation in Language Learning and Teaching*. Doi: 10.1080/17501229.2019.1615493

Teng, Feng Mark. 2019c. A comparison of text structure and self-regulated strategy instruction for elementary school students' writing. *English Teaching: Practice and Critique* 18 (3). 281–297.

Teng, Feng Mark. 2020. Young learners' reading and writing performance: Exploring collaborative modeling of text structure as an additional component of self-regulated strategy development. *Studies in Educational Evaluation*. Doi: 10.1016/j.stueduc.2020.100870

Teng, Feng Mark & Jing Huang. 2019. Predictive effects of writing strategies for self-regulated learning on secondary school learners' EFL writing proficiency. *TESOL Quarterly* 53. 232–247.

Tsui, Amy & Maria Ng. 2000. Do secondary L2 writers benefit from peer comments?. *Journal of Second Language Writing* 9 (2). 147–170.

van Lier, Leo. 2000. From input to affordance: Social interactive learning from an ecological perspective. In James P. Lantolf (ed.), *Sociocultural Theory and Second Language Learning*, 245–259. Oxford: Oxford University Press.

Victori, Mia. 1999. An analysis of writing knowledge in EFL composing: A case study of two effective and two less effective writers. *System* 27 (4). 537–555.

Wenden, Anita. 1998. Metacognitive knowledge and language learning. *Applied Linguistics* 19 (4). 515–537.

Zamel, Vivian. 1983. The composing processes of advanced ESL students: Six case studies. *TESOL Quarterly* 17 (2). 165–187.

Zhang, Zhe & Ken Hyland. 2018. Student engagement with teacher and automated feedback on L2 writing. *Assessing Writing* 36. 90–102.

Appendix

Please read the instructions on the writing task. Think about your experience of writing the paper and the writing processes. Several questions about your writing experience in this course will be asked.

1. How do you feel about doing this writing task?
2. How did you think of yourself as a writer in different stages of this writing task?
3. What was your confidence level in different stages of this writing task?
4. What kind of problems did you encounter while writing?
5. What do you know about the characteristics of a good paper for this writing task?
6. What do you know about the intended purpose and audience of this writing task?
7. What do you know about the different writing strategies, if any, that you used while doing this writing task? What were they? How did you use each?

Dureshahwar Shari Lughmani, Dennis Foung
Metacognitive strategy-focused instruction in a writing across the curriculum programme in a Hong Kong university: The impact on writing performance

Abstract: Writing across the curriculum (WAC) in the second language (L2) context requires careful instruction for both writing-to-learn and learning-to-write purposes. Instruction in metacognitive awareness has the potential to be an effective approach for improving writing in unfamiliar genres. This study describes the metacognitive strategies used as part of a university-wide WAC programme in a Hong Kong university. Researchers aimed to identify the most effective strategies, as well as L2 writers' usage and perceptions of these strategies. Data from 135 students were retrieved from a learning management system, including their use of various metacognitive tools, such as access to an assignment checklist and assignment guidelines, consultation attendance and student reflection, and student writing performance. The results showed that students used certain metacognitive strategies, e.g., assignment guidelines and student reflections, more than others. Correlation analysis and an independent sample *t*-test revealed a positive relationship between the use of certain metacognitive strategies (e.g., assignment guidelines and checklist) and writing performance.

Keywords: WAC, Genre-based Instruction, Writing in the Disciplines, Revision, Metacognition

1 Introduction

1.1 Hong Kong as a unique Chinese-speaking region

Among Chinese-speaking regions and cities, Hong Kong has a high proportion of English-medium universities, where L2 learners are required to read and write in English (Poon 2010). According to the University Grants Committee in Hong Kong (n.d.), the total number of such students was approximately 100,000 in 2017/18 in

---

Dureshahwar Shari Lughmani, The Hong Kong Polytechnic University
Dennis Foung, The Hong Kong Polytechnic University

https://doi.org/10.1515/9781501512643-007

eight publicly funded universities. Approximately 83% of these students were local L1 Cantonese Chinese, and 12% were from Mainland China with Mandarin as their native language. In this context, students faced language problems in English (Morrison and Evans 2018). Many of these students were not certain about the quality of their performance in writing assignments for the university, and did not think they could write well at this level (Morrison and Evans, 2018). Therefore, universities have adopted various approaches to enhance the writing capability of students, including Writing Across the Curriculum (WAC) programmes.

1.2 Writing across the curriculum

WAC as a movement has been operationalised through two complementary approaches which have been advocated for decades (e.g., Kuiper et al. 2017). The first approach, writing-to-learn, is based on constructivist theories of education. In this approach, student writers are more cognitively engaged, and they use writing as a tool to deepen learning, in addition to demonstrating what they have learned (Britton 1970). The second approach in WAC, which is also referred to as the rhetorical approach, considers writing as a means to communicate with the social or discourse communities of various academic disciplines (learning-to-write) (Maimon et al.1981). With the expansion of disciplines in an increasingly interconnected world, L2 writers need to be able to cope with complex social situations and at the same time participate in the construction of new knowledge through writing. Concerns about the increased cognitive load that this expansion of writing within the disciplines had on students led to one Hong Kong university's implementation of a substantial intensive writing component in their general education (GE) courses as a graduation requirement. This initiative is called the English Writing Requirement or EWR.

1.3 English writing requirement

The EWR requires all undergraduates to take a formal credit-bearing GE subject with an integrated writing assignment of 2,500 words that carries substantial weight (at least 40% of the overall course grade and varies across subjects). These EWR-embedded GE subjects requires the work of both subject teachers and writing teachers, and such collaborative approach has been successful in various contexts, such as that reported in Reynolds (2013). Students need to submit three drafts of their assignment: the first two drafts to language teachers and the last draft to the discipline teacher. The assignment needs to be written over a period of 13 weeks after receiving detailed feedback twice for their first two drafts. A score will be given after language teachers have read the second draft of the student. The final draft is then submitted to the discipline instructor at the end of the semester. The discipline instructor will also give a score to the student and the final score of the assignment is the sum of the score given by the language teacher and the discipline instructor. As university departments specialise in GE subjects and sub-disciplines, it is essential to ensure that language teachers and students understand the subject teachers' expectations and that students receive relevant, consistent, and constructive support from their language teachers. To facilitate L2 writers' progress in writing in new disciplinary genres, a systematic instruction of metacognitive strategies for genre awareness underpins this programme.

This systematic development and implementation of tools to facilitate metacognitive strategies aims at helping students understand the required writing assignment genres. Several tools were developed to systematically instruct metacognitive strategies, such as planning, monitoring, evaluating, and revising (Teng 2019a). In the present study, specific strategies included: 1) assignment orientations, 2) assignment guidelines, 3) checklists, 4) feedback reports, 5) consultations, and 6) student reflections. The tools were introduced to students via orientations, emails, and an online platform. The students were thus guided to promote their metacognitive writing strategies in the required genres. Details of these tools can be found in the Methodology section.

2 Literature review

Several previous studies have described and characterised metacognitive strategies. Flavell defined metacognitive strategies as language learners' knowledge and awareness of their own cognitive processes and outcomes, which includes the stages of planning, monitoring, evaluating, and revising. He defined the metacognitive strategies in cognitive terms and identified the four following dimensions: 1) metacognitive knowledge, 2) metacognitive experiences, 3) goals, and 4) actions to nurture "the active monitoring and consequent regulation and orchestration of cognitive processes to achieve cognitive goals" (Flavell 1979: 252). To enhance the role of metacognition in learning and solving problems, Mevarech and Kramarski designed a multi-dimensional method, called IMPROVE (Mevarech and Kramarski 1997). This acronym defines the metacognitive strategies involved in the process of writing, which are introducing new concepts, metacognitive questioning, practising, reviewing and reducing difficulties, obtaining mastery, verification, and enrichment. More recently, Kao and Reynolds explored cognitive strategies through empirical research (Kao and Reynolds 2017). Using factor analysis, cognitive strategies in writing were found to include cognition/preparation, compensation, affective, and social aspects. With these four latent constructs, a range of metacognitive strategies were operationalised and validated empirically, including planning the writing steps, using checklists, writing language diaries, and receiving feedback from teachers.

Other than the definitions of metacognitive strategies, various studies have also attempted to understand the role of metacognition and its significance in learning to write in a second language (Kasper 1997; Ong and Zhang 2013; Teng 2016). Writing is a process of externalising cognitive processes to make meaning. Hacker, Keener, and Kircher (2009) referred to writing itself as "applied metacognition" that involves "metacognitive monitoring" (awareness) and "metacognitive regulation" or control that results in the modification of behaviour (Hacker, Keener, and Kircher 2009: 157). Their study claimed that the act of writing has not been studied scientifically and therefore they explored a new methodology to arrive at a cognitive theory of the process of writing itself. This understanding was partly achieved through eye-tracking experimentation with students during their writing processes such as reading, deleting, and revising at the word and sentence level. Hayes and Flower in their 1980 model, which was later revised by Hayes in 1996, identified three basic components – task environment, cognitive processes, and writer's long-term memory. Among these, the cognitive processes included planning, translating, and reviewing, all coordinated by the writer who monitored this sophisticated process (Hayes 1996: 136). Bracewell further stressed the importance of the conscious control of writing sub-skills during the writing process, including problem solving skills (Bracewell 1983). More recently, Teng highlights the combination of text structure knowledge and metacognitive strategies for better self-regulated writing (Teng 2019b).

Due to the significance of metacognition in writing (Teng & Huang 2019), many studies have empirically investigated the role of metacognitive strategies in the development of writing. These strategies, in general, have a positive relationship with the writing development of students. A number of studies have found a positive relationship between the use of strategies and writing performance or perceived writing performance (Shields 2000; Gupta and Woldemariam 2011; Bai Hu and Gu 2014). Other studies have gone further to explore the nature of these strategies and how they are related to writing performance. For example, Teng, in his study in mainland China, posited that teachers need to explicitly instruct students on how to set goals, plan, and practise self-monitoring and adapting before the strategies can be effective (Teng 2016). The need for explicit instruction of strategies was echoed by Kasper (1997). Teng demonstrated that instruction in metacognition results in the "transfer of responsibility from the teacher to the students" in the development of writing (Teng 2016: 300). In other words, teachers take the lead by introducing the genre to students, students then gradually take a more active role in applying the strategies. In connection with the genre issues faced by university students, research has revealed that instruction in genre-related metacognitive strategies helps students become aware of disciplinary expectations, such as structure and moves in the context of university writing (Hadwin and Winne 1996; Lin, Newby, and Glenn 1994; Negretti and Kuteeva, 2011). Metacognition allows students to apply genre knowledge to their writing after they experience analysing the genres of academic papers (e.g., Dudley-Evans 1995; Hyland 2010; Johns 1997; Sasaki and Hirose 1996). Teng even suggested that metacognitive strategies related to genre aspects have a greater impact on writing performance than other strategies (Teng 2016). In sum, these studies provide sufficient theoretical justification for universities to introduce metacognitive strategies for developing the writing skills of their students.

2.1 The theoretical foundation of the EWR

The EWR is a clear illustration of how instruction in metacognition can be implemented in a university setting. The EWR uses a set of metacognitive tools to facilitate genre-awareness whereby students are guided and trained in the use of several strategies. The theoretical framework underpinning this instruction includes a combination of strategic approaches. Taking our lead from Flavell's model of metacognitive strategy instruction (1979), we extended our model to apply Winne and Hadwin's four-phase model of self-regulated learning (SRL) (1998) and included the five gateways of successful cognition or learning, as shown in Table 1 below. The table demonstrates how Winne and Hadwin's five gateways have been employed in the English Writing Requirement (EWR).

Table 1: Five Gateways to Successful Cognition (adapted to EWR process writing).

Gateway	Description	EWR framework equivalent
Register conditions	Does the learner identify conditions (If) and accurately instantiate their values?	Assignment Guidelines Assignment Orientation
Valid interpretation	Does the profile of conditions match an appropriate action?	Checklists
Capability	Can the learner execute the action (Then)?	Submission of drafts Genre-based feedback reports

Table 1 (continued)

Gateway	Description	EWR framework equivalent
Motivation	Will the learner expend resources to execute the action?	Revision and Reflection
Capacity + opportunity	Is there cognitive capacity and environmental opportunity to execute the action?	Genre-based feedback reports

The EWR programme features metacognitive strategy-focused instruction. EWR is designed to help students prepare their assignments at different stages. The writing process, in which students engage to produce a 2,500-word draft after three revisions over 13 weeks during a semester, draws inspiration from the models of metacognition in writing proposed by Flavell (1979) and Winne and Hadwin (1998). The EWR starts by developing "cognitive conditions" for students that cultivate "domain knowledge" and "knowledge of task". "Knowledge of study tactics and strategies" forms a major component of EWR metacognitive strategy training, and students are required to use the tools developed for the various stages in the writing process (Winne and Hadwin 1998: 127).

The four-phase model proposed by Winne and Hadwin in 1998, shown in Figure 1, extended Flavell's 1979 model of writing Winne and Hadwin (1998).

Winne and Hadwin (1998) provide the scaffolding for the systematic metacognitive strategy instruction framework developed in the EWR, as shown in Table 2 below.

The "definition of task" stage involves communicating with the subject experts to establish a clear understanding of the task, which is then conveyed to students through an assignment orientation [F2F] ("Face to Face"), so they can start their "planning". Students are also given assignment guidelines [online] and checklists (Drafts 1 and 2) [online] which have been prepared in close communication with the subject experts to reflect the genre and assist students in formulating their "goals and plans" "Study tactics" consist of making use of further metacognitive tools, such as analysing the first or second feedback report [online] and booking the first or second consultation [F2F]. "Adaptations" include controlling measures such as revising, rewriting, extending, and writing the student reflection [online] in the process of becoming aware of the genre-expectations and applying these to their writing.

The current study aims to explore whether the instruction of metacognitive strategies in the EWR was successful in helping students write and revise

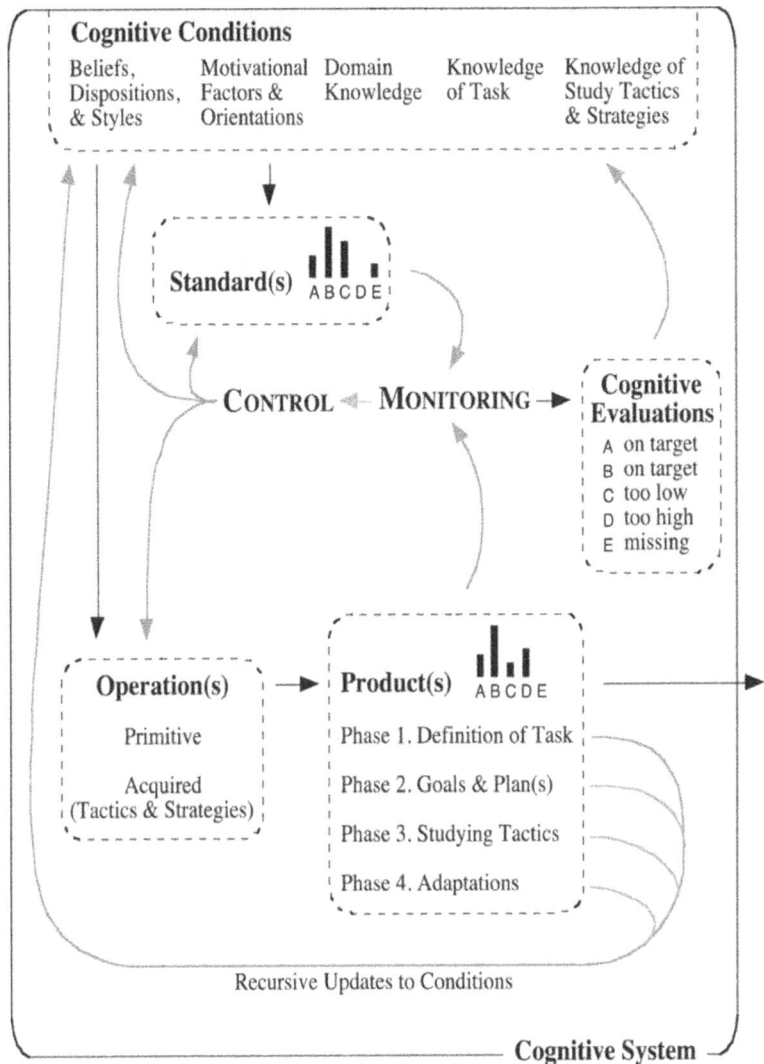

Figure 1: Winnie And Hadwin's (1998) four-phase model of self-regulated learning.

successfully, as indicated by their obtaining higher grades on the revision of their first drafts. Here are the specific research questions:

RQ1: How do students perceive these metacognitive strategies?

RQ2: Does the use of certain metacognitive strategies improve the writing performance of students? If so, which metacognitive strategies are effective?

Table 2: Mapping of the Framework – Winne and Hadwin (1998) vs. Flavell (1979).

Phases (Winne and Hadwin's 1998 four-phase model of SRL) as applied to metacognitive and cognitive processes in EWR	Flavell's (1979) equivalent metacognitive strategies as applied to EWR
[Definition of task]	[Planning] Assignment Orientation [F2F] Assignment Guidelines [Online]
[Goals and plans]	[Monitoring] Checklist (Draft 1) [Online]
[Studying tactics] Writing drafts, analysing and responding to feedback	[Monitoring] First Feedback Report [Online] First Consultation [F2F]
[Adaptations] Controlling through revising; rewriting, extending and reflection	[Evaluating and Revising] Student Reflection [Online] Checklist (Draft 2) [Online] Second Feedback Report [Online] Grading Revision through Rubric Including Criteria and Standards Second Consultation [F2F] Student Reflection [Online] Checklist (Draft 2) [Online]

3 Methodology

3.1 Metacognitive strategy-focused Instruction

While the previous section on the EWR outlines the theoretical foundations of, and rationale for the tools used in the programme, the section below describes how the tools are implemented in practice in each of the weeks in a semester. Table 3 provides an overview of the implementation.

3.1.1 Planning stage

During the planning stage, writing support tools are made available to the students. In weeks 3/4 (of a 13-week course), the discipline teacher offers a time slot for a writing teacher to give an assignment orientation during the lecture. The writing teacher introduces the assignment using the genre approach and suggests strategies for completing the assignment. Other support strategies (see

Table 3: Metacognitive Tools in English Writing Requirement Mapped According to Weeks.

Weeks	Tasks for students (Required)	Metacognitive Strategy Instructions provided (Flavell, 1979)
Week ¾		[Planning] Assignment Orientation [F2F] Assignment Guidelines [Online] [Monitoring] Checklist (Draft 1) [Online]
Around Week 6	First Draft Submission (to the writing teacher; 700 words) – Write the first few parts of the assignment	[Monitoring] First Feedback Report [Online] First Consultation [F2F] [Evaluating and Revising] Student Reflection [Online] Checklist (Draft 2) [Online]
Around Week 8	Second Draft Submission (to the writing teacher; 1500 words) – Revise the first 700 words – Expand the draft	[Evaluating and Revising] Second Feedback Report [Online] Second Consultation [F2F] Student Reflection [Online] Checklist (Draft 2) [Online]
Around Week 13	Final Draft Submission (to discipline teacher; 2500) – Revise the first 1500 words – Expand the draft	

Table 1 for details) are also introduced during this session. The orientation serves as an opportunity for students to receive face-to-face writing support during the planning stage. The orientation focuses on the task as an identifiable genre together with the sub-genres as indicated in Nesi and Gardner's framework (2012). The orientation is conducted by the writing teacher who has previously analysed the genre according to the mentioned framework, in close collaboration with the discipline teacher who serves as the subject expert.

The assignment guidelines are important for developing the students' metacognitive skills when writing in a virtual environment. Details of the assignment's genre and the respective strategies are presented in the orientation and summarised in an online document that students can download from their learning management system. The guidelines contain basic information about the assignment (e.g., genre and purposes), specific guidelines on organisational patterns, referencing and formatting requirements, excerpts for illustrating common student problems, and frequently asked questions (see Appendix 1 for a sample).

3.1.2 Monitoring stage

During the monitoring stage, students are reminded of the different strategies and receive feedback on the writing process; checklists and consultation sessions are also recommended. The Draft 1 checklist includes a list of items (approximately 10–15) on genre, language, and referencing that students can double check before submitting their first draft (see Appendix 2 for a sample). After submitting the first draft, students receive a feedback report from a language teacher (online PDF document), after which they can book a consultation to discuss their writing process with that teacher. The feedback report is a PDF document that consists of four to eight action points that students need to work on. Each action point focuses on one area for students to improve on and the writing teacher, in each action point, will name the problem, explain the nature of the problem, provide examples in students' text, list out resources for students to read more about that problem, and finally provide suggestions to fix the problem. The first feedback report/face-to-face consultation normally focuses on genre and writing organisation, and it may draw the students' attention to recurrent/systematic language and referencing errors.

3.1.3 Evaluation and revision stage

In the evaluation and revision stage, students revise their draft and prepare to submit a second draft. To help students evaluate their writing processes and strategies, they must reflect on the process by 1) rating their success in revising the first draft and 2) submitting a 50-word reflection to the writing teacher. In the second part of the reflection, students are presented with the following guiding questions and one textbox (in which to write their response?), but they are encouraged to write about any other aspects that they find useful for their learning.
1. What have you learned from revising your work?
2. What particular areas have you developed?
3. What areas would you like to develop more?
4. What were the challenges while revising your work?
5. Was the feedback report useful? In what ways?

In addition to reflection, students can also refer to the Draft 2 checklist for important items to review. After submission of the second draft, students receive a second feedback report, after which they can book another consultation session with their teacher. The second feedback report and consultation may still focus on genre and organisational issues, but at this stage the writing teacher is more likely to provide feedback on language, referencing issues, and aspects of genre. These instructional activities, which are intended to encourage students to evaluate their writing processes and to revise their work, underscore the importance of metacognitive instruction in helping the students compose a polished final paper.

3.2 Participants

Data from 135 students were retrieved for analysis. These students were taking a course as part of the GE requirement for their undergraduate programme which required them to fulfil the EWR (i.e., the WAC programme in question). Due to the design of the undergraduate programme, most of the students had already completed basic EAP training. The students were from different departments and programmes within the university. Most students had attained either a Level 3 (equivalent to the IELTS band 5.48–5.68) or Level 4 (equivalent to the IELTS band 6.31–6.51) on the Hong Kong Diploma of Secondary Education English Examination. As this study concerns with students' use of metacognitive strategies, students' differences in proficiency and study programme does not invalidate the current study.

The participants in the current study took four courses, Wearable Healthcare and Fitness Devices for Everyone, Fundamentals of Disaster Resilience, Chinese Art and Design, and Introducing Asian Popular Culture. Even though the writing assignments for these courses were academic essays, the required organisational patterns for each course were different. However, students should have received adequate guidelines and training through the metacognitive strategies provided, such as the assignment guidelines. It is also important to note that it is university policy to generally design these GE courses at the lowest level (Level 1), to allow all undergraduates to take the courses and ensure that the level of difficulty and the required expert knowledge in each course are comparable.

3.3 Outcome measures

To understand how the different stages of the metacognitive strategies affected the students, data were gathered from various sources (Table 4). These outcome measures were chosen on the basis of the validity of measuring the effectiveness of these metacognitive tools and the availability of data.

Table 4: Data Collected and Respective Data Sources.

Stage / Metacognitive Strategy tool	Outcome measures	Nature of data source
Planning Assignment Guidelines	No. of clicks on the assignment guidelines	Number – Count (0 to many)
Monitoring Use of Checklist in Draft 1 Feedback Reports Consultation One	Check marks on the Checklist Two Feedback reports prepared by the writing teacher Attended Consultation	Binary (i.e., YES/NO) Text Binary (i.e., YES/NO)
Evaluating and Revising Use of Checklist in Draft 2 Writing of Reflection Confidence in Revision	Check marks on the Checklist Student reflection Weighted average: Scores from radio buttons to indicate how well students think they have addressed an item on the feedback report – Can't revise at all (0) – Need to work harder (1) – Achieved to a certain extent (2) – Successful (3) – Very Successful (4)	Binary (i.e., YES/NO) Text Scale: 0–4
Consultation Two	Attended Consultation	Binary (i.e., YES/NO)
Overall Use of Checklist in any draft No. of Strategies Used	Check marks on the Checklist Counting: 1/ Use of Checklist in any drafts 2/ Attendance of Consultation 1 3/ Attendance of Consultation 2 4/ Writing of reflection	Binary (i.e., YES/NO) Number – Count (1–4)
Assignment Performance	Score	Scale 0–10

3.3.1 Assignment score

The assignment score is an indicator of students' performance. A rater assigned the score after he/she had read and commented on each student's second draft. The rater gave a score from 1 to 10 based on 1) task fulfilment, 2) organisation, 3) language, and 4) revision. The first three components were similar to other writing assessments and could be easily understood. "Revision" assessed the amount of revision that was completed on the second draft. Students were expected to read the rater's feedback and make revisions accordingly. If a student took all the suggestions offered in his/her feedback report, this individual would be scored high on this component. All assessment components were considered with equal weight. All eight raters in the current study were experienced in marking EWR assignments and were given sufficient information (e.g., assignment guidelines and checklists) to understand the assignment. They all received standardisation training (e.g. marker's briefing) and had at least one year of experience in marking similar student manuscripts before rating the manuscripts in the current study. After marking, an EWR team liaison member checked the raters' scores and moderated them when necessary. These procedures ensured that the assignment score was a valid and reliable indicator of a student's writing performance.

3.4 Data preparation and analysis

Because all the data were retrieved directly from both the learning management and the consultation booking systems, the data retrieved was considered complete without any missing components. Therefore, a missing cell reveals only that the student did not utilise a certain metacognitive strategy. For example, if students had not booked any consultation sessions, no data about their consultation would have been available in the consultation booking system.

The assignment score was an important indicator for this study, and various steps were taken to prepare this variable for analysis. At first, a visual inspection of a Stem-and-Leaf Plot and histogram indicated that the assignment score appeared to be normally distributed. However, a univariate outliner was then detected by examining the standard scores of the score (i.e., the Z score). One of them was > 3 and was removed from the dataset.

To answer RQ1 on students' perception of the metacognitive strategies, the feedback reports and reflection data were analysed to understand students' perceptions. The researchers compiled the student reflection entries and a small corpus with wordlists was created for further analysis. They then looked for keywords in the wordlists. These included high-frequency words that demonstrated the students' perceptions of the feedback report and other metacognitive tools and the development of their writing skills. After identifying these keywords, their concordances were examined carefully to identify common themes. Other than the students' reflections, two feedback reports for each student were analysed. The analysis was conducted by tagging the types of action points as "task fulfilment," "organisation," "language," or "referencing." Then, the mean number of action points for each component and the respective descriptive statistics were computed.

To answer RQ2 on how metacognitive strategies improve the writing performance, the means between those who had used a certain strategy and those who had not were compared by the researchers. The comparison was conducted by an independent samples *t*-test to explore differences between the two groups (Woodrow 2014). In this study, the points of interest were the assignment score (as an indication of students' writing performance) and the grouping variables (whether or not a student had used certain strategies). For example, the mean assignment scores of those who had used checklist 1 and those who had not were compared. This helped us understand whether students who had used a particular metacognitive strategy performed better than those who had not.

To further investigate RQ2, the researchers examined the correlation between the assignment scores with other numeric variables, such as the number of clicks on assignment guides and the number of strategies used. The aim of these analyses was to determine if there were any linear relationships between these variables. Correlation analysis was appropriate for exploring these relationships (Woodrow, 2014). IBM's Statistical Package for the Social Sciences (SPSS) 23 was used for the statistical analyses (an independent samples *t*-test and correlation analysis).

AntConc 3.43w was used to conduct the content analysis. After they submitted a second draft, 114 students wrote a short reflection paragraph. These short paragraphs were entered into AntConc 3.43w, and a Wordlist was generated. The research team went through the wordlist and identified content words that fit into six pre-defined categories: (1) Montent/genre/assignment, (2) Metacognitive strategies/EWR tools (Planning, monitoring, evaluating, and revising), (3) Use of sources, (4) Grammar and accuracy, (5) Structure (introduction, body, conclusion, topic sentence, paragraphs, etc.), and (6) Words of cognition and awareness. Then, the Concordance Lines of these words were examined to identify whether common themes existed. If a word or phrase with a similar meaning occurred more than once, it was identified as a theme for further analysis. All the words and phrases were identified as themes as long as they had details that were relevant to the pre-defined categories. No limitation was placed on the length of the words and phrases. Some themes were the result of the repeated occurrence of a word, but some were identified after examining several words and phrases with similar meanings.

3.5 Ethical clearance

The Ethical Review for Teaching/Research involving Human Subjects of this project was approved by the Departmental Research Committee and recorded on the university's Human Subjects Ethics Application Review System. In practice, the student data retrieval process was supervised by the coordinator of the WAC programme. All student and teacher identities were removed during the data retrieval process (by an administrator) and student data was anonymized. During the data analysis process, all data files were stored on a password-protected computer. After the data analysis stage, all data files were deleted.

4 Results

Generally, the students chose various tools. The descriptive statistics for each tool are summarised in Table 5. The most popular strategy was the use of assignment guidelines, with 90% of the students accessing them. Writing reflection was also a popular tool (84%). The least popular tool was attending consultation 2, with an attendance rate of only 11%. In addition to accessing the assignment guidelines, 66% of the students used at least two of the tools provided. These results show that the students exercised their right to choose their preferred tools. Even though some of the tools seemed to be more popular (e.g., assignment guidelines), none were entirely unused.

The performance indicators show that students did well but were conservative in their reflections on their confidence. The mean assignment score out of 10 was 6.73 with a score of "6" considered satisfactory and a score of "7" considered good. The students, therefore, did fairly well. However, their description of success in addressing the teachers' feedback comments (i.e., confidence in revision) was relatively modest. Their mean score for confidence was 2.38 (out of four), which was between "achieved to a certain extent" and "successful'."

4.1 Impact of metacognitive strategies

Certain strategies were used by only some students, so it was of interest to determine whether the students who used certain strategies scored significantly higher on the assignments. There were six strategies as follows: 1) using the draft 1 checklist, 2) attending consultation 1, 3) attending consultation 2, 4) writing a reflection, 5) accessing the assignment guidelines, and 6) using any checklist. The size of one group for accessing the assignment guidelines and attending consultation 2 was too small ($n = 13$ or $n = 15$) to be statistically robust, so no comparisons were made for these groups. Independent samples t-tests were performed on the remaining four strategies. Multiple hypothesis

Table 5: Descriptive Statistics for Metacognitive Provided.

Stage / Metacognitive Strategy tool	Data Source	Descriptive Statistics
Planning		
Assignment Guidelines	No. of clicks on the assignment guidelines	Mean 12.33 Median 10.00 SD 9.80 Min 0 Max 42 No (10%; No click) Yes (90%; One click+)
Monitoring		
Use of Checklist in Draft 1	Check marks on the Checklist	No 49 (37%) Yes 85 (63%)
Consultation One	Attended Consultation	No 109 (81%) Yes 25 (19%)
Evaluating and Revising		
Writing of Reflection	Student reflection	No 21 (16%) Yes 113 (84%)
Confidence in Revision	Weighted average: Scores from radio buttons to decide how well students think they have addressed an item on the feedback report – Can't revise at all / No attempt (0) – Need to work harder (1) – Achieved to a certain extent (2) – Successful (3) – Very Successful (4)	Mean 2.38 Median 2.75 SD: 1.22 Min 0 Max 4
Consultation Two	Attended Consultation	No 119 (89%) Yes 15 (11%)
Overall		
Assignment Score	Score (0–10)	Mean 6.73 Median 7.00 SD 1.246 Min 3 Max 10
Use of Checklist in Any Draft (same as: Use of Checklist in Draft 2)	Check marks on the Checklist	No 38 (28%) Yes 96 (72%)

Table 5 (continued)

Stage / Metacognitive Strategy tool	Data Source	Descriptive Statistics
No. of Strategies used	Counting: 1/ Use of Checklist in any drafts 2/ Attendance of Consultation 1 3/ Attendance of Consultation 2 4/ Writing of reflection	0 7 (5%) 1 38 (28%) 2 64 (48%) 3 18 (13%) 4 7 (5%)

tests were administered at the same time; therefore, Bonferroni corrections were made, and the critical value was reduced to 0.05/4 = 0.025. The results of these tests are summarised in Table 6.

Table 6: Mean Differences – Metacognitive Tools.

Metacognitive Strategies / Tool	Mean for YES	Mean for NO	Mean Difference	t (df)	Effect Size **(Cohen's d)
Using Draft One Checklist	6.98	6.31	+0.670*	3.096 (132)	0.545 (Medium)
Attendance at Consultation 1	7.08	6.65	+0.429	1.560 (132)	NA
Writing of Reflection	6.81	6.72	+0.09	0.312 (132)	NA
Using Checklist	6.94	6.21	+0.727*	3.146 (132)	0.576 (Medium)

* p<0.025
** Cut-off points used are based on Cohen (1988)

The results show that the metacognitive strategies may have helped the students with their writing. Among the four strategies, the students who used one or more strategies scored higher than those who did not use any strategies. The students who used the checklist for both drafts or only for Draft 1 had statistically significant higher scores than those who did not. Those who used the Draft 1 checklist scored higher by 0.67 (on a ten-point scale), and the effect size was medium. Similarly, those who used the checklist for either Draft 1 or Draft 2 scored higher by 0.727, and the effect size was medium. These results suggest that all the strategies may have had a positive impact, and the use of checklists seemed to have had clearer impacts than the other strategies.

Pearson correlation analyses were used to explore the relationships between the variables. The assignment guidelines were positively correlated with the assignment scores ($r = 0.201$, $p < 0.05$). In other words, the more the students clicked on the assignment guidelines, the higher their scores. These scores refer to the scores obtained on the revision of Draft 1, as given by the ELC teachers. Even though the strength of the relationship (i.e., correlation coefficient) was weak, this relationship deserves further discussion.

4.2 Corpus-driven content analysis of student reflections

To further answer RQ2 and understand the students' perceptions, corpus-driven content analyses of the student reflections and teacher feedback reports were conducted. This section presents the analysis of the student reflections. The purpose of the analysis is to explore how the students perceived the revision process and what elements captured their attention. After incorporating the student reflections into Antdoc, a wordlist of 1,037 words was generated. Next, the research team examined the words to identify whether they fell into the six pre-defined categories and found that 41 words were directly relevant. The concordance lines of these 41 words were reviewed to identify the common themes. Table 7 lists the commonly found words in the content.

Table 7: List of Commonly Found Content Words and Themes.

Categories	Related Words	Frequency		Common Themes (occurrence)
		Individual words	Sub-total	
Content/Genre/ Assignment	Essay (First content word: rank = 10) Content	Not Applicable	134	Better essay (29) Awareness: My essay → not good (6) Organise my essay (5) Reminder for future essay (4) Challenges of essay writing (5) improve my content (8)

Table 7 (continued)

Categories	Related Words	Frequency		Common Themes (occurrence)
		Individual words	Sub-total	
Metacognitive Strategies / EWR Tools (Planning, Monitoring, Evaluating, and Revising)	Feedback Report (62) Draft (53) Revising Skills Style Tone revision	Not Applicable	264	Useful feedback (68)
Use of Sources	References / Referencing Reference Citation APA	Not Applicable	95	Preparing a reference list (15) Problems of referencing (10) Improve the skills in referencing (6) Guidelines / Referencing machine (4) Correct format of reference list (3) Not familiar with referencing (3)
Grammar and Accuracy	Grammar / Grammatical Mistakes Errors	Not Applicable	137	Grammar problems (32) Awareness → Checking for grammar issue (6)
Structure (Intro, Body, Conclusion, Topic Sentence, Paragraphs, etc.)	Structure Sentence Introduction Paragraph Sentences Subheadings Organisation Organise	18 20 13 12 11 11 8 8	93	Better structure (2) Awareness in structure (4) [Some refer to the sentence structure] Improve the introduction (7) Improve the paragraph (6) Topic / concluding sentences (6) More / fewer / re-writing sentences (5)

Table 7 (continued)

Categories	Related Words	Frequency		Common Themes (occurrence)
		Individual words	Sub-total	
Words of Cognition and Awareness	Learn/t /ed	66	332	*learned* to paraphrase / structure / cite *better* express my views / understand / organise
	Better	38		
	Think	38		
	Improve	32		I *think* I know how / the feedback is useful
	Help	25		
	Develop(ed)	33		*Improve* the subheadings / my performance / organisation / writing
	Correct	19		
	Know	16		
	Revise	14		*Help* me write an essay with richer content / from ELC staff / me to explain my ideas
	Attention	12		
	Difficult	10		
	Challenge/ing	18		*Develop(ed)* my essay/ the skills / the review / my organisation / my English writing / the sentence structure
				Correct APA style/ errors / way of referencing
				Know that I have to change . . . / the mistakes / my weaknesses / better
				Revise my writing / the grammar / my work / my essay / my draft
				Attention to structure/ to errors/ the linkage between paragraphs / to referencing
				Difficult to add an overview / part of revising work / to handle . . .
				Challenge that I encountered / is grammar /

As Table 7 shows, an analysis of the reflection data revealed six major themes, namely, content, metacognitive strategies and tools, use of sources, grammar and language, structure, and words of cognition and awareness. The most frequent reflection themes related to the use of metacognitive tools (n=264), such as feedback and revision in improving the students' essays, and to the use of words related to cognition (or lack thereof) (n=332), indicating a significant awareness about the use of the strategies and, as a result, becoming, or wanting to become, more cognisant of the various aspects of the writing task. The next most frequent were two important themes for second language learners, grammar and accuracy (n=137), followed closely by content and genre-related themes. As the EWR feedback was heavily geared towards metacognitive strategies and the structure of the assignment, students were more concerned about their grammatical accuracy, as witnessed in the reflection analysis.

The next two themes most reflected upon were the use of sources (n=95) and the structure (n=93). One reason that these items were least frequent may have been because ample online support was provided through the metacognitive strategies, and most writers felt they had adequate information about the assignment structure in terms of the sections. The students appeared to be more concerned about sentence-level cohesion. Among the aspects of structure, the introduction stood out. Students seemed to be aware of their problems with the introduction, or perhaps since the introduction is a required section in most genres, it is a popular theme that students need to reflect on.

4.3 Analysis of teacher feedback reports

This section presents the results of the analysis of the teacher feedback reports. To supplement the analysis of student perceptions and performance, only a general picture is presented below to illustrate what types of feedback were given to students. Table 8 presents the mean number of action points given in each report for each aspect (and the total score).

Table 8: Types of Action Points in Each Report.

	Mean No. of Action Points on				Mean No. of Action Points in Report
	Task Fulfilment	Organisation	Language	Referencing	
Draft 1 Report	0.56	1.30	0.85	1.00	4.14
Draft 2 Report	0.65	1.30	0.98	0.96	4.49

Note. *Each feedback report is prepared by one teacher and should consist of four to six action points.* Each student will receive one Draft 1 Report and one Draft 2 Report, so the figures from the above table represent 135 Draft 1 Report and 135 Draft 2 Report.

Generally, the number and distribution of action points given is quite similar in the two reports, with a total of four action points. Action points on organisation were the most popular (with approximately 1.3 action points in each report), followed by language/referencing and task fulfilment. Typically, a teacher gave one or two action points on organisation, followed by a point on language and another point on referencing. Task fulfilment may be an item that is present if necessary.

5 Discussion

This study explored 1) students' perceptions of metacognitive strategies and 2) the use of certain metacognitive strategies that had an impact on improving students' writing performance. The results section identified the assignment guidelines and reflections as the most frequently used metacognitive tools. The students also indicated that the feedback reports provided were useful in their writing assignment. In addition to perceptions, there is a potential positive impact of the assignment guidelines and checklists on writing performance. These will be further discussed below.

5.1 Student perception of the tools

To study students' perceptions of the metacognitive strategies (RQ1), the researchers noted from the quantitative data that the assignment guidelines and student reflections were popular among students. The reason that assignment guidelines were the most frequently used tool could be the realisation that they were the most fundamental document setting the extent of the assignment. Assignment guidelines constitute a metacognitive strategy as they provided a list of strategies and reminders for developing the assignment. They also included a range of resources that may have triggered the use of other metacognitive strategies that underpin the others and are therefore introduced at the beginning of the semester. In fact, Morrison (2014) reported that their studies with Hong Kong students clearly illustrated that students need "a framework for the structure of the assignment" (Morrison (2014: 153). As the assignment guidelines (See Appendix 1) address this need, it is no surprise that it is such a popular tool. Frequent reference to the assignment guidelines also testifies to students' awareness of the importance of this metacognitive tool in ensuring that their work is relevant to the genre and to the discipline teacher's expectations. The students' prioritisation of this tool can be attributed to the "authority-seeking" behaviour of Chinese students (Cortazzi and Jin 1996), as the assignment guidelines are always presented as a collaboration between the discipline teacher and the writing teacher. Students are therefore interested in hearing advice from the "authorities," i.e., the discipline teacher and the language teacher.

Reflection was the second most frequently used strategy, even though it does not have a significant relationship with the assignment scores. The importance of this strategy is in line with Teng's argument that when student writers "are more self-regulated (e.g., more organized and reflective in actively monitoring and evaluating the composition process), they are more skilled in writing" (Teng 2019c: 11). Reflection primarily enabled students to evaluate and articulate their own writing development (e.g. Waschle et al. 2015). This was shown in the thematic analysis of the reflections where students demonstrated their ability to evaluate their own performance and identify errors/problems that they had already made. Students were aware of their writing improvement and the implications for their future as well. However, the reflection may not have helped them improve the current draft or the current assignment. In fact, language diaries (as an affective construct), described in a study by Kao and Reynolds (2017), were found to have the weakest correlation with writing performance (among other metacognitive strategies). Perhaps it is too soon to evaluate the immediate impact of writing reflection, as this neglects the potential impact of this tool on the students' writing development in the future.

Other than assignment guidelines and student reflections, the students also found the feedback reports to be useful, as indicated in the thematic analysis of the students' reflections. Feedback reports are purposely based on the assignment guidelines and checklists in such a manner that they reflect the genre. These could, therefore, be treated as teachers' tools for guidance on metacognition tools in writing. Therefore, the usefulness of the feedback report is reflected through the usefulness of the assignment guidelines and checklists discussed earlier. Other than these, feedback itself is dialogic in nature (e.g. Steen-Utheim and Witteck 2017); i.e., a platform for students and teachers to discuss the writing assignment. Such an interaction process is important in the writing development of students (Reynolds and Anderson 2015).

5.2 Impact on students' writing performance

In response to RQ2, we have established that instruction and use of certain metacognitive strategies, such as assignment guidelines and checklists, are associated with better writing performance (Teng 2016; Teng 2019a). Generally, the positive impact of metacognitive strategies on writing performance is not surprising (Shields 2000; Gupta and Woldemariam 2011; Bai, Hu and Gu 2014). To further explore the relationships, the assignment guidelines and checklists are the most explicit form of instruction of genre knowledge compared to the other metacognitive strategies introduced because they specifically outline what the assignments require. The guidelines present the genre guidelines in the planning stage, and the checklists present the same sets of genre requirements in the monitoring stage (Flavell 1979). In other words, students understand clearly what they need to do through these tools. This perhaps echoes what Teng (2016) discussed, namely that the instruction of genre-related metacognitive strategies is more beneficial to students than other strategies, and explicit instruction is necessary to make the strategies effective. Foung and Lughmani have chronicled the development of a similar open access support platform (with a genre guide and genre checklist) that is equally useful both offline and online and has flexibility for various types of WAC writers for a "flexible genre learning experience" (Foung and Lughmani 2018: 129). All these suggest that assignment guidelines and checklists are the most important metacognitive strategies.

5.3 Implications for writing teachers

The results of this study have two important implications for writing teachers. First, teachers should provide students with writing assignment guidelines so that students are able to structure their work more effectively and confidently. If guidelines are provided by an authoritarian source (i.e. teacher), students will be more confident as they complete their assignments. As they tend to trust the materials provided by the teacher, they save time from evaluating online writing resources prepared by a source they are not familiar with. Also, an interactional / dialogic feedback process was shown to be effective for providing writing feedback in this study. In the current study, writing teacher does not just give one-way summative feedback to assess the performance of students, but facilitate a dynamic feedback process to help students improve their writing skills. Writing teachers start by providing assignment guidelines to students and students respond by preparing their assignments based on the guidelines. Teachers then react to students' attempt with the feedback reports and students responded to the feedback reports via reflection and their second draft. Some students may even drive the interaction process further with consultation session(s). With such an interactional approach, students will not only know the existence of their problems, but they will also receive clarity about a problem that may not have been understood in a one-way feedback process. Once the students understand their writing problems, they are more likely to avoid similar problems in their future writing.

6 Conclusion

The current study discussed the implementation of metacognitive strategies in a university-wide WAC programme in a Chinese-speaking region, Hong Kong. The study found that explicit genre instruction through assignment guidelines and student reflections is popular among students, while assignment guidelines and checklists are positively associated with their writing performance. The findings of this study extend those of previous studies on the use of metacognitive strategies and showcase the full implementation of metacognitive strategies in a WAC setting. This study is a significant contribution to the field because until now most WAC programmes or support measures with metacognitive strategies have been optional; however, our study explored the use of a full range of metacognitive strategies in university credit-bearing courses with an embedded WAC component.

The present study has several limitations, and readers should interpret the results with caution. First, the sample size of this study was small, and the proportion of students (not) using certain strategies may have been different if the sample size had been larger. The corpus used in the analysis consisted only of a small number of student reflections and feedback reports. This means that some other representative keywords may not have been highlighted in this small corpus. The researchers also acknowledge that the frequency of the use of metacognitive strategies and student performance was correlative, which is not necessarily causative. It is possible that those students who used strategies more frequently were already better writers. All these factors could affect the reliability of the current study. Other than the methodological limitations, this study provides a more complete picture of the students' strategy use, performance, and perceptions.

Research into genre-based metacognitive strategy instruction needs to consider the social conventions of disciplinary discourse communities and equip L2 writers with the tools to succeed in entering these communities through writing. Communication in writing-across-the-curriculum contexts can be successful only if we give novice writers some tools and support measures to discover the rules of written communication through metacognitive strategies, thus enabling them to gradually take control of their own writing. The question of identifying more appropriate metacognitive strategy instruction models for different novice writers' needs and contexts remains unexplored; this could be a direction for future research in this area.

References

Abba, Katherine A., Zhang Shuai Steven, & R. Joshi. 2018. Community college writers' metaknowledge of effective writing. *Journal of Writing Research, 10*(1), 85–105.

Bai, Rui, Guangwei Hu, & Peter Yongqi Gu. 2014. The relationship between use of writing strategies and English proficiency in Singapore primary schools. *The Asia-Pacific Education Researcher, 23*, 355–365.

Bracewell, R. J. (1983). Investigating the control of writing skills. In P. Mosenthal, L. Tamor, & S. A. Walmsley (Eds.), *Research on writing: Principles and methods*. New York: Longman.

Britton, James. 1970. Language and learning. London, UK: Penguin Books.

Morrison, Bruce. 2014. Challenges faced by non-native undergraduate student writers in an English-medium university. *The Asian ESP Journal, 1*, 137–172.

Morrison, Bruce., & Stephen Evans. 2018. Supporting non-native speaker student writers making the transition from school to an English-medium university. *Language Learning in Higher Education, 8*(1), 1–20.

Cohen, Jacob. 1988. *Statistical power analysis for the behavioral sciences*. New York, NY: Routledge Academic.

Cortazzi, Martin., & Lixian Jin. 1996. *Cultures of learning: language classrooms in China*. In Hywei. Coleman, (Ed.), Society and the Language Classroom (169–206). Cambridge University Press, Cambridge.

Dudley-Evans, Tony. 1995. Common-core and specific approaches to the teaching of academic writing. In Diane Belcher & George Briane (Eds.), *Academic writing in a second language: Essays on research and pedagogy* (293–313). Norwood, NJ: Ablex.

Flavell, John. H. 1979. Metacognition and cognitive monitoring: a new area of cognitive-developmental inquiry. *American Psychologist, 34*, 906–911.

Foung, Dennis., Dureshahwar Shari Lughmani. 2018. A comprehensive CALL solution for writing in the disciplines. In Seda Khadimally (Ed.), *Technology-Assisted ESL acquisition and development for nontraditional learners* (108–132). Hershey, PA: IGI Global.

Gupta, Deepti., & Getachew Seyoum Woldemariam. 2011. The influence of motivation and attitude on writing strategy use of undergraduate EFL students: Quantitative and qualitative perspective. *The Asian EFL Journal, 13*, 34–89.

Hacker, Douglas J., Matt C. Keener, & John C. Kircher. 2009. Writing is applied metacognition. In D. J. Hacker, J. Dunlosky, & A. C. Graesser (eds.). *Handbook of metacognition in education (pp. 154–172.)* New York, NY: Routledge.

Hadwin, Allyson Fiona, & Philip H. Winne. 1996. Study strategies have meager support: A review with recommendations for implementation. *The Journal of Higher Education, 67*(6), 692–715.

Hayes, J. R. (1996). A new framework for understanding cognition and affect in writing. In R. Indrisano & J. R. Squire (eds.). *Perspectives on writing: Research, Theory, and practice*. UK: Routledge.

Hyland, Ken. 2010. English for professional academic purposes: Writing for scholarly publication. In D. Belcher (Ed.), *English for specific purposes in theory and practice* (83–105). Ann Arbor: University of Michigan Press.

Johns, Ann. 1997. *Text, role, and context: Developing academic literacies*. Cambridge, UK: Cambridge University Press.

Kao, Chian-Wen, and Barry Lee Reynolds. 2017. A study on the relationship among Taiwanese college students' EFL writing strategy use, writing ability and writing difficulty. *English Teaching & Learning, 41*(4), 31–67.

Kasper, Loretta F. 1997. Assessing the metacognitive growth of ESL student writers. *TESL-EJ, 3* (1), 1–20.

Kuiper, Cindy, Jantien Smit, Lieve De Wachter, & Jan Elen. 2017. Scaffolding tertiary students' writing in a genre-based writing intervention. *Journal of Writing Research, 9*(1), 27–59.

Lin, Xiaodong., T. Newby, & N. Glenn. 1994. *Embedding metacognitive cues into hypermedia systems to promote far transfer problem solving*. Paper presented at the National Convention of the Association for Educational Communications and Technology.

Maimon, Elaine P., Gerlad L. Belcher, G. W. Hearn, B. F. Nodine, & F. W. O'Connon. 1981. *Writing in the Arts and Sciences*. Cambridge, MA: Winthrop.

Mevarech, Zemira, & Shimon Fridkin. 2006. The effects of IMPROVE on mathematical knowledge: Mathematical reasoning and meta-cognition. *Metacognition and Learning, 1*, 85–97.

Mevarech, Zemira R., & Bracha Kramarski. 1997. IMPROVE: a multidimensional method for teaching mathematics in heterogeneous classrooms. *American Educational Research Journal, 34*(2), 365–394.

Negretti, Raffaella, & Maria Kuteeva. 2011. Fostering metacognitive genre awareness in L2 academic reading and writing: a case study of pre-service English teachers. *Journal of Second Language Writing, 20*, 95–110.

Ong, J., & Zhang, L. J. (2013). Effects of the manipulation of cognitive processes on EFL writers' text quality. TESOL Quarterly, 47(2), 375–398.

Ong, Justina. 2014. How do planning time and task conditions affect metacognitive processes of L2 writers? *Journal of Second Language Writing, 23*, 17–30.

Poon, Anita Y.K. 2010. Language use, and language policy and planning in Hong Kong. *Current Issues in Language Planning, 11*(1), 1–66, DOI: 10.1080/14664201003682327

Reynolds, Barry Lee. 2013. A web-based EFL writing environment as a bridge between academic advisers and junior researchers: A pilot study. *British Journal of Educational Technology, 44*(3), E77–E80. doi:10.1111/j.1467-8535.2012.01344.x

Reynolds, Barry Lee, & Tom A.F. Anderson. 2015. Extra-dimensional in-class communications: Action research exploring text chat support of face-to-face writing. *Computers and Composition, 35*, 52–64.

Sasaki, Miyuki, & Keiko Hirose. 1996. Explanatory variables for EFL students' expository writing. *Language Learning, 46*(1), 137–168.

Shields, R. N. 2000. *Writing strategies as predictors of student scores on the Pennsylvania system of school assessment writing test* (Doctoral dissertation, Widener University). Retrieved from https://www.education.pa.gov/Documents/K-12/Assessment%20and%20Accountability/PSSA/Technical%20Reports/2018%20PSSA%20Technical%20Report.pdf

Steen-Utheim, Anna, & Anne Line Wittek. 2017. Dialogic feedback and potentialities for student learning. *Learning, Culture and Social Interaction, 15*, 18–30.

Teng, Feng. 2016. Immediate and delayed effects of embedded metacognitive instruction on Chinese EFL students' English writing and regulation of cognition. *Thinking Skills and Creativity, 22*, 289–302.

Teng, Feng. 2019a. Tertiary-level students' English writing performance and metacognitive awareness: A group metacognitive support perspective. *Scandinavian Journal of Educational Research*. doi: 10.1080/00313831.2019.1595712

Teng, Feng. 2019b. A comparison of text structure and self-regulated strategy instruction for elementary school students' writing. *English Teaching: Practice and Critique*. DOI: https://doi.org/10.1108/ETPC-07-2018-0070

Teng, Feng. 2019c. The role of metacognitive knowledge and regulation in mediating university EFL learners' writing performance. *Innovation in Language Learning and Teaching*. https://doi.org/10.1080/17501229.2019.1615493

Teng, Feng., & Huang, Jing. 2019. Predictive effects of writing strategies for self-regulated learning on secondary school learners' EFL writing proficiency. *TESOL Quarterly, 53,* 232–247.

Wäschle, Kristin, Anja Gebhardt, Eva-Maria Oberbusch & Matthias Nückles. 2015. Journal writing in science: Effects on comprehension, interest, and critical reflection. *Journal of Writing Research, 7*(1),41–64.

Winne, Phili. & Allyson F. Hadwin. 1998. Studying as self-regulated learning. In Hacker, Douglas J., John Dunlosky, & Arthur C. Graesser. (Eds.), *Metacognition in educational theory and practice* (277–304). Mahwah, NJ: Lawrence Erlbaum Associates.

Woodrow, L. (2014). Writing about quantitative research in applied linguistics. New York, NY: Springer.

Appendix 1 – Sample assignment guidelines

The English writing requirement

Assignment guidelines

Subject title	Introducing Asian Popular Culture
Credit value	3
Weighting of the writing requirement assignment	40% (10% from ELC + 30% from CAR teacher)
Word limit	Draft 1: 700 words Draft 2: 1,500 words Draft 3: 2,500 words (not more than 3000 words)
Genre	**Analytical Academic Essay**
Writing instructions for students Please, include writing assignment instructions. Consider the following questions:	In this assignment, students write on an aspect of Asian popular culture often manifested in films, TV dramas, comics and pop music. Their writing should demonstrate their knowledge and understanding of cultural theories, the socio-cultural contexts, and issues and themes about Asian popular culture covered in the lectures. Through the essay, students demonstrate their skills in effectively: 1. conducting library and web-based research skills; 2. describing, explaining, and analysing the cultural issue (e.g. Hong Kong movies, Korean dramas, Cantopop) or phenomenon (e.g. Korean celebrities' suicides, Korean Wave, Japan anime) chosen for discussion 3. drawing on scholars' theories, views, or arguments to fully answer the question set out.

(continued)

Role of reading	Students are expected to read extensively and in-depth on scholarly works written on the issue that they have chosen to write on. They should take notes of the scholars' viewpoints when they read. Chinese sources are acceptable, but a minimum of five ENGLISH books and academic journal articles are required. Media NOT ALLOWED: Wikipedia, HKGolden, Baidu Baike, Zhihu
Organisational pattern	As with any academic essays, there should be an Abstract, keywords, introduction, body paragraphs, and conclusion. The **introduction** should contain relevant background information about the practical dreamer you have chosen to write on. Then, clearly write out the aim of the essay, either by posing a question or by using a statement of thesis. This will make the scope of your essay clear to the reader. Include an **overview** of what the different parts of your essay will be about. In the **body paragraphs**, write out the different sections in the same order as you have said in your overview. Write a **conclusion** to tie up (summarise) all the different parts in your essay. Here, you restate what you said you will discuss in your introduction. Headings and/ or subheadings are highly recommended. What should be included in Draft 1 and 2? Draft 1 (700 words): Draft 2 (1500 words): – **Introduction** – **Introduction** – **Body paragraphs** – **Body paragraphs** Include at least citations from two sources Include at least citations from four sources – **Conclusion** (optional)
References / Formatting style	– APA referencing style is preferred – Footnotes covering further explanations are accepted. – Graphics/media in the assignment are accepted
Submission deadlines Please indicate when and how the final draft will be submitted.	**Submission of first draft to ELC**: 23 July (Mon) 23:59, Week 9 **Submission of second draft to ELC**: 30 July (Mon) 23:59, Week 10 **Submission of final draft to CAR teacher**: 9 August (Thur) 23:59 **Mode of submission for final draft:** via TURNITIN/ hard copy / other (please specify): _____
Plagiarism	Once plagiarism is detected, the WHOLE COURSE will be marked FAIL.

(continued)

Marking criteria	ELC's: Task fulfilment (25%); Organisation (25%); Language (25%); Revision (25%) CAR teacher's: Argumentation (55%); Structure (10%); Sources (15%); Literacy (10%); Presentation (5%); General style (5%)
Generic features	– In-depth elaboration of ideas In order to strengthen your overall argument, apart from references to outside sources, you need to evaluate the ideas cited and elaborate your own view points. The excerpt below shows how the main idea in a paragraph can be discussed in a thorough manner, with reference to literature. "Another factor that has caused the decline of Cantopop is the rise of Korean music. According to Chan et al. (2016), 75% of the respondents have never listened to Cantopop. The lack of knowledge of Cantopop may affect Hong Kong people's identities. Some of the people interviewed chose not to listen to Cantopop after they started to listen to Korean music and mentioned how this affected their perceptions of their identities as Hongkongers (Wong, 2017)." ← Topic sentence / Sub-points supporting the topic sentence with citations and elaboration of ideas. – How to synthesise cited materials when discussing the definitions? Example Text 1: *Some of the researchers consider culture as the beliefs, behaviors, and characteristics that are common to the members of a particular group.* — Topic sentence bringing out the main idea *According to Davidson (2015), in ancient languages the origin of the meaning of "culture" in ancient languages means the building of cities.* — Support your idea with source materials *An example showcasing this is Shiroishi city, Miyagi prefecture, in northern Japan, and its connection with the video game and television anime Sengoku BASARA.* — Explain/Elaborate the ideas of the source materials / Support with an example

(continued)

	– Inclusion of visuals It is common to include visual aids like graphs or maps from books or the internet to help illustrate ideas in this assignment. Refer to the FAQs at the bottom on what visuals to cite, and how to cite them. – Hedging techniques An objective and cautious tone should be exercised to avoid assertiveness, especially in Discussion, where strategies to improve disaster resilience are proposed. Students should avoid over-generalizing with expressions like "it is obvious that . . ." or "Without a doubt", or strong words like "the government must". For example, 1) Another factor that has caused the decline of Cantopop **is** the rise of Korean music. (without hedging) vs. 2) Another factor that has caused the decline of Cantopop **seems to be** the rise of Korean music. (with hedging) For more on hedging techniques, visit: XXX

30-minute EWR Video Orientation to be conducted by the CAR teacher in Week 9
"Introducing English Writing Requirement": https://www.youtube.com/embed/bQlk7zawMVA
Would you like the EWR liaison to attend the lecture to offer in-class support? ☐ YES ☐ NO

30-minute Assignment Orientation to be conducted by the EWR liaison before first draft submission
ELC liaison in-class support preferred?   ☐ YES ☐ NO
(please fill up the information below if support preferred)

Date:	17 JULY
Time:	10:30
Venue:	BC201

Policy Note
In order to pass the subject, students must pass the writing component assessment, i.e., attain a minimum grade D in the writing component.
To pass the Writing Requirement component, students are required to:
(i) Study the online learning materials on meeting the Writing Requirements developed by ELC found on XXXX and complete the online writing activities in XXX.
(ii) Submit the Writing Requirement tasks assigned by the ELC instructor according to schedule, and perform satisfactorily in those tasks.

Frequently asked questions about analytical argumentative essay

1. Q: How many sentences should there be in each body paragraph?

A: Each body paragraph should focus on ONE main point, followed by a series of sentences that support it. In other words, a typical paragraph in the body section consists of four elements: 1. Transition, 2. Topic sentence, 3. Elaboration and analysis (including sufficient evidence to support your views), and 4. Concluding sentence. If you only have two or three sentences in a paragraph, it could mean that one or more of these four elements are missing. It may also suggest that your elaboration and analysis are insufficient and need further strengthening. For details of the four-element-structure, please refer to: https://owl.english.purdue.edu/owl/resource/724/02

2. Q: I am told my paragraphs are too short. What should I do?

A: If you find that most body paragraphs in your draft seem too short and scattered, try to make an outline based on what you have written so far – i.e., write down on a piece of paper the main idea presented in each written paragraph. This can help you visualize the problem in your structure, and re-organize your ideas in a more logical way. For instance, think about whether the short paragraphs can be combined – or whether you can add details to support each point and thus make each into a more fully developed paragraph.

3. Q: Can online sources be used?

A: In your essay it is okay refer to relevant reports available on credible websites. Meanwhile, websites such as Wikipedia, HKGolden, Baidu Baike, Zhihu are not appropriate sources to cite because they lack quality assurance, since you cannot be certain who wrote them. If you are not sure whether to use an online source, please consult your CAR subject teacher(s).

4. Q: What kind of visual aids should I include?

A: Include images or graphics **only when necessary**. This is an academic paper and not a magazine article. Do not overwhelm your reader with images or pictures that are irrelevant to your essay for decorative purpose. You should include only those visual materials that can enhance the audience's understanding of your text.

5. Q: How do I cite images from website?

A: All images including graphs, charts, maps, drawings and photographs are referred to as figures. You need to label the image as a figure and place a caption (i.e. a brief explanation of the figure) directly below the image, which includes any acknowledgement that the image is reprinted/adapted from another source. For example:
- Figure 1. Images of Geisha women. Retrieved from http: https://sora news24.com/2014/01/20/36-historical-photographs-of-geisha-and-apprentice-geisha-beauties/
  The in-text citation would be like this:
- Figure 1 shows the . . .
  Your reference would be as follows:
- Rogers, K. (2014, Jan 20). 36 historical photographs of geisha and apprentice geisha beauties. Soranews 24. Retrieved from https://soranews24.com/2014/01/20/36-historical-photographs-of-geisha-and-apprentice-geisha-beauties/
- (For more on APA referencing, please refer to the ELC referencing guide: XXX)

Appendix 2 – Sample checklist

An introduction to Asian popular culture

Checklist for your academic essay

Before you submit your 1st or 2nd draft, check that it meets the requirements listed below.

	Your draft
☐	submit it together with the assignment cover and this checklist
☐	is 700 words long (for draft 1) **Or**
☐	is 1,500 words long (for draft 2)
☐	include headings and subheadings as recommended
☐	include in-text citations (for both drafts) and a reference list for draft 2
	Introduction
☐	give relevant facts about Asian culture-related issue you have chosen to write on
☐	pose a question that limits your subject: the answer to the question is your essay, **Or**
☐	contain a simple statement of thesis that limits your subject
☐	give an overview of the structure of the essay
	Body paragraphs
☐	answer the question you have posed in your introduction
☐	use citations to introduce views, or theories from scholars, and integrate them in your discussions
☐	use plenty of signposting to help your reader follow your discussions
☐	include one main idea, at most two, in each paragraph
☐	**Conclusion** (optional for 1st draft)
☐	bring your discussions together to show how you have answered the question you raised in your introduction, **Or**
☐	bring your discussions together to show that they have supported the thesis you stated in your introduction
	The APA referencing style is . . .
☐	used for in-text citations
☐	used to present the list of references
☐	used correctly

Note: For this assignment, your teacher suggests that you use APA referencing style. To check the format, refer to [. . .]

Anora Yu

A narrative inquiry into washback of high-stakes and low-stakes testing on second language English writing in Hong Kong higher education

Abstract: Washback, the impact of testing on teaching and learning, is a prominent notion in language testing and assessment. Many renowned testing and assessment researchers have demonstrated positive and/or negative washback effects. Although several studies have been conducted on the relationship between tests and teachers' and/or learners' attitudes and behaviour, very few have used narrative inquiry to study teachers' practical personal experiences. This research explored the washback effect on second-language (L2) English writing teaching and learning through a narrative inquiry into the experiences of an L2 English teacher at a self-financed higher education institution in Hong Kong. The participant taught English courses with both high-stakes and low-stakes tests. The study reports on the different teaching approaches used by the participant to deal with high-stakes and low-stakes tests, making meanings of these choices through the teacher's first-hand accounts. Using narrative inquiry, the researcher's voice was foregrounded while attending to the participant's stories and at times it was interwoven through the participant's experiences to make new discoveries. The data were analysed to illuminate the teacher's stories with reference to the washback of high-stakes and low-stakes testing on L2 English writing at the tertiary level in Hong Kong.

Keywords: washback, high-stakes and low-stakes testing, L2 English writing, higher education, narrative inquiry

1 Introduction

The concept of washback is prominent in applied linguistics research on language testing and assessment. According to Messick (1996: 241), *washback* refers to "the extent to which the introduction and use of a test influences language teachers and learners to do *things* [emphasis added] they would not

Anora Yu, Independent Researcher

https://doi.org/10.1515/9781501512643-008

otherwise do that promote or inhibit language learning". Messick's definition of washback was strongly influenced by that of Alderson and Wall (1993: 117), who suggested that testing leads teachers to "do *things* [emphasis added] they would not necessarily otherwise do". As a teacher of English as a second language (L2) in a self-financed higher education institution in Hong Kong for over 20 years, I was intrigued by the concept of washback. Hong Kong is known for its exam-oriented education system. Many teaching and learning activities revolve around assessment, especially when they come to high-stakes testing. I would like to explore if alternative teaching approaches are available. In addition, as an L2 English teacher in Hong Kong, I fully understand that many frontline teachers struggle with student writing with little satisfaction (Lee 2009). Therefore, I conducted this narrative inquiry with another L2 English teacher to explore the *things* done and not done by an L2 teacher when administering high-stakes and low-stakes tests in L2 English writing in a higher education institution in Hong Kong.

Narrative inquiry was selected as the methodology because it allowed me to understand my participant's practical personal experiences in depth and make meanings from the stories as well as resorting to my lived experiences to interpolate where necessary to make new discoveries. The study aimed to analyse the *things* that bring about positive washback effects, i.e., the promotion of language learning, as informed by Messick (1996), from his study of two L2 English teachers' lived experiences. A broader aim of this study was to offer practical pedagogical implications to make teaching and learning of L2 English writing more meaningful and rewarding.

This narrative inquiry reports on three interesting vignettes that countered general notions of washback of high-stakes and low-stakes testing on L2 English writing in Hong Kong higher education. It is hoped that the findings contribute to knowledge of washback, casting light on its particularities, subjectivity, subtlety, and complexity. The narrative inquiry also seeks to create resonance with and offer insights for L2 teachers and other readers.

2 Interrelation between teaching/learning and assessment – Which comes first?

As an L2 English teacher working in a self-financed higher education institution in Hong Kong, I have my own beliefs, values, and worldviews regarding teaching and learning approaches. Ideally, assessment should follow teaching and learning, as presented below:

A. Identify the learners.
Who are the target recipients? What are their backgrounds (socio-economic, religious, educational, cognitive, etc.)? What do they already know? What do they want to know?
B. Set the teaching objectives and content.
What do educators want to teach during the course? Are the teaching objectives in line with the broader aims and objectives of the programme/institution/community/nation?
C. Decide on the learning outcomes.
What do educators want learners to have achieved upon completion of the course?
D. Determine the pedagogical approach.
What kinds of teaching and learning methodologies and approaches should be deployed to carry out Steps A, B, and C?
E. Select assessment methods.
What kind of assessment (formative/summative; norm-referenced/criterion-referenced, etc.) will best reflect Steps A, B, C, and D?

If assessment in an educational context is taken as an outcome or end-product of teaching and learning, it is known as assessment of learning. Carless, Joughin, and Mok (2006: 395) termed this "assessment as certification". It is used by educators and learners to reflect on the effectiveness of teaching and learning. Based on this rationale, assessment – or the assessment of learning – should be driven by teaching and learning objectives and led by teaching and learning methodologies.

This conceptual framework of "assessment of learning" can be illustrated in linear form, as in Figure 1 below.

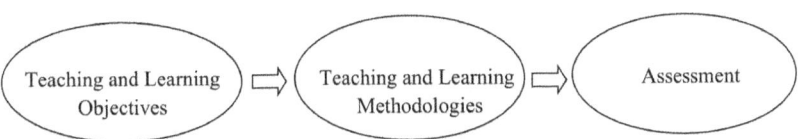

Figure 1: Linear representation of assessment of learning.

However, the relationship between teaching/learning and assessment may also be circular; the practices influence each other, as evidenced in the dynamics of assessment for learning (Latham 2011; Chappuis 2015), assessment as learning (Carless, Joughin, and Mok 2006; Earl 2013) and learning-oriented assessment (Carless 2006, 2007, 2014) as suggested in Figure 2.

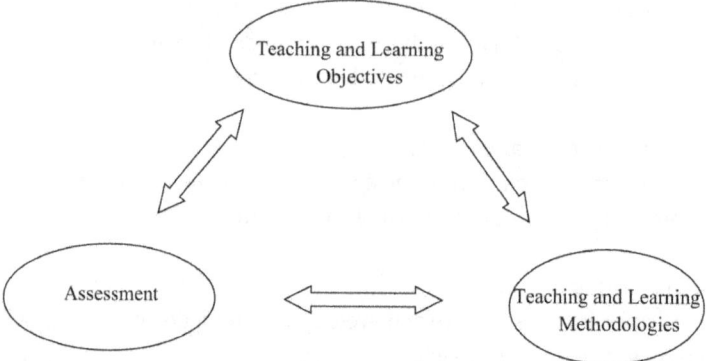

Figure 2: Circular representation of assessment for learning.

Based on the above, assessment can be defined as an inquiry-based process used by teachers and learners to make informed decisions about teaching and learning (Serafini 2000), rather than an end-product of teaching effectiveness and/ or the learning process. The essence of assessment is believed to be learning rather than measurement (Carless, Joughin, and Mok, 2006). Teaching and learning objectives, methodologies, and assessment methods should be inextricably linked. Although teaching and learning occur in stages, the movement between these stages can be modelled in three dimensions, as a spiral, as shown in Figure 3.

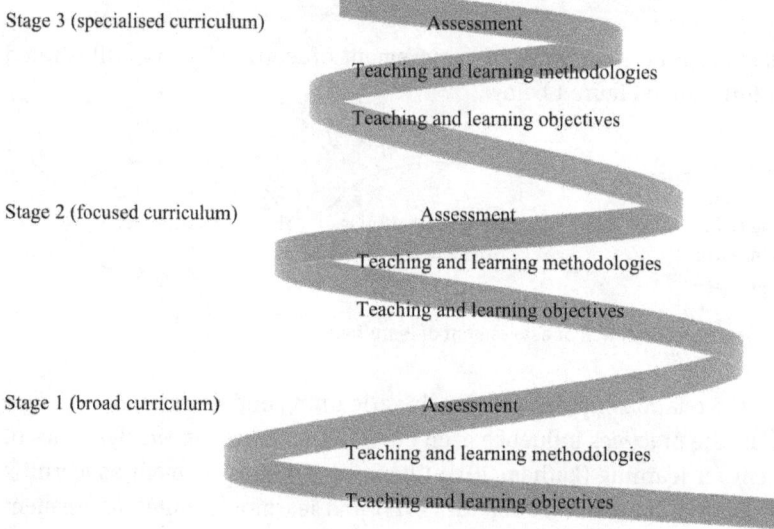

Figure 3: Spiral representation of assessment to foster lifelong teaching and learning.

The first stage, or the fundamental stage, features a broad base of teaching and learning activities whereby both teachers and learners develop their own teaching and learning capacity based on the interplay of teaching and learning objectives, methodologies, and assessment. Drawing on the process of inquiry-based assessment, teachers and learners are able to make informed decisions about their further teaching and learning progress, leading to the second stage – a focused curriculum. By building the teachers' capacity to teach and learners' capacity to learn, both teachers and learners can develop their metacognitive awareness and take responsibility for their future teaching and learning journey by, for example, planning the teaching and learning process, activating these plans, and evaluating their own effectiveness. Carless, Joughin, and Mok (2006: 395) termed this process "assessment to foster lifelong learning". I would look at it as being reciprocal – assessment to foster lifelong teaching and learning – as this process benefits teachers as much as it does learners. Accordingly, the upward movement may be developed in stages, becoming more specialised and on-going.

In real life, however, assessment always comes before teaching and learning, especially within a highly competitive educational system. The abovementioned sequence is normally reversed – beginning with Step E – and one-way, with the selection of teaching and learning methodologies led by assessment. Green (2007a: 1) described this as "[the tail] wagging the dog", wherein *tail* refers to assessment and *dog* refers to teaching and learning objectives and methodologies. This sequence can be illustrated in linear form, as shown in Figure 4.

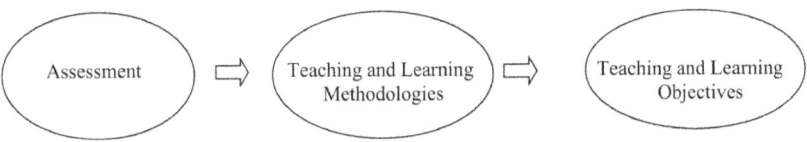

Figure 4: Linear representation of assessment-driven learning.

As an L2 English teacher working in Hong Kong, I have witnessed the implementation of a great deal of assessment-driven educational practices. Unsurprisingly, the design of some public examination coursebooks is driven entirely by the examination syllabus. In some examination-oriented courses, past examination papers are the only teaching and learning materials used.

In such cases, teachers teach to the test and learners learn to the test. They over-drill in certain examination formats, such as multiple-choice questions from past examination papers. Some teachers and learners study the examination syllabus at great length, and certain teaching and learning activities revolve around past papers or model answers. Similarly, many reference books available in bookshops contain primarily model examination answers, and Hong Kong's burgeoning "tutorial schools" offer good illustrations of assessment-driven teaching and learning approaches. Some researchers have even asked whether simply changing methods of assessment would change teaching and learning at all (Zhan and Andrews 2014).

3 Rationale for the study

The impact of assessment on teaching and learning is known as washback or backwash. Washback can be positive or negative. Washback effect differs between courses with high-stakes and low-stakes tests. Therefore, this study aims to explore an L2 English teacher's interpretation of high stakes and low-stakes testing. The focus of the research is L2 English writing. Writing is chosen as I have been impacted by Lee (2009: 34): "In many teaching contexts, first language or second language (L2), teachers are still slaving over student writing". I am curious whether there are any alternative teaching approaches, and/or teachers' perceptions towards teaching/learning and assessment to make teaching and learning L2 English writing more enjoyable and less "slaving", hence generating positive washback.

Since I am also an experienced L2 English teacher in Hong Kong, I consider myself a rich source of data. I would like to make use of my own lived experiences. By conducting a narrative inquiry with an L2 English teacher, I would be able to interpolate my own experience into my research participant's to co-construct new meanings and new knowledge.

In addition, Alderson and Hamp-Lyons (1996: 280) offered the following interesting caveat: "simple forms of washback hypotheses are too naïve: influences on what happens in class are much more complex than unexamined beliefs about washback allows". The postmodern epistemological assumption that the social world is value-laden, complex and contingent is becoming increasingly popular. Therefore, a method of exploring washback that accommodates its particularity, subjectivity, subtleties and nuances is needed. The aim of this study is to fill this research gap by conducting a narrative inquiry into the teaching strategies used by an L2 English teacher at a self-financed higher education institution in Hong Kong to deal with high-stakes and low-stakes writing tests.

The research question guiding this study is as follows:

> What teaching approaches are used by an L2 English teacher at a self-financed higher education institution in Hong Kong to deal with high-stakes and low-stakes writing tests?

4 Literature review

In this section, I review the body of literature concerning key terms such as high-stakes testing, low-stakes testing, positive washback, negative washback, and related studies.

4.1 High-stakes testing versus low-stakes testing

Cheng (1998) provided a reader-friendly definition of a high-stakes test. Good results in high-stakes tests yield future academic and employment opportunities. Such tests are usually public examinations or large-scale standardised tests. As well as considering the impact of high-stakes tests on test-takers, or in Bachman and Palmer's (1996: 29–30) words, at the "micro" level, Smith (1991: 9) extended the definition of a high-stakes test to stress its impact at the "macro" level, i.e., affecting members of a wider community, such as teachers, education institutions, regions, cities, and even countries.

> [The results of high-stakes tests] are used to trigger actions or decisions such as passing or failing a grade, graduating or not, determining teacher or principal merit, or assuming responsibility for a failing district by a state agency.

Scores in high-stakes tests are used not only to judge students' competence, but also to make important decisions about teachers' performance. Graduates' test scores are often compared with those of graduates from other institutions. The results are published yearly and made publicly available, resulting in a branding effect. The results testify not only to the quality of teachers, but also to that of education institutions and cities at large. As Smith (1991: 9) noted, "the publication of test scores produces feelings of shame, embarrassment, guilt, and anger in teachers and the determination to do what is necessary to avoid such feelings in the future". As a symbol of status, test scores are used by education institutions to show off and as a tool to impose certain values on teachers. They invariably drive teachers to seek to exceed previous years' test scores and break records. In some cases, institutions' reputation, accreditation, and external funding are contingent on students' test scores – high stakes indeed. This is a never-ending rat race. An example from the Hong Kong educational context is the Diploma of Secondary Education Examination, which takes place after six years of secondary schooling and is recognised by all government-funded universities and self-financed higher education institutions in Hong Kong. Another example is the International English Language Testing System (IELTS) test, which is used by many local and overseas higher education institutions as an entrance and/or exit requirement, and by some organisations for career screening.

Low-stakes tests, in contrast, have little to no personal consequences associated with test-talkers' scores (Barry et al. 2010). At the abovementioned macro level, low-stakes tests have few significant consequences, whether for learners themselves or for other stakeholders, such as teachers, education institutions, regions and countries. Examples include in-class quizzes, grammar workshops offered in schools and non-credit-bearing modules offered in colleges. Perhaps because of such conventional beliefs that low-stakes testing has low, or no impact on teaching and learning stakeholders, low-stakes tests have received little currency. However, most studies regarding low-stakes testing are related to test-takers' motivation. For example, Barry el al. (2010), and Wise (2009) presumed that student test-taking motivation is related to the stakes of the test. Swerdzewski, Harmes, and Finney (2011: 163) held similar claims: "With high-stakes tests such as SAT, ACT, and GRE, student test-taking motivation has traditionally not been an issue", and "Students do not put forth effort on low-stakes tests introduce a potential source of construct-irrelevant variance into test data" (Swerdzewski, Harmes, and Finney 2011: 183).

The body of literature suggests that high-stakes and low-stakes testing has always had very clear-cut definitions. I wanted to explore if frontline teachers also share such beliefs and perceptions when dealing with high-stakes and low-stakes testing.

4.2 Washback or backwash?

It can be assumed that teachers do or do not do certain *things* when dealing with high-stakes and low-stakes tests (Alderson and Wall 1993). In the domain of testing and assessment, this influence of testing on teaching is known as washback. Alderson and Wall (1993) noted that examinations often come at the end of a course, so the influence of testing and assessment is seen working in a backward direction, hence the term "washback". Conversely, Spolsky (1994: 55) termed the unintended and accidental side effects as "backwash". Similarly, Wall and Hughes (2012) described the impact of testing on teaching and learning, such as the development of teaching materials and classroom management, as backwash. They found this effect to be more common in general education. Hughes (2012: 1) offered the following account of the phenomenon:

> The effect of testing on teaching and learning is known as *backwash*, and can be harmful or beneficial. If a test is regarded as important, if the stakes are high, preparation for it can come to dominate all teaching and learning activities.

4.3 Positive washback versus negative washback

In the applied linguistics literature, Hughes (2012) defined "positive washback" as testing with a beneficial effect on teaching and learning, and "negative washback" as that with a harmful effect. Positive washback occurs when tests impact areas of teaching such as syllabus revision, the design of new textbooks and the development of innovative teaching and learning methods and techniques that stress the purposeful and interactive use of authentic English.

In addition, some educators have suggested that certain tests enhance motivation to teach and learn, improve student achievement (Watanabe 2001) and increase the time devoted to teaching and learning. Their washback is thus positive. However, Watanabe (2001) argued that once a high-stakes test such as a final examination has been taken, motivation is very difficult to sustain.

According to Wall (2000: 500), a test with negative washback "invariably leads to cramming; narrows the curriculum; concentrates attention on those skills amenable to testing . . . constrains the creativity and spontaneity of teachers and students and finally demeans the professional judgement of teachers". Alderson and Hamp-Lyons (1996: 280) investigated washback in a Test of English as a Foreign Language (TOEFL) context, and reported concerning findings, such as "unnatural teaching," "TOEFLese," and "students taking TOFEL courses instead of 'real' English courses".

Some teachers feel anxious about and stressed by the publication of their students' test scores, which may discourage them from trying new *things* in the classroom. For example, presentations, which are pivotal to students' future studies and careers, are often neglected, as presentation skills are not tested in public examinations. Eventually, the curriculum may narrow as a result; as Purpura (2009: 305) established, "students might place undue importance on learning how to answer multiple-choice grammar questions, rather than learning how to communicate in the target language".

One of the most severe critics of negative washback was Wall (2000: 500–501), who claimed that measurement-driven instruction is "nothing more than psychometric imperialism"; that "teachers always 'teach to the test'"; that, more ominously, a high-stakes test "transfers control over the curriculum to the agency which sets or controls the exam"; and worse still, that test developers have "commercial rather than educational interests at heart". Based on the above notions from the literature, this study seeks to explore whether anything can be done to promote positive washback.

4.4 Washback research conducted in various contexts

A large number of studies have been conducted on washback in language testing and assessment. Research areas include teacher factors and washback (Cheng 2005; Wall and Horak 2006), learner factors and washback (Watanabe 2001), and test preparation behaviour (Stoneman 2005). Various research methods have been used. Many studies, such as that of Cheng (2005), have combined quantitative data from questionnaires with qualitative data based on interviews and classroom observation. In a study conducted in Taiwan, Pan (2014) used student questionnaires and a comparison of test scores before and after the introduction of English exit tests, the General English Proficiency Test and the Test of English for International Communication, to explore learner washback, and investigated the influence of exit tests on learners' motivation, learning strategies, and test performance. Pan (2014) reported that English certification exit requirements appeared to promote the "assessment of learning" rather than "assessment for learning," which treats assessment as a means, not an end.

The study closest to the current research was carried out by Green (2007a), who empirically investigated the washback of the IELTS Academic Writing test on English for Academic Purposes (EAP) provision. Green (2007a) concluded that the EAP competencies required to study effectively at university were not well addressed in IELTS preparation courses. What is different from the present research is that the research context of Green (2007a) was limited to the United Kingdom, and the researcher used a combination of quantitative and qualitative methods. The present study used narrative inquiry as a methodology and the focus was on collecting teacher's stories on washback effects. In addition, Estaji and Tajeddin (2012) conducted an empirical study on the washback of the IELTS Academic Writing test in Tehran, the capital of Iran. They focused on learner factors and adopted a mixed methodology comprising questionnaires, observations, and interviews to explore learners' perspectives on their motivation, test-taking anxiety, test-taking strategies, and expectations for their courses. They concluded that washback is complex and context-oriented. A similar study of washback was conducted in Vietnam by Barnes (2017), who explored the attitudes, beliefs and teaching practices of four teachers teaching a TOEFL iBT preparation course and General English classes. In this qualitative case study, Barnes (2017) reported that the test preparation course focused primarily on the product of learning, whereas the General English classes were more concerned with the process.

A review of the literature on the washback effects of testing and assessment reveals that few studies have focused on the context of L2 English writing in self-financed higher education institutions in Hong Kong. Cheng (2010) conducted a study similar to the current narrative inquiry on washback and teaching in Hong Kong, but focused on secondary schools. In addition, the public examination explored in Cheng's (2010) study, the Hong Kong Certificate of Education Examination, has since been phased out and replaced by the Diploma of Secondary Education Examination. Cheng, Andrews, and Yu (2011) used questionnaires to explore both students' and parents' perspectives on school-based assessment in Hong Kong, and reported that the washback effect was related to students' self-rated English proficiency. Chinese students who considered their English ability to be high were more likely than their counterparts with less confidence in their English ability to engage in intense test preparation.

Swerdzewski, Harmes, and Finney (2009: 190) studied students' perceptions on low-stakes tests. They suggested attaching more importance to the test by increasing the stakes of the test and making "what was once low-stakes now high-stakes". This study offered me some inspiration as I also wanted to know if the stakes can be crafted or modified by teachers. In addition, I was also interested in whether the stakes are a determining factor to motivate learning.

5 The study

5.1 Context of the study

In 2009, an educational innovation known as the 3-3-4 educational structure was implemented in Hong Kong, mandating that all students receive three years' junior secondary and three years' senior secondary schooling. After completing the Sixth Form, students are required to take the Hong Kong Diploma of Secondary Education Examination to proceed to four years' studies at a local higher education institution or to study overseas. Hong Kong's higher education institutions are divided into two main types: government-funded (i.e., funded by the University Grants Committee) universities and self-financed institutions. In mid-2018, degree courses were offered by eight government-funded universities and 12 self-financed higher education institutions in Hong Kong, of which one is a statutory university and the other is a private university.

The study context was a self-financed higher education institution in Hong Kong (henceforth the College) that offered degree programmes. At the time of the study, the College was offering around 20 degree programmes, all of which had been accredited by the Hong Kong Council for Academic and Vocational Qualifications (HKCAAVQ) through a stringent institutional review and programme validation exercises mandated prior to the launch of all official academic programmes in Hong Kong. After scrutinising documents submitted by the College and the findings of numerous on-site visits by a panel of local and overseas reviewers, the HKCAAVQ issued an accreditation report containing recommendations and suggestions for the College. The College fulfilled all the recommendations and suggestions within the required time, allowing it to launch the academic degree programmes.

The College's Department of English offers a Bachelor of Arts in English programme and an English Language Teaching (ELT) Unit. The ELT Unit provides a wide range of credit-bearing English courses for the whole college, such as General English, Academic English, Business English, and English for Specific Purposes. In collaboration with the English Language Centre, it also runs non-credit-bearing courses such as an English enhancement course, an IELTS preparation course and several workshops and consultation sessions.

Three years ago, the College introduced an English language exit requirement. To graduate, all students are required to attain at least an overall Band 6 in the International English Language Testing System (IELTS) test, although no requirements exist for individual sub-scores in the four sections – listening, reading, writing and speaking. Students who fail to meet the English language exit requirement (i.e., fail to attain at least an overall Band 6 in the IELTS) can enrol on an English course named English Exit offered by the ELT Unit for a fee. Passing the English Exit course is equivalent to fulfilling the College's English language exit requirement.

5.2 Participant

The participant in this study, Hannah (pseudonym), was an L2 teacher at the ELT Unit in the College's Department of English. At the time of the study,

Hannah had more than 10 years' teaching experience. She was responsible for teaching credit-bearing courses such as Academic English. She also took up the English Exit course. In addition, she held language-related short courses and workshops for the English Language Centre. She was considered an ideal research participant as she taught courses involving both high-stakes and low-stakes tests. For example, passing the high-stakes English Exit course allows students to graduate from the College, whereas a fail defers graduation. In contrast, workshops organised by the English Language Centre are regarded as low-stakes since they carry no credits, and enrolment is voluntary.

5.3 Methodology

Narrative inquiry was conducted to explore the lived experiences reported by Hannah, an L2 English teacher, of the washback of high-stakes and low-stakes testing on L2 English writing at a self-financed higher education institution in Hong Kong.

As I am also an L2 English teacher, with a teaching background and experience similar to Hannah's, I regarded myself as a rich source of data, where *data* refers to "observable information" on or "direct experience" of the context (Punch 2009). When collecting data from the participant, I also sought to gain insights into my own teaching approaches. I thus took the dual role of researcher and research subject, reporting on what the participant and I were "up to" (Alvesson 2002: 175). I believe that personal involvement is a rich resource for inquiry (Alvesson 2003). Therefore, I sought to thicken the participant's narrative by integrating my own personal practical experiences with the participant's stories.

Narrative inquiry has been defined as the study of experience as story (Connelly and Clandinin 2006). However, I would instead define narrative inquiry as "the study of experience *through experience* as story" (Yu 2017: 60, original emphasis). "In narrative inquiry, experience, rather than theoretically informed research questions . . . tends to be the starting point" (Trahar 2011b: 48). This is why I did not develop a framework of testing and assessment theories at the beginning of this chapter. The nature of the reality under study was contingent on the meanings that the participant and I ascribed to our contexts, and these meanings were central to understanding human behaviour and the social world.

The study had only one official participant. I sought to explore Hannah's first-hand lived experiences and to understand how she made meanings and connected these meanings with the social world around her. I, as an insider researcher, could also be considered a participant. I hoped that combining my subjectivity with the participant's experiences would generate new knowledge as the co-constructed stories unfolded. Narrative inquiry is usually appropriate when studying a small number of participants, as it permits attention to subtleties and nuances. I did not seek to make generalisable claims.

5.4 Data collection

Before conducting the interviews, I explained the objectives of the narrative inquiry to the participant, Hannah. After gaining Hannah's initial consent, I sent her a formal invitation outlining the research title, objectives, data collection method, and details of the interviews. Hannah was assured that her anonymity and confidentiality would be protected throughout the research. She understood that she would be given a pseudonym and some sensitive information would be removed or masked. Hannah was also assured of her right to withdraw from the narrative inquiry at any stage. Hannah signed an informed consent form on the same day that she received the formal invitation.

I conducted two one-on-one face-to-face interviews with Hannah at her workplace in 2017 with plenty of small talk before and after the interviews. Each interview lasted for around 2 hours. The interviews were audio-recorded. They were conducted in Cantonese – both Hannah's and my first language – the use of mother tongue in the interviews could encourage my participant to tell me more nuanced experiences freely. I conducted narrative interviewing, seeking "to *understand* rather than to *explain*" (Fontana and Frey 2005: 706, original emphases). Narrative interviews are unstructured in-depth interviews with specific features (Jovchelovitch and Bauer 2000); for example, they may be "non-standardardised" and "open-ended" (Punch 2014: 147). The merit of this approach is that it does not impose an "a priori categorisation which might limit the field of inquiry" (Punch 2014: 147). I stressed the importance of the participant's and my own experiences, seeking to excavate her particularities and subtleties (Fontana 2003), but did not aim to look at causality. I also attempted to "reach a mutual understanding and intimacy of feelings with the interviewee" (Fontana 2003: 54). I did not prepare many questions or seek to elicit certain answers; nor did I ask many questions during the interviews. I merely listened attentively to my participant's stories and sought to re-present as many rich and valuable stories as possible.

5.5 Data analysis

I conducted the transcription myself, which is important for narrative researchers, as it ensures that no nuances and subtleties are neglected by an uninvested third party. Jovchelovitch and Bauer (2000: 65) described the transcription process as "the first step of analysis" . I listened to the audio recordings repeatedly. I attempted to eliminate all of my ingrained presumptions and attended actively to Hannah's stories. Riessman's (2008) dialogic/performance analysis was used to re-present the co-constructed stories. My dialogue with the participant was presented in a conversational format. Dialogic/performance analysis closely resembles performance rather than conversation. It fundamentally problematises the way in which dialogue is interactively produced and performed as narrative. It stresses the influence of the researcher, the context, and the social circumstances. In carrying out dialogic/performance analysis, I played an important role in the interview process and became an active presence in the text. Whereas many researchers claim to be objective, I honoured my own subjectivity in this inquiry. Therefore, in addition to my participant's voice, my own voice was fully presented in a form of reflexivity (Trahar 2011a).

6 Findings and discussion

As the stories unfolded, I discovered three unexpected vignettes, as follows:

6.1 Vignette 1: "What are the two types of assessment?" – High-stakes or low-stakes testing: It is all contingent on a teacher's take

Many researchers, such as Hamp-Lyons (2017), Inbar-Lourie (2013), and Scarino (2013), have called for acknowledgement of the importance of assessment literacy. Assessment literacy has been defined as "a basic understanding of educational assessment and related skills to apply such knowledge to various measures of student achievement" (Xu and Brown 2016: 149). Teachers' experience and knowledge of assessment are widely believed to impact their teaching. However, during the inquiry, I discovered quite the contrary: Hannah did not rigidly fulfil conventional criteria for assessment literacy. She was not even able to distinguish between formative and summative assessment. The former refers to the "formal and informal processes teachers and students use to gather evidence for the purpose of informing next steps in learning," whereas the latter provides "evidence of student achievement for the purpose of making a judgement about student competence or programme effectiveness" (Chappuis 2015: 3–4).

> Hannah: It's like what the academics call . . . . What is it? . . . Sum . . .
>
> Researcher: Formative and summative?
>
> Hannah: [Chuckling] Oh yes . . .

Hannah seemed unable to identify the two most common types of assessment, and was not cognisant of the processes and procedures involved in developing learning-oriented assessment in response to high-stakes and low-stakes testing. Instead, she used her intuition.

> Hannah: Well, . . . you may think that the English Exit course has high stakes . . . Um . . . for me, it is not . . . on paper, . . . it is a graduation requirement . . . in the future, no matter what jobs they take, they will need to be able to write in English . . . I relate the use of English to their workplace . . . I do not show them the marking scheme . . . do not pressurise them . . . I try to make the classroom atmosphere relaxing . . . it's summertime after all . . . Meanwhile, people may think that the Personal Statement workshop has low stakes . . . in a sense that it doesn't offer credit . . . I don't use marks as bait . . . as no marks are given . . . say that if they want to transfer to a government-funded university or find a good job upon graduation, or participate in an exchange programme . . . and suggest [that the test has an] immediate impact and [a] long-term impact . . . my definitions of high-stakes and low-stakes are different from those of academics . . .

Interestingly, this vignette reveals that Hannah taught a course with a high-stakes test course as if it had had low stakes, and vice versa. Hannah believed that even low-stakes testing has an impact on students' futures.

> Hannah: I believe that, to a large extent, stakes are crafted by the teacher. Of course, the marks available are indicated in the module outline, e.g., how many marks or what percentage can be gained in a writing task . . . but if no marks are given for certain writing tasks, they are [still] influential . . . and have an impact . . . the definition of stakes is fluid . . . I use the impact to tempt . . . or guide the students . . . [grinning] . . .

Hannah reminded her students that if their personal statements were not well written, the consequences could be severe. The stakes, defined as "the gain or loss the test-taker may get from taking the test" (Hamp-Lyons 2017), were crafted by her. She believed that the results of even a low-stakes test would affect students' futures, whether sooner or later. She thus taught courses with low-stakes tests as if they had high stakes and linked the results obtained in these tests with the students' further studies and future employment, the College's two major indicators of success. Hannah explained that she thus believed even the Personal Statement workshop to have high stakes. Whilst Hannah did not seem to possess assessment literacy, she seemed aware of Markus and Nurius's (1986, as cited in Zhan and Andrews 2014) concept of "possible selves". She enabled the students to portray themselves in possible future states, involving thoughts, images, and senses (Zhan and Andrews 2014). She brought her own values and meanings to the Personal Statement workshop by connecting its outcomes with long-term goals, which resembles the abovementioned principles of an ideal self and possible selves.

Hannah also sought to convince her students that the English Exit course was "relaxing". This echoes Bailey's (2005) claim that although teachers have little control over high-stakes tests, they do have the power to generate positive washback by creating a positive learning atmosphere. Watanabe (2004) stated that when teachers have negative beliefs about assessment, their teaching may be negatively affected, resulting in negative washback. Labelling a test negatively may be more detrimental to teaching and learning than the effects of the actual test. In the same vein, Hannah believed that labelling a test positively could bring favourable results. Her teaching approaches were based on her own beliefs about the stakes of different tests.

6.2 Vignette 2: "Teaching writing versus teaching a piece of writing" – Is writing a means or an end?

Hannah: In the writing paper of the English Exit course, I teach writing, whereas in the speaking course, students are asked to submit a piece of written rhetorical analysis. But I treat [the latter] assignment as teaching a piece of writing . . . [giggling]

Researcher: What do you mean? Writing is submitted in a speaking course?

Hannah: Yes, students are asked to submit one piece of writing in the speaking course . . . named rhetorical analysis . . .

Researcher: So it's not all about speaking . . .

Hannah: Well . . . the English Exit course writing paper is more regimented . . . students are expected to demonstrate their ability to complete writing tasks, show logical thinking, use the language items . . . and the use of discourse markers for better coherence . . . I stress a lot about the requirements . . . I tell the students about the marking scheme . . . and refer to the rubric and marking criteria . . . Well, for the rhetorical analysis component of the speaking course . . . students are asked to analyse a piece of speech of their choice . . . the focus is on the rhetorical appeals . . . I use another set of strategies . . . I . . . put aside the writing requirements and even grammar . . . free writing basically . . . marking is totally different . . . I do not mark intensively . . . I do not correct their grammatical mistakes in detail . . . but comment on their efficiency . . . I don't want to frustrate them . . . credit is given to students who attempt a task . . . I value most their analytical thinking and creativity . . . .

Researcher: Yes, you are right . . . efficiency is seldom assessed in high-stakes testing . . .

This vignette reminded me of the two major approaches to teaching writing: the product approach and the process approach (Basturkmen 2014). The product approach involves stages of familiarisation, controlled writing, guided writing, and free writing (Steele 2004). Instruction in grammar, vocabulary, and sentence structure is followed by students' "imitation of the input" (Badger and White 2000). Students are gradually allowed more autonomy over their writing. The process approach places less emphasis on aspects of linguistic knowledge such as grammar and vocabulary (Badger and White 2000). Instead, the focus is directed towards planning, idea generation, problem solving, self-reflection, and self-evaluation (Graham and Sandmel 2011).

The different teaching and learning approaches adopted by Hannah to teach writing were not driven by the stakes of the tests per se, but by her intuitive assessment. Some researchers have claimed that when stakes are high, teaching and learning occur in line with the test rather than around the language itself (Andrews 2004; Matoush and Fu 2012). The English Exit course writing paper taught by Hannah had been designed as a make-up course for students who had been unable to meet the College's English language exit requirement. The assessment criteria were heavily guided, consciously or subconsciously, by the four categories of the assessment criteria used in the IELTS test, namely task achievement, coherence and cohesion, lexical resources, and grammatical range and accuracy. The teaching content was also heavily governed by the assessment criteria. These criteria seemed to be imprinted on Hannah's mind, as evident in her spontaneous recital of the teaching elements. These assessment criteria must have been ingrained enough to form a set of standards, albeit with room for change. To a large extent, the criteria had circumscribed her teaching. Her teaching approaches, she conceded, were fairly regimented and conventional, and revolved around the assessment criteria and methods. This is akin to the "tell-show-do" approach suggested by Cheng and Curtis (2004: 15). Hannah's teaching approach was best categorised as the product approach, which is more linear and teacher-oriented than the process approach. In a sense, then, Hannah taught to the test and her students wrote to the test.

However, Hannah allowed more flexibility in both content and teaching approach when the students came to write rhetorical analyses during the speaking course. She focused on the delivery of creative ideas, perceptive observations and soft skills such as efficiency. Less concern was paid to linguistic accuracy or the use of academic lexicons. This approach can be categorised as the process approach. This is consistent with Carless's (2007) findings that the product approach is far more common than the process approach among writing teachers in Hong Kong, and that the delivery of knowledge is thus privileged over the development of communication skills.

Interestingly, Hannah taught writing in the writing course – a "direct test", as in Weigle's (2002) term – relatively conventionally, but taught "a piece of writing" in a speaking course – an "indirect test" (Weigle 2002) – more creatively and flexibly. She explained that in the writing course, writing is an end product, whereas in the speaking course, writing is a means to an end for delivering a product. Effort, observation and creativity, qualities rarely measured in formal high-stakes testing, are more highly valued during speaking courses, as noted by Ayers (1993: 16):

> Standardised tests can't measure initiative, creativity, imagination, conceptual thinking, curiosity, effort, irony, judgement, commitment, nuance, good will, ethical reflection, or a host of other dispositions and attributes. What they can measure and count are isolated skills, specific facts and functions, content knowledge, the least interesting and least significant aspects of learning.

Some washback researchers, such as Cheng (2010: 52), have claimed that examinations are not the "be-all and end-all" of education. "They are not an end in themselves" (Cheng 2010: 52). The same applies to the teaching of writing. Some students find writing frustrating as they believe they will never reach the level of proficiency to which they aspire. Some teachers also find the teaching and marking of writing tedious and unrewarding (Lee 2009). If teachers can encourage more initiative, creativity and imagination, as suggested by Ayers (1993), or efficiency, as stressed by Hannah, writing will become less daunting and more pleasurable. In addition, teachers should take note of Hannah's approaches to teaching the writing of rhetorical analysis, in which she sought to make writing a means to an end instead of an end in itself. If teachers focus more on the writing process than the writing product, the results of high-stakes or low-stakes tests can ensure a positive washback effect.

6.3 Vignette 3: "My student left the room with the listening test writing task unfinished" – Motivation to succeed or motivation to avoid failure?

One of the positive washback effects suggested in the literature is that certain tests can enhance motivation (Watanabe 2001). As an L2 English learner and teacher in Hong Kong, I share this belief. Hannah also held this belief:

> Hannah: As a teacher, I am pragmatic. I put myself in my students' shoes. If a test carries no marks, I do not take it seriously . . . when I was a student, I was alert to this . . . GPA . . . even professors are concerned about scores . . .

However, Hannah also offered a surprising counterexample.

> Hannah: I'll share with you an episode this summer during the English Exit course . . . a male student . . . in a listening paper with a writing task from a TED talk . . . [the task was to] evaluate the speaker's style . . . the student left halfway through the listening paper . . . refused to complete the writing task . . . he emailed me afterwards . . . he said he was sick of doing this kind of task after so many years of writing . . . he was fed up with writing tests . . . but he felt sorry about leaving . . . he felt like he was going to explode if he continued to do it . . . but when he left he looked very embarrassed. I then received his email when I returned to my office . . .
>
> Researcher: What did you feel about this event?
>
> Hannah: It just struck me, really . . .

Some washback researchers, such as Green (2007b), Tsagari (2009), and Zhan and Andrews (2014), have suggested that examinations motivate students to learn. It is widely believed that if examinees consider the test important, they will put in effort (Barry et al. 2010). According to Watanabe (2001), once a high-stakes test such as a final examination is over, motivation is difficult to sustain. However, the above episode shows that motivation had ceased even before the examination had ended. The intended learning outcome was not achieved despite the student's awareness that the test had high stakes – its scores would determine whether he was able to graduate. The student's reaction to the writing test was inconsistent with the claim that high-stakes testing can generate a positive washback effect on students' learning motivation. When motivational efforts exceed an optimal point, a negative effect such as a decline in performance may occur; this phenomenon is known as the Yerkes-Dodson law (Alderson and Wall 1993: 119). High-stakes tests administered to motivate students can produce unintended negative washback when students' stress levels become unmanageable. The stress, anxiety and "associated guilt, shame, or embarrassment" (Alderson and Wall 1993: 118) brought about by such tests can be considered side effects or by-products. In the above episode reported by Hannah, the writing task motivated the student not to succeed, but to seek to avoid failure. With hindsight, Hannah offered a thought-provoking insight into the student's behaviour:

> Hannah: Our students' backgrounds should be taken into account . . . their language proficiency is not high . . . their interest in learning is low . . . I constantly remind myself . . . give them a sense of achievement . . . they need to taste the sweetness of success . . . If the same writing task had been set in a workshop, the students would not have escaped . . . [sigh] . . .

Grades are motivating for some students, especially high-flyers who see their learning bear fruit. However, grades can be demotivating for those who do not perform well and those who wish to avoid failure. This may also explain why some students become "avoiders" (Swerdzewski, Harmes, and Finney 2009) or drop out of school.

7 Implications of the study

This narrative inquiry explored the teaching strategies implemented by an L2 English teacher at a self-financed higher education institution in Hong Kong to deal with high-stakes and low-stakes English writing tests. Many researchers defined high-stakes and low-stakes testing rather rigidly. Some teachers' teaching styles and methodologies were to some extent driven by the stakes of tests. However, the distinction between stakes could be as flexible as Hannah indicated in the first vignette. She attached her own set of values and meanings to her teaching and justified the stakes positively. The alternative way in which Hannah perceived a test, i.e., as high-stakes or low-stakes, had a big impact on her choice of teaching style and methodology.

The second vignette showed that Hannah used a product approach to teaching writing, especially when teaching courses with high-stakes tests. This may be due to the strong influence of the IELTS writing paper, as the writing course in question was designed as an equivalent exit requirement. However, Hannah used a process approach to teach "a piece of writing" in a speaking course. This vignette invites teachers to rethink their own teaching styles. Communicative language ability (McNamara 1996) could be adopted as an alternative, stressing social variables such as creativity, a sense of humour, and originality in students' writing, and rejecting the use of stock phrases and regurgitation of ideas or "model" essays. In Hannah's words, teaching "a piece of writing" emphasised the process over the product. This may explain why some

L2 English teachers find essay marking less daunting than their peers do (Lee 2009). To make the teaching and learning of L2 English writing more effective and enjoyable, writing should not be taken as a subject or a content-based course, but instead as a real-life learning process aiding communication.

In addition, Hannah's comments in the third vignette offered good implications for teachers with regard to motivation for learning. The provision of a sense of achievement is of utmost importance in sustaining students' interest in learning, especially when teaching students of average or lower ability. Hannah constantly informed her students of what they had done well to offer them "the sweetness of success", without pointing out what they had not been able to accomplish. Teachers may consider praising their students' writing not purely in terms of writing assessment rubrics, which are written by assessors with a clear picture of the ideal performance of the majority. Teachers are advised not to use a "one-size-fits-all" teaching and learning approach, or assessment method. They may evaluate students' progress relative to their own previous writing performance. Students are more motivated if their progress and achievement are emphasised, but they may become demotivated if they experience defeat when comparing themselves to more successful peers (Stiggins 2001). Instead of providing students with summative feedback alone, "feedforward" (Carless, Joughin, and Mok 2006) can be offered to advance their learning. This kind of reinforcement and confidence building is especially useful in encouraging students to take risks and go beyond their comfort zones (Earl 2006). Assessment practice will thereby realise all of its goals, as proposed by Carless, Joughin, and Mok (2006): assessment as certification (as suggested in Figure 1), assessment as learning (as suggested in Figure 2) and assessment to foster lifelong teaching and learning (as suggested in Figure 3).

8 Limitations and further study

The study had only one official participant, and the data related only to her teaching experience. I could be regarded as a second, unofficial participant. Although in narrative research, the narrative researchers are regarded as in the field (Trahar 2009), "a member of the landscape" (Clandinin and Connelly 2000: 76) and therefore rich in data, the official data were collected from two narrative interviews. Nevertheless, given the small number of participants and the complexity of washback effects, I did not seek to make generalisable claims. Nor did I wish to oversimplify the interplay between factors, such as learner qualities, education policies and cultural characteristics. I concur with Cheng (2008: 359) that future washback studies should be designed "to investigate the consequences of language testing need to be multiphase, multimethod and longitudinal". Accordingly, future researchers could carry out repeated observations of classroom teaching, investigate the effects of policies and curricula, and/or interview the learners to understand the various factors inducing washback.

9 Conclusions

The main aim of this study was to gain an understanding of the washback effect through exploration of an L2 English teacher's use of different approaches to teaching writing for high-stakes and low-stakes tests to students at a Hong Kong self-financed higher education institution. Narrative interviews were used to solicit the participant's stories. Three interesting vignettes were observed during the inquiry. The first vignette has not supported the claim that assessment literacy, or test awareness, is conducive to teaching and learning and thus has a positive washback effect. As an experienced L2 English teacher, Hannah had developed her own definitions and thus her own interpretations of high-stakes and low-stakes testing. She crafted her own purposes for the tests and made meanings based on her own beliefs about the tests. She explained that the meanings she communicated to her students were rather different from the conventional definitions in the literature. The second vignette suggested that Hannah adopted a process approach when teaching "a piece of writing" during a speaking course. She focused on the writing process, with particular attention to analytical thinking, creativity and efficiency, rather than on the products of writing. The third vignette contradicted the common belief that high-stakes tests enhance learners' motivation. It countered the definition of washback as the way in which tests influence teachers and learners "to do *things* [emphasis added] they would not necessarily otherwise do because of the test" (Alderson and Wall 1993: 117). Surprisingly, one of Hannah's students left a test incomplete despite its high stakes.

This narrative inquiry shed light on an L2 English teacher's practical personal knowledge and first-hand experiences of teaching L2 English writing. The study also sought to create resonance with and offer insights for L2 teachers and other readers, and its findings are expected to add to knowledge of washback. Most importantly, the study can offer practical pedagogical implications for teachers to problematise their own teaching approaches in relation to assessment and contest their ingrained assumptions of conventional practices. It is hoped readers can be informed of alternative pedagogical approaches to L2 English writing and make teaching and learning of L2 writing more meaningful and rewarding.

References

Alderson, Charles & Hamp-Lyons, Liz. 1996. TOEFL preparation courses: A study of washback. *Language Testing* 13. 280–297. doi:10.1177/026553229601300304

Alderson, Charles & Wall, Dianne. 1993. Does washback exist? *Applied Linguistics* 14 (2). 115–129. https://doi.org/10.1093/applin/14.2.115

Alvesson, Mats. 2002. *Postmodernism and social research*. Buckingham: Open University Press.

Alvesson, Mats. 2003. Methodology for close-up studies: Struggling with closeness and closure. *Higher Education* 46 (2). 167–193. https://doi.org/10.1023/A:1024716513774

Andrews, Stephen. 2004. Washback and curriculum innovation. In Liying Cheng, Yoshinori Watanabe & Andy Curtis (eds.), *Washback in language testing: Research contexts and methods*, 37–50. Mahwah, NJ: Lawrence Erlbaum Associates Publishers.

Ayers, William. 1993. *To teach: The journey of a teacher*. New York: Teachers College Press.

Bachman, Lyle & Palmer, Adrian. 1996. *Language testing in practice*. Oxford: Oxford University Press.

Badger, Richard & White, Goodith. 2000. A process genre approach to teaching writing. *ELT Journal* 54 (2). 153–160. https://doi.org/10.1093/elt/54.2.153

Bailey, Kathleen. 2005. Looking back down the road: A recent history of language classroom research. *Review of Applied Linguistics in China* 1. 6–47.

Barnes, Melissa. 2017. Washback: Exploring what constitutes "good" teaching practices. *Journal of English for Academic Purposes* 30. 1–12. doi:10.1016/j.jeap.2017.10.003

Barry, Carol, L., Jeanne S. Horst, Sara J. Finney, Allison R. Brown & Jason P. Kopp. 2010. Do examinees have similar test-taking effort? A high-stakes question for low-stakes testing. *International Journal of Testing* 10 (4). 342–363. doi:10.1080/15305058.2010.508569

Basturkmen, Helen. 2014. *Ideas and options in English for specific purposes*. Mahwah, NJ: Lawrence Erlbaum Associates Publishers.

Carless, David. 2006. Learning-oriented assessment: Principles and practice. *Assessment and Evaluation in Higher Education* 31 (4). 395–398. https://doi.org/10.1080/02602930600679043

Carless, David. 2007. Learning-oriented assessment: Conceptual bases and practical implications. *Innovations in Education and Teaching International* 44 (1). 57–66. doi:10.1080/14703290601081332

Carless, David, Gordon Joughin & Magdalena Mok. 2006. Learning-oriented assessment: Principles and practice. *Assessment and Evaluation in Higher Education* 31 (4). 395–398. https://doi.org/10.1080/02602930600679043

Chappuis, Jan. 2015. *Seven strategies of assessment for learning* (2nd edn.). Upper Saddle River, NJ: Pearson.

Cheng, Liying. 1998. Impact of a public English examination change on students' perceptions and attitudes toward their English learning. *Studies in Education Evaluation* 24 (3). 278–310. https://doi.org/10.1016/S0191-491X(98)00018-2

Cheng, Liying. 2005. *Changing language teaching through language testing: A washback study*. Cambridge: Cambridge University Press.

Cheng, Liying. 2008. Washback, impact and consequences. Encyclopedia of Language and Education 7. 349–364.

Cheng, Liying. 2010. How does washback influence teaching? Implications for Hong Kong. *Language and Education* 11 (1). 38–54. https://doi.org/10.1080/09500789708666717

Cheng, Liying, Stephen Andrews & Ying Yu. 2011. Impact and consequences of school-based assessment (SBA): Students' and parents' views of SBA in Hong Kong. *Language Testing* 28 (2). 221–249. https://doi.org/10.1177%2F0265532210384253

Cheng, Liying & Curtis, Andy. 2004. Washback or backwash: A review of the impact of testing on teaching and learning. In Liying Cheng & Yoshinori Watanabe (eds.), *Washback in language testing: Research contexts and methods*, 3–18. Mahwah, NJ: Lawrence Erlbaum Associates Publishers.

Clandinin, D. Jean & Connelly, F. Michael. 2000. *Narrative inquiry: Experience and story in qualitative research*. San Francisco: Jossey- Bass.

Connelly, F. Michael & Clandinin, D. Jean. 2006. Narrative inquiry. In Judith L. Green, Gregory Camilli & Patricia B. Elmore (eds.), *Handbook of complementary methods in educational research*, 477–488. Mahwah, NJ: Lawrence Erlbaum Associates Inc.

Earl, Lorna M. 2013. *Assessment as learning: Using classroom assessment to maximise student learning*. London, England: Sage.

Earl, Lorna M. 2006. *Rethinking classroom assessment with purpose in mind: Assessment for learning, assessment as learning, assessment of learning*. Manitoba,: Manitoba Education, Citizenship and Youth.

Elshawa, Niveen R. M., Swee Heng Chan, Ain Nadzimah Abdullah, & Sabariah Rashid. 2016. Teachers' assessment literacy and washback effect of assessment. *International Journal of Applied Linguistics and English Literature* 5 (4). 135–141. doi:10.7575/aiac.ijalel.v.5n.4p.135

Estaji, Masoomeh & Tajeddin, Zia. 2012. The learner factor in washback context: An empirical study investigating the washback of the IELTS academic writing test. *Language Testing in Asia* 2 (1). 5–25. doi:10.1186/2229-0443-2-1-5

Fontana, Andrea. 2003. Postmodern trends in interviewing. In Jaber Gubrium & James Holstein (eds.), *Handbook of interview research*, 849–876. Thousand Oaks, CA: Sage.

Fontana, Andrea & Frey, James. 2005. The interview: From neutral stance to political involvement. In Norman K. Denzin & Yvonna S. Lincoln (eds.), *The Sage handbook of qualitative research*, 695–727. Thousand Oaks, CA: Sage.

Graham, Steve & Sandmel, Karin. 2011. The process writing approach: A meta-analysis. *The Journal of Educational Research* 104 (6). 396–407. https://doi.org/10.1080/00220671.2010.488703

Green, Anthony. 2007a. *IELTS washback in context: Preparation for academic writing in higher education*. Cambridge: Cambridge University Press.

Green, Anthony. 2007b. Washback to learning outcomes: A comparative study of IELTS preparation and university pre-sessional language courses. *Assessment in Education: Principles, Policy & Practice* 14 (1). 75–97.

Hamp-Lyons, Liz. 2017. Why is assessment literacy important and to whom? Retrieved from https://www.youtube.com/watch?v=DAXID0-aZQU

Hughes, Arthur. 2012. *Testing for language teachers*. Cambridge: Cambridge University Press.

Inbar-Lourie, Ofra. 2008. Constructing a language assessment knowledge base: A focus on language assessment courses. *Language Testing* 25 (3). 385–402. https://doi.org/10.1177%2F0265532208090158

Inbar-Lourie, Ofra. (2013). Guest Editorial to the special issue on language assessment literacy. *Language Testing* 30 (3). 301–307. doi:10.1177/0265532213480126

Jovchelovitch, Sandra & Bauer, Martin W. 2000. Narrative interviewing. In Martin W. Bauer & George Gaskell (eds.), *Qualitative researching with text, image and sound: A practical handbook*, 57–74. London: Sage.

Latham, Gloria. 2011. Assessment for learning. In Gloria Latham, Mindy Blaise, Shelley Dole, Julie Faulkner & Karen Malone, *Learning to teach: New times, new practices* (2nd edn.). South Melbourne: Oxford University Press. 262–284.

Lee, Icy. 2009. Ten mismatches between teachers' beliefs and written feedback practice. *ELT Journal* 63 (1). 13–22. https://doi.org/10.1093/elt/ccn010

Matoush, Marylou M. & Fu, Danling. 2012. Tests of English language as significant thresholds for college-bound Chinese and the washback of test-preparation. *Changing English* 19 (1). 111–121. doi:10.1080/1358684X.2012.649176

McNamara, Tim F. 1996. *Measuring second language performance*. Harlow: Longman.

Messick, Samuel. 1996. Validity and washback in language testing. *Language Testing* 13 (3). 241–246. doi:10.1177/026553229601300302

Pan, Yi-ching. 2009. A review of washback and its pedagogical implications. *Journal of Science, Foreign Languages* 25. 257–263. https://js.vnu.edu.vn/FS/article/view/2441

Pan, Yi-ching. 2014. Learner washback variability in standardized exit tests. *The Electronic Journal for English as a Second Language* 18 (2). 1–30. Retrieved from http://www.tesl-ej.org/wordpress/issues/volume18/ej70/ej70a2/

Punch, Keith. 2009. *Introduction to research methods in education*. London: Sage.

Punch, Keith. 2014. *Introduction to social research: Quantitative and qualitative approaches*. London: Sage.

Purpura, James E. 2009. The impact of large-scale and classroom-based language assessments on the individual. In Lynda Taylor & Cyril J. Weir (eds.), *Language testing matters*. Cambridge: Cambridge University Press. 301–325.

Riessman, Catherine K. 2008. *Narrative methods for the human sciences*. Thousand Oaks, CA: Sage.

Scarino, Angela. 2013. Language assessment literacy as self-awareness: Understanding the role of interpretation in assessment and in teacher learning. *Language Testing* 30 (3). 309–327. doi:10.1177/0265532213480128

Serafini, Frank. 2000. Three paradigms of assessment: Measurement, procedure and inquiry. *The Reading Teacher* 54 (4). 384–93. https://www.jstor.org/stable/20204924

Smith, Mary L. 1991. Put to the test: The effects of external testing on teachers. *Educational Researchers* 20 (5). 8–11. https://doi.org/10.3102%2F0013189X020005008

Spolsky, Bernard. 1994. The examination of classroom backwash cycle: Some historical cases. In David Nunan (ed.), *Bringing about change in language education*, 55–66. Hong Kong: University of Hong Kong, Department of Curriculum Studies.

Steele, Vanessa. 2004. Product and process writing: A comparison. Retrieved from http://www.teachingenglish.org.uk/article/product-process-writing-a-comparison.

Stiggins, Rick J. 2001. *Leadership for excellence in assessment: A powerful new school district planning guide*. Portland, OR: Assessment Training Institute.

Stoneman, Bernadette. 2005. *An impact study of an exit English test for university graduates in Hong Kong: Investigating whether the status of a test affects students' test preparation activities*. Hong Kong: Hong Kong Polytechnic University doctoral dissertation. http://hdl.handle.net/10397/2720

Swerdzewski, Peter. J., Christine J. Harmes & Sara J Finney. 2009. Skipping the test: Using empirical evidence to inform policy related to students who avoid taking low-stakes assessments in College. *The Journal of General Education* 58 (3). 167–95. https://doi.org/10.1353/jge.0.0043

Swerdzewski, Peter J., Christine J. Harmes & Sara J Finney. 2011. Two approaches for identifying low-motivated students in a low-stakes assessment context. *Applied Measurement in Education* 24 (2). 162–188. doi:10.1080/08957347.2011.555217

Taylor, Liz. 2009. Developing assessment literacy. *Annual Review of Applied Linguistics* 29. 21–36.

Trahar, Sheila. 2009. Beyond the story itself: Narrative inquiry and autoethnography in intercultural research in higher education. *Forum: Qualitative Social Research* 10 (1). Art. 30.

Trahar, Sheila. 2011a. "Burt's story reminded me of my grandmother": Using a reflecting team to facilitate learning about narrative data analysis. In Sheila Trahar (ed.), *Learning and teaching narrative inquiry: Travelling in the borderlands*, 141–56. Amsterdam,: John Benjamins Publishing Company.

Trahar, Sheila. 2011b. Changing landscapes, shifting identities in higher education: Narratives of academics in the UK. *Research in Education* 86 (1). 46–60. https://doi.org/10.7227/RIE.86.5

Tsagari, Dina. 2009. *The complexity of test washback*. Frankfurt: Peter Lang Publishing.

Wall, Dianne. 2000. The impact of high-stakes testing on teaching and learning: Can this be predicted or controlled? *System* 28 (4). 499–509. doi:10.1016/S0346-251X(00)00035-X

Wall, Dianne & Horak, Tania. 2006. *The impact of changes in the TOEFL examination on teaching and learning in Central and Eastern Europe: Phase 1, The baseline study. TOEFL Monograph Series 34*. Prinston, NJ: Educational Testing Service. https://onlinelibrary.wiley.com/doi/pdf/10.1002/j.2333-8504.2006.tb02024.x

Watanabe, Yoshinori. 2001. Does university entrance examination motivate learners? A case study of learner interviews. In Akita Association of English Studies (ed.), *Trans-equator exchanges: A collection of academic papers in honour of Professor David Ingram*, 100–110. Akita City, Japan: Akita.

Watanabe, Yoshinori. 2004. Teacher factors mediating washback. In Liying Cheng & Yoshinori Watanabe (eds.), *Washback in language testing: Research contexts and methods*, 19–36. Mahwah, NJ: Lawrence Erlbaum Associates Publishers.

Weigle, Sara C. 2002. *Assessing writing*. Cambridge: Cambridge University Press.

Wise, Steve L. (2009). Strategies for managing the problem of unmotivated examinees in low-stakes testing programs. *The Journal of General Education* 58 (3), 152–166. doi:10.1353/jge.0.0042

Xu, Yueting & Brown, Gavin T. 2016. Teacher assessment literacy in practice: A reconceptualization. *Teaching and Teacher Education* 58. 149–162. doi:10.1016/j.tate.2016.05.010

Yu, Anora. 2017. *Being, becoming and belonging – Identity ambiguity or identity demystification? A narrative inquiry into the professional identities of an associate department head of a higher education institution in Hong Kong*. Bristol: University of Bristol doctoral dissertation.

Zhan, Ying & Andrews, Stephen. 2014. Washback effects from a high-stakes examination on out-of-class English learning: Insights from possible self-theories. *Assessment in Education: Principles, Policy & Practice* 21 (1), 71–89. doi:10.1080/0969594X.2012.757546

(Luna) Jing Cai
Preparing Chinese novice writers for academia: An integrated genre-based approach for writing research articles

Abstract: With the rapid development of, and pressing requirements for international publication in China, there has never been such an urgent need among Chinese graduate students and scholars for improving their English academic writing skills. In this chapter, a text-focused genre-based approach was developed to provide comprehensive scaffolding to novice writers. From the top down, this approach integrates two traditions of genre-based pedagogies, namely that of the English for Specific Purposes (ESP) School as well as the Sydney School Teaching and Learning Cycle. In this regard, a strong emphasis is placed on using guided analyses for understanding prototypical research article genre structures. From the bottom up, this approach applies a corpus-informed lexical approach where academic lexical phrases are utilized as the building blocks of academic prose. Application of this approach as a case study conducted in a tertiary institution yielded very positive feedback from Chinese graduate students. This feedback evidenced an increased level of genre awareness in students after instruction. Particularly, the moves/steps as well as handy linguistic tools (e.g., lexical phrases) were found to provide an effective solution to students' common problem during the preliminary stages of research article writing: "not knowing what to write about in each section".

Keywords: genre-based approach, writing research articles, lexical phrases, Chinese graduate students, course evaluation

1 Introduction: The context of EAP in China

With the internationalization of research and publication, China has become one of the largest producers of research output in recent years. According to data provided by the Institute of Scientific and Technical Information of China (2017), China ranks second as the source for the number of citations

---

(Luna) Jing Cai, Guangdong University of Foreign Studies

https://doi.org/10.1515/9781501512643-009

worldwide.[1] However, it was not until the beginning of this decade that a major shift in instructional focus from general English proficiency to English for academic purposes occurred in the College English programs in Chinese universities (Cai, 2014). This means, that for many decades before this reform, Chinese students were given little guidance on academic literacy in general. As a result, the research and teaching of academic writing is still in its infancy, according to a comprehensive review published in China (Xu, 2015).

Many EAP writing courses in Chinese tertiary institutions still adopt a "textbook" approach. Some of them do not have tailor-made curriculum or up-to-date course materials (including the institution where this study carried out). The results of a large scale needs analysis across institutions in Shanghai (Cai, J.G., 2012) have shown that, 86.2% of the 927 students indicated their strong needs in the knowledge of searching for relevant research articles and understanding them, due to lack of academic literacy. This was especially the case when it came to genre knowledge of the academic discourse and specific language features therein. With research publication having become a graduation requirement for many majors, postgraduate students in China have been forced to learn how to write research papers, but primarily on their own, particularly in terms of language use (Cai, J. L., 2013). In addition, they lack clear guidance in research ethics, which means insufficient knowledge about the definition of "plagiarism", paraphrasing and summarizing skills (Cai, J.G., 2014). These, together with the lack of linguistic devices, have contributed to the high percentage of plagiarism exhibited in the graduation theses written by Chinese students (Qu, 2016). Under such context, this study sets out to develop a localized approach to teaching academic writing for publication. This approach will be aimed toward equipping novice writers, particularly postgraduate students, with basic skills on the research genre as well as academic language to participate as members of academia.

2 Dominant genre-based approaches to teaching academic writing

Theoretical insights from genre studies have informed genre-based approaches to writing. The term "genre" has been used in a range of educational contexts to refer not only to types of literary texts, but also to any distinctive type of spoken or

---

[1] http://www.istic.ac.cn/tabid/640/default.aspx

written category of discourse, with or without literary aspirations (Swales, 1990). Genre approaches provide an effective writing pedagogy, by "making explicit what is to be learnt, providing a coherent framework for studying both language and contexts" (Hyland, 2007, p. 149). According to Hyon (1996), the impact of genre in educational contexts is evident primarily in three major traditions of research studies: 1) the English for Specific/Academic Purposes (ESP/EAP) School, 2) the Sydney School, and 3) the New Rhetoric (NR) approach. A fairly new direction would be critical EAP (Benesch 1999; Pennycook, 1997) and Academic Literacies (e.g., Lillis & Scott, 2007). It is worth noting that Coffin and Donohue (2012) categorized these various traditions of research into a continuum. Placement along this continuum will depend on the starting point of analysis in instruction, namely whether the work is text-focused or writer-focused. The ESP School and the Sydney School are more text-focused in that students are directed to explicitly analyze well selected "genre exemplars" to understand common practices in the discourse community. In contrast to this, followers of the NR and Academic Literacies approaches, as well as critical EAP schools, have all criticized such static and normalized approaches. Rather, they will emphasize that writing functions as a social practice that builds on the power relationships, identity, social roles, and epistemology involved in writing.

The Academic Literacies approach and the critical EAP approach have been prevalent in the west, especially in English as a Second Language (ESL) contexts (e.g. Chun, 2015; Corcoran & Englander, 2016). However, researchers like Tribble and Wingate (2013) noticed the inadequate support provided in EAP courses offered by universities in the UK. These universities will most often exclusively cater to a narrow set of target groups, such as advanced native speakers. These researchers (Tribble & Wingate, 2013; Wingate, 2012; Wingate & Tribble, 2011) published a series of articles proposing a "mainstream pedagogy" that works by integrating different genre theories to fit novices of "all backgrounds", because "all students, regardless of background, are novices in the discourses and conventions of their chosen academic disciplines" (2013, p. 307). They argued that beginners, especially the large growing body of international students learning English as a second language (L2), struggle at the initial stage of academic writing, that is to understand and control the *text*. Likewise, in the English as a Foreign Language (EFL) context, Huang's (2014) research strongly supported this argument. Through tracking a research student's journey of genre knowledge development in a genre-based writing course, his findings suggested that *explicit instruction* on genre, moves, and linguistic features provide enormous help to shape novice writers' knowledge of writing for publication. Similarly, in mainland China, the primary concern for the EFL writers is whether they can understand and master relevant academic texts. Some students have limited exposure to authentic research articles in English, while some others have insufficient access to these articles (partly due to the lack of knowledge of academic searching), not to mention being "critical" in interpretation. For this study, a comprehensive approach that integrates the traditions *within* the text-focused approaches is proposed to help scaffold novice Chinese writers from both the top down and the bottom up. This proposed pedagogy is similar to Tribble and Wingate's (2013) in terms of its text-based orientations, but it also differs from their study in context (i.e., the EFL context as opposed to the ESL where elements of critical EAP were involved). The embedded lexical phrases instruction was also an important addition to this approach.

3 An integrated genre-based approach: Theoretical framework

In order to provide EFL students in mainland China with comprehensive scaffolding, this study adapted and integrated three traditions of linguistic studies. The first is the ESP genre-based approach, useful for top-down research in discourse analysis, taken originally from the Swalesian tradition. The second is the EAP-related lexical bundle studies, which serves as an important language feature in academic discourse, helping students develop their skills from the bottom up. Third and lastly is the Sydney School genre-based pedagogy, which helps embed the two aforementioned traditions in a comprehensive context for structured teacher-student interactions as well as tasks.

Now each of these approaches will be detailed and reviewed The ESP genre-based approach is first of all the overarching framework adopted in the present study. Researchers in the field of ESP have long been interested in genre as a tool for analyzing and teaching both the spoken and written language in academic as well as in professional settings. Swales' groundbreaking studies (1988, 1990, 2004) were seminal in shaping genre theory in ESP. Specifically, his research focuses on genre in academic settings, with an emphasis on genre analyses applied to the introductory sections of research articles. According to Swales' (2004) conceptualization of research article genre analysis, there are three layers of analysis subsumed under the genre of research article, namely part-genre, move/step analysis, and language features. The sections in the research articles are called part-genres, which constitute the macro-organization. For example, the most conventional macro-organization for a research article is introduction, method, results, and discussion (I-M-R-D).

Under part-genres, the smallest unit of discourse that carries a communicative function is called a move/step. The most prominent move/step, typically found in a paper's introductory section, was identified by Swales in the "creating a research space" (CARS) model. The CARS model includes several obligatory steps, such as "establishing the territory" and "identifying the gap", as well as optional steps, such as "stating the purpose and outlining the current research" (Swales & Feak, 2012, p. 331). This model has been one of the most frequently cited in genre analysis literature (e.g., Kwan, 2006). Underneath this move/step analysis, one finds linguistic verbalization or realization of the communicative purposes expressed in said moves. These verbalizations come in the form of "language features". This pioneering model of genre analysis has promoted a considerable number of findings on research articles descriptions across various disciplines. Discoveries have also been made on a variety of part-genres, including the literature review section (Kwan, 2006), discussion (Peacock, 2002), results (Brett, 1994), and even abstract (Lorés, 2004) sections of research articles. These conceptualizations have subsequently been used as effective resources in teaching.

Secondly, lexical bundles (i.e., academic lexical phrases) can be conceptualized as specific linguistic features within the ESP genre-based framework. Along with other general language features, these academic lexical phrases function as the bottom-up building blocks of academic discourse (Biber, Conrad, & Cortes, 2004). "General" features refer to those language features specific to the *academic register* in general, such as hedging, imperatives, directives, cohesive devices, and general academic writing styles (the use of formal vocabulary, punctuation, and summary words). General linguistic features are applicable to all forms of academic writing, regardless of generic or disciplinary contexts. Specific features are the ones specific to the *research genres* (e.g., dissertation, grant proposal, research article). Examples include reporting verbs in reviews, metadiscourse (e.g., Hyland & Tse, 2004) which shows the interpersonal dimension of academic writing and interactions between the author and audience, and "evaluative *that*" (Hyland & Tse, 2005) as important means of providing author comment and evaluation.

For this study, lexical bundles are highlighted as a major component of language features in genre analysis in nearly every lesson. There are three reasons for this practice. First, lexical bundles constitute a large portion of discourse (Schmitt & Carter, 2004), and they appear repeatedly as fixed units. In other words, language is often processed as chunks and not as individual words. Second, lexical bundles are defining markers of fluent and professional writing that meet the expectation of the academic community. Third, they represent the lexico-grammatical underpinnings of a language so often revealed in corpus studies but much harder to detect through analysis of individual texts (Coxhead & Byrd,

2007). Corpus-informed explicit instruction was embedded in the pedagogy to teach these bundles. The explicit teaching materials were selected from concordance lines, and the task design takes into consideration the three psychological processes necessary for successful vocabulary learning in the literature (Nation, 2001): noticing, generating, and retrieving. Note that these processes are compatible with the genre-based Teaching and Learning Cycle (TLC), which emphasizes raising rhetoric and language awareness through the guided reading of model texts, especially during the sentence making stage (Rose & Martin, 2012).

Thirdly, Sydney School genre-based pedagogy is useful in its systematic linguistics theory and its corresponding conceptualizations regarding the learning process. There are three levels of teaching and learning cycles under the conceptualization of language as a whole, from context to text in "compositional hierarchies" (Rose, 2010, p. 258). The three levels of support, presented in Figure 1, help students enhance acquisition of "written language patterns through experience of instances in context" (Rose, 2010, p. 263). The social goals of a text are achieved by the sequencing from the genre stages down to the letters. In the context of this pedagogy, the outer circle deals with the text in its entirety, while the middle circle focuses on sections or paragraphs of the text, and the inner circle covers sentences, words, and letters. However, the components in each circle are not applied in chronological order. For example, "Preparing for Reading", "Joint Construction" and "Individual Construction" in the outer circle are not in the same pedagogical

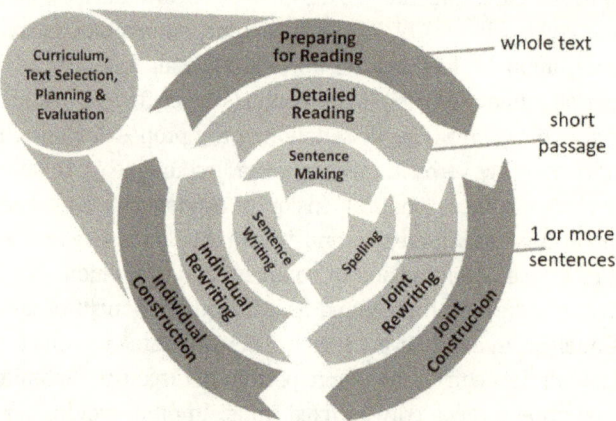

Figure 1: The Teaching and Learning Cycles for Curriculum Contexts–Three Degrees of Scaffolding Support.
Note. Adapted with permission from Rose, D. & Martin J.R. (2012) *Learning to Write, Reading to Learn: Genre, Knowledge and Pedagogy in the Sydney School.* by, 2012, Sheffield (UK) and Bristol (USA): Equinox, p. 147.

stage. This means that the teaching may start by preparing students for reading the whole text, then move to the "Detailed Reading" of certain paragraphs in the middle circle, and then down to the sentences and letters in the inner circle, and finally return to the rewriting in the middle circle and the construction of a complete text in the outer circle. In traditional language education, language will be taught in systemic separate contrasts moving from the lower level system (such as sounds and letters), to the higher system (such as grammar) in separate language activities from different classes and courses. For example, learners need to acquire meaningless phonics and letter-sound relationships before they are able to move on to words and sentences. The Sydney School considers this sequence of teaching as "bottom-up" (Rose, 2010). The teaching cycle from the Sydney School is, in contrast, simultaneously from both the "top down" and the "bottom up". It is able to integrate all levels and systems of language from the larger social context to the lowest level of realizations as each structural feature may instantiate "multiple intersecting systems" (Rose, 2010, p. 2). By experiencing repeated instances in context with modelling and scaffolding of the complete social construction of writing, the learning of language systems is not isolated.

Figure 2 presents the pedagogical framework of this study. The ESP approach sets the overarching framework: the teaching context (advanced learning for academic or professional purposes), and provides the theoretical basis of descriptive analysis of the research article genre. This means that the curriculum and the genre analysis tasks in class follow the schematic structure of a research article and the general principles outlined in Swales and Feak's (2004) pioneering textbook "Academic Writing for Graduate Students", as well as other reference materials published in ESP journals. Thus, the course consisted of four units of instruction which were devoted to the RA part-genres, "Introduction and Review", "Methods", "Results", and "Discussion and Conclusion". The middle circle in Figure 2 visualizes that almost every lesson in

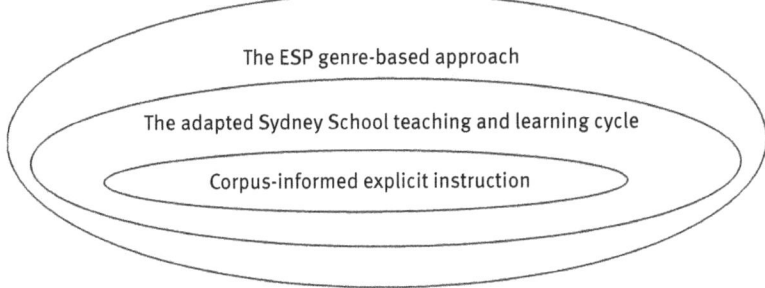

Figure 2: Pedagogical Framework of This Study.

the four units, the Sydney School TLC was adapted into the general ESP curriculum in order to systematically guide students through the genre analysis in class. From the top down, the students' attention was drawn towards the two dimensions of important building blocks, the discourse level and lexicogrammatical level. Moves, steps, and lexical phrases were brought to students' attention in the context of "Detailed Reading" (Rose & Martin, 2012) in the TLC. Furthermore, corpus-informed explicit instruction on lexical bundles was also incorporated into the inner circle with "Sentence Making" and "Sentence Writing" tasks to help scaffold students from the bottom up.

In the subsequent sections, I further explain the actual course design, and use the third week of class as a typical example to demonstrate how the principles were implemented. Finally, I report the evaluation of the course using multiple data sources.

4 Implementation of this approach: Example of a writing course for the Applied Linguistics discipline

The course where this approach was implemented was called "Writing Applied Linguistics Research Papers". It was designed for first-year graduate students majoring in applied linguistics. This course was built into the key compulsory content-based course "Second Language Acquisition" (offered by the same professor), as an adjunct course, where they shared the same writing assignment. For the professor, this design was optimal because students could integrate the contents learned in the core course with the linguistic aspects in the writing course and produce one coherent piece of work, instead of writing two separate research papers. I, the researcher, played dual roles as both an insider and an outsider: I designed the intervention and the course materials with comments and insights from the professor (the instructor of the course); during the instructional period, I was the observer who monitored the implementation of this approach and collected relevant data for evaluation.

4.1 Course material development

In this 16-week course, each lesson took 80 minutes. All the genre exemplars for genre analysis tasks in class were drawn from a self-compiled professional research article corpus in the discipline. It is a 480 thousand-word corpus comprising 50 SSCI research articles published in the last ten years, most of which were empirical studies covering the major topics in applied linguistics. Several articles were required readings from the SLA core course. Before the actual intervention, a pilot study was conducted with several students of varying proficiency from the previous year. These students provided insights for the selection of genre exemplars in Detailed Reading: first of all, the part-genre in the article should be written with clarity and an appropriate length (around 10 minutes of reading time); second, these exemplars show some prototypical genre structures and language features, probably with some unconventional features (for non-prescriptive, critical reading); third, the text difficulty was moderate, so weaker students were able to handle the reading without too much stress. The weaker students in the pilot study also pointed out where Chinese translations may be needed in the exemplar. Each lesson's tasks followed the principles and theories in the pioneering resource book on ESP genre-based pedagogy by Swales and Feak (2004), in addition to a series of follow-up textbooks using the same approach (Swales & Feak, 2009, 2011). However, the original tasks and texts from the textbook were not fully adopted and modifications were made on the form and content. Multi-disciplinary genre exemplars were changed to be discipline-specific. More importantly, this course chose *one* coherent exemplar per lesson for all the tasks related to the same part-genre, opposed to different text extracts for tasks of different purposes. This fit in the Sydney School TLC which suggested using one major text in one lesson to contextualize students for the Detailed Reading. Other genre analysis references such as those published in *Journal of ESP* were also used, for extended discussions based on the major exemplar.

Another important use of the self-compiled corpus was the selection of target lexical bundles for teaching. I used the frequency-driven approach (Biber, Conrad, & Leech, 2002) to compare a learner corpus with the professional corpus and generated a list of 45 four-word target lexical bundles using Antconc (Anthony, 2008). The learner corpus consisted of 55 theses written by the previous cohorts of students. It is of similar size (around 400 thousand words) to the professional corpus. Setting up cut-off frequency for retrieval and the process of tidying up the inflation in the bundle list basically follow what has been described in Hyland (2008) and Chen & Baker (2010). Additionally, other move-specific phrases for explicit teaching and awareness raising were also selected from the corpus by performing genre analysis. Most phrases related to moves were selected from the "language focus" sections from Swale and Feak's (2004) book as well as online resources such as the Academic Phrasebank compiled by the University of Manchester (2005). Text extracts in the form of concordance lines were used in the explicit teaching tasks on the bundles.

4.2 Assignments

The assignments consisted of two parts, the genre analysis tasks and the rewriting task. The purpose of the genre analysis tasks was to evaluate how well the students had learned about genre knowledge in class and to further train them in conducting self-directed genre analysis. Students were guided to engage in five genre analysis tasks after class, which were similar to what they had been doing in class. Each task was designed to correspond with the instructional content of that section (i.e., the part-genre in focus).

Individual Rewriting, originally a learning activity (Rose & Martin, 2012) following Joint Rewriting, was adapted as an assignment task. It helped students to recontextualize their genre knowledge already learned. Through this guided rewriting assignment, students could choose to rewrite one of the poorly written research papers the professor had selected for them. They were written by the previous students. The basic requirement was the paper needed to be rewritten into an acceptable/publishable piece of work, from the discourse level to the word level. Students were encouraged to apply the typical genre structure and phrases which had been introduced in class. They had to annotate their rewriting by showing where they had made the changes. This is called "rewriting the content" in the Sydney School pedagogy. This task was broken down into several sections as an on-going assignment. The rewriting of each section was due after the completion of each unit.

4.3 Week 3 example

This week was selected to illustrate a typical lesson that covers the basic moves/steps of a part-genre, such as the introduction section, for a research article. The goal of this lesson was to understand the CARS model (Swales, 1990) and relevant linguistic realizations through genre analysis. It involved several stages as follows:

Stage 1. "Preparing for Reading": The teacher prepared students for reading the introduction section of the selected sample paper by guiding them to think about why scholars need to "create a research space" (CARS) in the community (Swales & Feak, 2004, pp. 242–243). Then students were presented with an overview of the current unit – the move/steps in the CARS model, and how they were expected to be manifested in the selected paper. This stage also included a general introduction on the content of the paper to prepare them for Detailed Reading. The sample paper for genre analysis in class was selected from the journal *Applied Linguistics* about language attrition. According to Rose and Martin (2012), the teacher had to pre-analyze the text before teaching, and then students would engage in the guided "Detailed Reading" of the genre exemplar from the top down – from identifying the three basic moves to the steps and to the lexico-grammatical level of language features.

Stage 2. "Detailed Reading" and "Rewriting" are the turbo-charged engines of the TLC. In Stage 1, the focus of "Preparing for Reading" is on the global structure and meaning of texts, genre, and stages. In contrast, "Detailed Reading" and "Joint Rewriting" use scaffolding classroom interactions to focus on patterns of language within and between sentences of short passages. There were two tasks embedded in the Detailed Reading process. The first task was a discovery-based activity of the three moves of CARS model in the sample paper following Swales and Feak's task format (2004, p. 244). Instead of completing the task questions and looking for the right answers from the text, the teacher would guide the students into the Detailed Reading line by line (Rose & Martin, 2012). For example, the teacher would guide the students progressively in analyzing the moves and steps, asking questions on the rhetorical purposes and reasons for such organization, and drawing students' attention to the prototypical lexical phrases. In Task 2, special attention was directed to the steps in Move 1. First of all, Step a (claiming centrality) was introduced through the awareness raising of specific language features signaling the step. Some content-based questions were also directed to in-depth group discussions, such as "what are the general processes and variables affecting attrition?". The questions could then be summarized through the careful reading of Move 1 Step b (a brief review of the literature). At this stage, the classroom interactions, or the "curriculum genre" plays an essential role for scaffolding. In the Sydney School, it typically involves five moves: "prepare", "focus", "propose" "evaluate (affirm or reject)" and "elaborate" (Rose & Martin, 2012, p. 157). This can be seen as a modified version of the traditional pedagogical exchange analysis "IRF" (Initiation-Response-Feedback). For each round of "evaluation" and "elaborate", new knowledge is meaningfully constructed in the social context. Through careful planning of the teacher's focus questions, most students could receive affirmative evaluation which can promote learning. The following excerpt gives a taste of how the teacher scaffolded students line by line through pedagogical exchange patterns mentioned above.

[Excerpt from "Detailed Reading" in Week 3 (24:04–27:00)]

T: Okay, now let's turn to explore the first move "establishing a research territory" together in the text. We have just studied the conventional CARS model. The first step in the first move is usually "claiming the centrality". What centrality is being claimed? Can you guess what is meant by "claiming centrality"? What is "centrality"? Where does the word come from? [prepare, and focus]
S: Central. [propose]
T: Yes! Very good! It means that it deserves our special attention. Claiming centrality is simply a more professional way of saying it: to show that the general research area is important, central, interesting, problematic, etc. In short, it is *worthwhile* to do this research. So can you find this step in the sample paper? What study is central and important? Can you tell me? [affirm, elaborate, focus]
Ss: "Language attrition"! [propose]
T: Yes, and "both L1 and L2 attrition". How does it tell you that it is claiming centrality? [affirm, focus]
Ss: "have been subjected to rigorous examinations throughout the past couple of decades . . ." [propose]
T: So what does "rigorous examination" mean here? [focus]
S: (Searching for words)
T: Can you put it into a verb phrase? If I want to say, "L1 and L2 attrition have been . . . "[focus]
Ss: (Some murmuring)
T: What is the main verb here? "Rigorously" . . . [focus]
S: "Rigorously examined"! [propose]
T: Yes! Can you make that into a complete sentence? [affirm and focus]
S: "L1 and L2 attrition have been examined rigorously . . . " [propose]
T: Great! As you can see, we change lots of verbs into nouns like "rigorous examination" in academic writing. That's what we call "nominalization". And "rigorously" can mean "strictly" and "accurately". [affirm and elaborate]
T: Can you tell me any other phrases that give you hints regarding the purpose of "claiming centrality"? [focus]
Ss: "giving rise to its present status as a recognized field of" . . . [propose]
. . .

Stage 3. "Joint Rewriting" stage: After understanding the overall rhetorical organization, the language features of the specific steps, and the incidental instruction on other language features, students were encouraged to collect more phrases and "Jointly Rewrite" with the guidance of the teacher. Students needed to come up with alternative phrases to describe Step a (claiming centrality) using the key content words written on the blackboard by the teacher for brainstorming. This is called "rewriting the language" (same content, different language), according to Rose and Martin (2012). As for "rewriting the content" (using the same language to write about different content), it was applied in important sessions, such as rewriting the results section and also as a final assignment. For example, in Week 12, students were asked to use the rhetorical structures and phrases learned from the sample paper to rewrite a new paragraph reporting inferential statistics from an unfamiliar table. Self-directed learning after class was also encouraged.

Stage 4. Sentence making stage: Finally, as shown in the inner cycle in Figure 2, corpus informed explicit instruction was incorporated into the inner circle of TLC. Three target lexical bundles were chosen for this lesson and were explicitly studied through activities such as corpus concordance reading, collocation, and sentence construction exercises. The exploration of each phrase involved the same bottom-up scaffolding process: First, the corpus extracts provided an input-rich situation where the processing of meaning and usage of the phrase was reinforced; then they studied the collocation and other alternatives for expressing the same meaning of the phrase. Next, the grammatical structure and rhetorical functions were discussed, as well as the part-genres where the phrase can be used. Finally, they were asked to rewrite sentences or create a sentence of their own using the target phrase.

Due to limited space, the original teaching materials from week 3 and other supplementary materials are not provided in the appendices, please contact the corresponding author for more information.

4.4 Evaluation of the course

An evaluation of the course was conducted throughout the whole process of instruction for 16 weeks. The following three major research methods were used:

1) Evaluation survey: The questionnaire covers six major issues, utilizing a 5-point Likert scale. The content involves students' evaluation on the instructional approach, teaching materials and assignments, syllabus, and impact of this course on reading and writing research papers. The last three questions are open-ended ones without a word limit, including questions with topics like: what impressed them most about the course, suggestions on how to improve it, and other readings they have read outside of class. The survey was distributed to all the participants who attended the course.

2) Student interviews: A one-to-one follow-up interview was held each week after class for 16 weeks with four selected students (two with relatively high baseline English proficiency and two with low proficiency). Each interview lasted about an hour. The semi-structured interviews contained three major parts: the in-class uptake, self-assessment on learning, and suggestions about

the lessons. The interviews were supplementary to the survey data and aimed to understand the needs and uptake of students at different starting levels.

3) Classroom observations and other ethnographic data: The author/researcher was the observer of the course. An observation protocol was developed in which notes were taken on students' responses to and participation in the classroom activities conducted, teacher's delivery, and explanation of knowledge. Other ethnographic data on site was also collected as supplementary information, including face to face informal chats with the teacher and random students after class or via QQ (a social networking software popular in China).

5 Results of the course evaluation

A total of 84 participants returned the questionnaire survey. After calculating the mean scores, descriptive statistics of the findings were calculated and are shown in Table 1. On a scale of 1–5, 1 indicates "unsatisfactory" (or "least helpful") and 5 indicates "satisfactory" (or "very helpful"). The mean scores of all the evaluation

Table 1: Results of Course Evaluation Survey (N = 84).

Survey items		Mean	SD
Overall impression of the entire course		4.53	0.67
Evaluations on the teaching approach		4.35	0.78
Teaching materials and assignments		4.45	0.70
Quality of syllabus		4.58	0.62
The teacher's delivery		4.42	0.66
Impact of the course on academic reading (helpfulness)		4.64	0.63
Impact of the course on academic writing (helpfulness)	General organization	4.68	0.64
	Genre structures (move/steps)	4.61	0.73
	Specific language features	4.54	0.65
	Lexical bundles	4.46	0.85

items were above 4, and most scores are around 4.50. The overall impression score of the course is 4.53 out of 5, which clearly shows students' positive attitude towards the course. In particular, they found the course most helpful for academic reading (M = 4.64, SD = 0.63), the organization of academic writing (M = 4.68, SD = 0.64), as well as the prototypical rhetorical structures of research paper genre (M = 4.61, SD = 0.73). Interestingly, the students were more satisfied about the content and teaching materials than the teaching approach (M = 4.35, SD = 0.78). From the open-ended questions included in the survey, participants specified that the teacher-student interaction was not as effective as it should be due to the large class size. This prevented the teacher from interacting with the students who sat in the back of the classroom. Those who responded more actively usually sat in the front rows. However, they also pointed out that compared with other courses having too many group discussions instead of teacher-student interactions, this teaching approach is more intense in terms of information density, leading to students gaining more. This explains the high score on "teaching materials". I reported elsewhere (Cai, 2016) in greater detail about the quantitative findings of pre- and post-tests of the intervention, which shows that the instruction has significantly improved the genre awareness and the acquisition of lexical bundles for students of all starting levels. The overall writing assignment score is not reported here, as there is no pre-test of paper writing for comparison, so the evaluation is unable to show the effectiveness of the instruction in terms of change in overall ability in writing.

6 Students' perspectives on the impressive part of the course (triangulations from other sources of data)

A sample pool of 70 participants responded to the open-ended questions offered at the end of the survey. The first question asked students what they thought was the most impactful part of the course. After a thorough analysis, three major themes emerged. Most strikingly, genre structure was mentioned most frequently, comprising up to 85% of the total responses. On the other hand, 40% of the respondents indicated that learning of bundles left the deepest impression, and that they would like to make use of them in future writing. Lastly, 30% of them noted that they found learning specific language features most useful, such as move-specific lexical phrases, the specific verbs, tenses, and vocabulary relevant to the genre.

The strong implication of this course on genre awareness raising was further confirmed in the classroom observation and interview data, where students constantly indicated their opinions in the conversations and casual chats. One of the focal participants stated how in previous courses she had taken, they were only instructed on the general formality and required sections for writing a research paper, and she realized that these were simply part-genres of a research article. There was no mentioning of more specific moves and steps to guide them in writing sections of academic papers. What was taught in this new course was like "a walking stick"([guaizhang]) that helps her notice something she could not have known but through a large amount of reading. Another critical aspect constantly mentioned by the participants was the reckoning of "reading for different purposes", especially rhetorically. One of them said:

> I gradually learned to read a paper for different purposes: reading for language and reading for content. <u>Language and content can be separated, or I should say that I found it difficult to concentrate on both at the same time when reading, but in this course we were given more time to focus on the language and the purpose behind these linguistic choices.</u> In other courses, we were only required to read for information. After becoming more informed about genre structure, it has become easier for us to read other research papers with similar structures as well! Sometimes I subconsciously highlight and achieve greater awareness in reading for language and genre when going about detailed reading myself. After collecting more useful language features, I become more confident in my ability to write like a scholar.
> [Casual chat with Participant 25 (a mid-level achiever) via QQ, original in Chinese, 15 Jan. 2012]

The language training that Chinese students had received for years focused primarily on grammar and vocabulary, or on how to understand the content of the reading materials – either "focus on form" or "focus on content" only. Little analysis was carried out on the "writing process" of the exemplar, or to think like a writer. These findings imply that teachers need to draw students' attention to the fundamental social purposes of academic writing as well. After this course, students were transformed from being "information readers" (Hirvela, 2004, p. 115), or language readers, to "rhetorical reader/miners" (Hirvela, 2004, p.119).

More proof of such improvement could be seen in the remarkable initiative students took in their subsequent rewriting and annotation tasks. Many students were incredibly devoted to making annotations on their rewriting assignments. In the guidelines of the rewriting task, no specific instructions were given on how students should go about completing the task. Regardless, the students seemed very interested. They both creatively and voluntarily used colors, tables, and textboxes as useful tools in the processes of their rewriting, covering a variety of aspects, as shown in Figure 3. For example,

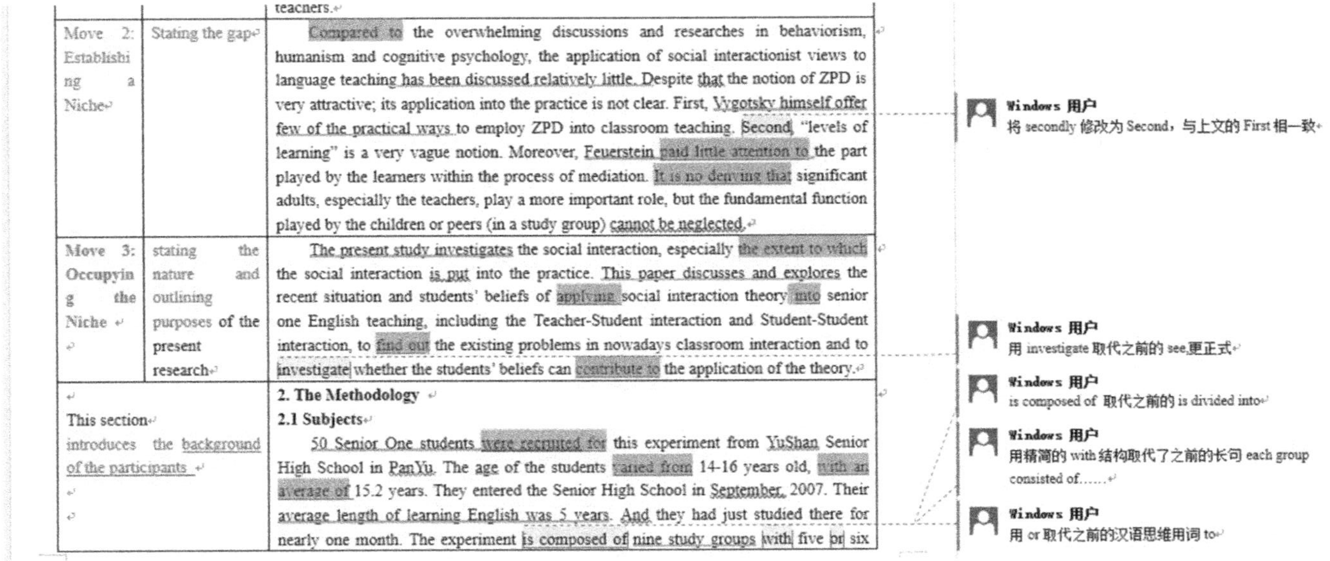

		teachers.
Move 2: Establishing a Niche	Stating the gap	Compared to the overwhelming discussions and researches in behaviorism, humanism and cognitive psychology, the application of social interactionist views to language teaching has been discussed relatively little. Despite that the notion of ZPD is very attractive, its application into the practice is not clear. First, Vygotsky himself offer few of the practical ways to employ ZPD into classroom teaching. Second, "levels of learning" is a very vague notion. Moreover, Feuerstein, and little attention to the part played by the learners within the process of mediation. It is no denying that significant adults, especially the teachers, play a more important role, but the fundamental function played by the children or peers (in a study group) cannot be neglected.
Move 3: Occupying the Niche	stating the nature and outlining purposes of the present research	The present study investigates the social interaction, especially the extent to which the social interaction is put into the practice. This paper discusses and explores the recent situation and students' beliefs of applying social interaction theory, into senior one English teaching, including the Teacher-Student interaction and Student-Student interaction, to find out the existing problems in nowadays classroom interaction and to investigate whether the students' beliefs can contribute to the application of the theory.
		2. The Methodology
		2.1 Subjects
	This section introduces the background of the participants	50 Senior One students were recruited for this experiment from YuShan Senior High School in PanYu. The age of the students varied from 14-16 years old, with an average of 15.2 years. They entered the Senior High School in September, 2007. Their average length of learning English was 5 years. And they had just studied there for nearly one month. The experiment is composed of nine study groups with five or six

Comments (right margin):
- Windows 用户: 将 secondarily 修改为 Second, 与上文的 First 相一致
- Windows 用户: 用 investigate 取代之前的 see 更正式
- Windows 用户: 取代之前的
- Windows 用户: 用措辞简洁 取代之前的长句 each group consisted of ……
- Windows 用户: 用 or 取代之前的汉语思维错用词 to

Figure 3: Example of Student Annotations in Rewriting.

students were found to have annotated their reconstruction of the move/steps in the paper, the specific features and bundles used, and at the same time they provided reasons for why they did so. They indicated the new content they had added, the data they had re-analyzed with new tables generated for clearer demonstration. They even corrected the mistakes in grammar, punctuation, as well as inappropriate wording that they found. These observations suggest that students enjoyed these activities considerably, and that students genuinely believed that this practice would be helpful for them in future writing tasks. With new technology, this rewriting or editing practice could be done online using a text-chat, so that a large number of students could collaborate with each other and the instructor in real time. In Reynolds and Anderson's (2015) study, students gave positive responses to similar practice.

Further evidence of the application of genre knowledge and phrases are reflected in students' final rewriting products. After a discussion on the coding scheme by the raters and the complete coding of all the 66 pieces of rewriting, a very encouraging picture was observed. On average, each participant voluntarily used 31.42 (SD = 14.22) *new* instructed move-specific phrases (indicating the start of the new moves) appropriately in writing, excluding the re-used phrases. Students' awareness of using these move-specific phrases, however, varied greatly from learner to learner. This is exhibited in the high *SD* scores. The least competent student used only six move-specific phrases appropriately in the writing, while the most competent student used up to 58 move-specific phrases. Those who preferred to use move-specific phrases noted that they regarded these phrases as signals for the genre structure whenever they wanted to start a new move, and they are "must-have" linguistic devices for writing up different sections of a research paper. Students in this study even consider these move-specific phrases more pragmatic than the lexical bundles with general academic functions, as the bundles are incomplete grammatical units, more abstract in nature, optional, and less predictable in where they are to be placed.

7 Students' suggestions for improving the course

Based on the results of the open-ended questions of the survey as well as the student interviews, three major points can be summarized from analyzing the content and themes therein. First of all, time limits stand out as the greatest constraint for students. It was found that students prefer more discussion regarding a given task after the guided detailed reading activity, time and class size permitting (e.g., Respondent 54, 60, and 77). However, a paradox was found in that some other students wrote that the time spent on the detailed reading activities for each text extract was not sufficient *before* carrying out a group discussion (e.g., Respondent 20 and 36). Simply put, students need more time for both stages. In reflecting on the major issues addressed in the Sydney School genre-based pedagogy, there has always been a problem regarding time constraints. A solution suggested by Rose (2010) is that a full cycle can be completed once in two weeks, as opposed to once every week.

Secondly, as the text extracts of each lesson are divided into segments taken individually from sample research papers, students (e.g., Respondent 35) will sometimes lack a holistic understanding of the research papers in their handouts. As such, there is a constant need to remind the students of the connection between the part-genres already covered in class as well as those being currently covered. This is necessary in order to create a comprehensive perspective for navigating the knowledge to be gained in class from the top down. Moreover, it was found that some students were not effective in synthesizing materials and knowledge covered across lessons, further adding to the difficulties presented by a syllabus divided by the part-genres of various research articles. To remedy this, more time can be devoted to reviewing past lessons in order to reinforce such connections (e.g., Respondent 10, 43, 57, and 61).

Finally, it must be noted that some students asked about the variability of the move/steps they noticed in their after-class readings, wondering whether they *should* follow a prototypical move/step or not. This reveals that some students are in fact already set to begin the subsequent stage: developing critical genre knowledge from the academic literacies and critical EAP traditions. The professor in this course did indeed emphasize that critically reading schematic structures in class, but still suggested the students to learn to walk with the "walking stick" before throwing it away.

8 Conclusion

This study has presented an integrated genre-based approach to academic writing. It takes into consideration the EFL novice writers' lack of exposure to authentic academic texts, as well as the writers' needs of understanding and controlling the texts during the initial stage of academic writing. This text-focused approach utilizes the strengths of different traditions of research, namely the research article genre analysis taken from the ESP School and the pedagogy of the Sydney School. The recent research findings of lexical bundles and phrases were also integrated into the study's model in order to serve as building blocks for supporting the writing skills of novices from the bottom up. It was found that this approach was very well received by the participants in the applied linguistic discipline, and it was shown to be very promising for disciplinary-specific academic writing courses. When applying this approach to other disciplines, subject experts could collaborate with the linguistics teachers by providing the professional text exemplars in the discipline for greater focus on content teaching in the core courses, while the linguistic teachers adopt the current framework in designing an adjunct writing course that draws students' attention to the linguistic aspects of writing in the discourse community.

Acknowledgement: I want to thank Guangdong University of Foreign Studies for providing the funding and platform for the research. My appreciation also goes to the editors and the anonymous reviewers for their insightful suggestions which helped improve the manuscript in several rounds of revision. I also want to extend my gratitude to the participants who agreed to commit themselves in the complicated data collection process.

References

Anthony, Laurence. 2008. AntConc (3.2.2) [Computer Software]. Tokyo, Japan: Waseda University. Available from http://www.antlab.sci.waseda.ac.jp/ (June, 1, 2010.)
Benesch, Sarah. 1999. Needs analysis and curriculum development in EAP. *TESOL Quarterly* 18 (4). 313–327.
Biber, Douglas, Conrad, Susan., & Cortes, Vivian. 2004. *If you look at . . .* : lexical bundles in academic lectures and textbooks. *Applied Linguistics* 25. 371–405.
Biber, Douglas, Conrad, Susan, & Leech, Geoffrey. (2002). *Longman student grammar of spoken and written English*. Harlow: Pearson.
Brett, Paul. 1994. A genre analysis of the results section of sociology articles. *English for Specific Purposes* 13. 47–59.
Cai, Jing L. 2013. Students' Perceptions of Academic Writing: A Needs Analysis of EAP in China. *Language Education in Asia* 4(1),5–22.
Cai, Jing L. 2016. An exploratory study on an integrated genre-based approach for the instruction of academic lexical phrases. *Journal of English for Academic Purposes* 24. 58–74.
Cai, Ji-gang. 2012. Academic English: Needs Analysis Teaching Methods ["学术英语"课程需求分析和教学方法研究]. *Foreign Language Learning Theory and Practice* [外语教学理论与实践] 2. 30–35.
Cai, Ji-gang 2014. English for academic purposes and quality foreign language education [学业用途英语、学术用途英语及优质外语教育]. *Computer-assisted Foreign Language Education* [外语电化教学] 3. 3–8.
Chen, Yu-hua, & Baker, Paul. 2010. Lexical Bundles in L1 and L2 Academic Writing. *Language Learning & Technology* 14(2). 30–49.

Chun, Christian. 2015. *Power and meaning making in an EAP classroom*. Bristol: Multilingual Matters.

Coffin, Caroline. & Donohue, James P. 2012. Academic literacies and systemic functional linguistics: How do they relate? *Journal of English for Academic Purposes* 11(1). 64–75.

Corcoran, James. & Englander, Karen. 2016. A proposal for critical-pragmatic pedagogical approaches to English for research publication purposes. *Publications* 4(6). 1–10.

Coxhead, Averil. & Byrd, Pat. 2007. Preparing writing teachers to teach the vocabulary and grammar of academic prose. *Journal of Second Language Writing* 16(3). 129–147.

Hirvela, Alan. 2004. *Connecting reading and writing in second Language writing instruction*. Ann Arbor: University of Michigan Press.

Huang, Ju-chuan. 2014. Learning to write for publication in English through genre-based pedagogy: A case in Taiwan. *System* 45. 175–186.

Hyland, Ken. 2007. Genre pedagogy: Language, literacy and L2 writing instruction. *Journal of Second Language Writing* 16. 148–164.

Hyland, Ken. 2008. Academic clusters: text patterning in published and postgraduate writing. *International Journal of Applied Linguistics* 18(1). 42–62.

Hyland, Ken, & Tse, Polly. 2004. Metadiscourse in academic writing: A reappraisal. *Applied Linguistics* 25(2). 156–177.

Hyland, Ken, & Tse, Polly. 2005. Hooking the reader: A corpus study of evaluative that in abstracts. *English for Specific Purposes* 24(2),123–139.

Hyon, Sunny. 1996. Genre in three traditions: Implications for ESL. *TESOL Quarterly* 30 (4), 693–722.

Kwan, Becky. 2006. The schematic structure of literature reviews in doctoral theses of applied linguistics. *English for Specific Purposes* 25, 30–55.

Lillis, Theresa, & Scott, Mary. 2007. Defining academic literacies research: Issues of epistemology, ideology and strategy. *Journal of Applied Linguistics* 4(1),5–32.

Lorés, Rosa. 2004. On RA abstracts: From rhetorical structure to thematic organization. *English for Specific Purposes* 23(3),280–302.

Nation, Paul I. S. 2001. *Learning Vocabulary in Another Language*. Cambridge: Cambridge University Press.

Peacock, Matthew. 2002. Communicative moves in the discussion section of research articles. *System* 30(4). 479–497.

Pennycook, Alastair. 1997. Vulgar pragmatism, critical pragmatism, and EAP. *Pergamon* 16(4). 263–69.

Qu, Jing-jing. 2016. A cross-sectional comparative analysis of plagiarism in student theses in China [论文抄袭对比研究]. *Education Teaching Forum [教育教学论坛]* 3. 168–170.

Reynolds, Barry L. & Anderson, Tom A.F. 2015. Extra-dimensional in-class communications: Action research exploring text chat support of face-to-face writing. *Computers and Composition* 35. 52–64. doi:10.1016/j.compcom.2014.12.002

Rose, David. & Martin, Jim R. 2012. *Learning to Write, Reading to Learn: Genre, knowledge and pedagogy in the Sydney School*. Sheffield (UK) and Bristol (USA): Equinox.

Rose, David. 2010. Learning in linguistic contexts: Integrating SFL theory with literacy teaching. In Yan Fang and Canzhong Wu (Eds.), *Challenges to Systemic Functional Linguistics: Theory and practice*, 258–263. Beijing: 36th ISFC Organizing Committee.

Schmitt, Norbert, & Carter, Ronald. 2004. Formulaic sequences in action. In N. Schmitt (Ed.), *Formulaic sequences*, 1–22. Amsterdam/Philadelphia: John Benjamins.

Swales, John M. 1988. Discourse communities, genres and English as an international language. *World Englishes* 7(2). 211–220.
Swales, John M. 1990. *Genre analysis: English in academic and research settings*. Cambridge: Cambridge University Press.
Swales, John M. 2004. *Research genres: Explorations in academic and research settings*. Cambridge, UK: Cambridge University Press.
Swales, John M. & Feak, Christine B. 2004. *Academic writing for graduate students: Essential tasks and skills (Second Edition)*. Ann Arbor, MI: University of Michigan Press.
Swales, John M. & Feak, Christine. B. 2009. *Telling a research story: Writing a literature review*. Ann Arbor: University of Michigan Press.
Swales, John. M. & Feak, Christine. B. 2011. *Creating contexts: Writing introductions across genres*. Ann Arbor: University of Michigan Press.
Swales, John. M. & Feak, Christine B. 2012. Academic Writing for Graduate Students: Essential Tasks and Skills. Ann Arbor, MI: University of Michigan Press.
Tribble, Christopher. & Wingate, Ursula. 2013. From text to corpus: A genre-based approach to academic literacy instruction. *System* 41. 307–321.
University of Manchester 2005. Academic Phrasebank [online]. Retrieved from: http://www.phrasebank.manchester.ac.uk/. (September 10, 2015.)
Wingate, Ursula. 2012. Using academic literacies and genre-based models for academic writing instruction: A literacy journey. *Journal of English for Academic Purposes* 11(1). 26–37.
Wingate, Ursula & Tribble, Christopher. 2011. The best of both worlds? Towards an English for academic purposes/academic literacies writing pedagogy. *Studies in Higher Education* 37(4).1–15.
Xu, Fang. 2015. A literature review on English academic writing in China. [学术写作研究述评]. *Foreign Language Teaching and Research* [外语教学与研究] 47(1). 94–105.

Appendix A: Course evaluation survey

Directions:
Please indicate your preference on a scale from 1 to 5. You can choose to circle, highlight or underline your choice.

1. What is your overall impression of the course?
   你對這個課程整體滿意度？
   Unsatisfactory-------------------------------satisfactory
   不滿意------------------------------------很滿意
   1   2   3   4   5
2. What do you think of the curriculum?
   你對課程設置各方面的滿意度？
   – Regarding teaching method (Do you like the task-based "reading to learn" approach?)

   教學方法的实施方面（你觉得教师引导的任务和读写教学方式效果如何？）

Unsatisfactory-----------------------------Satisfactory
不滿意-----------------------------很滿意
1   2   3   4   5
- Regarding teaching materials and assignments (the clarity and content in the materials)
  上課材料及作業方面（上課的材料和作業清晰易懂內容豐富嗎？）
  Unsatisfactory-----------------------------Satisfactory
  不滿意-----------------------------很滿意
  1   2   3   4   5
- Regarding the syllabus (Has the teacher taught what you wanted to learn?)
  課程安排方面（上課的內容是你們需要的和想學的嗎？）
  Unsatisfactory-----------------------------Satisfactory
  不滿意-----------------------------很滿意
  1   2   3   4   5
- The teacher's delivery 教師的表達
  Unsatisfactory-----------------------------Satisfactory
  不滿意-----------------------------很滿意
  1   2   3   4   5

3. What impact has the course had on your academic reading and writing
   對論文閱讀和論文寫作的幫助？
   A. Helpfulness to **academic reading**
      對你閱讀論文的幫助
      Least helpful-----------------------------very helpful
      沒什麼幫助-----------------------------很有幫助
      1   2   3   4   5

   B. Helpfulness to **academic writing (i.e. research paper writing)**
      對你自己論文寫作的幫助有多大？

      a) Organization 文章內容組織
         Least helpful-----------------------------Very helpful
         沒什麼幫助-----------------------------很有幫助
         1   2   3   4   5
      b) Genre structures: Move/Step 文體結構
         Least helpful-----------------------------Very helpful
         沒什麼幫助-----------------------------很有幫助
         1   2   3   4   5

c) Specific language features 特殊語言特徵
   Least helpful------------------------------Very helpful
   沒什麼幫助------------------------------很有幫助
   1   2   3   4   5

d) Lexical bundles 词块
   Least helpful------------------------------Very helpful
   沒什麼幫助------------------------------很有幫助
   1   2   3   4   5

4. What aspect of the course has been most influential toward your learning?
   這門課對你最大的幫助和影響在哪裡?
5. Have you done any **academic reading in English** besides the assignments in the course (including any reading from other courses)? If so, can you please briefly explain what kind of books or papers you have read?
   除了這門課的作業以外, 在課後有沒有閱讀一些學術方面的文章文獻或者書籍 (包括其他課程的內容)?
6. Do you have any suggestions or comments regarding the course? Both positive and negative comments are welcome.
   你有什麼其他意見嗎? 好的或者不好的都可以。

Appendix B: Prompts for retrospective interview with student cases

(Week 3 sample)

Instructions: In this half an hour to one hour, you are expected to **recall what just happened in the classroom.** Please **do not** look at your classroom handouts when you are doing the recall. Please treat the following questions as **prompts** for your recall and never feel restricted by them. You are **free to add** anything you think important and worthwhile to report and please do not hesitate to initiate any new topic to discuss.

I. A review of teaching materials and classroom activities in this class

a. How do you think of the teaching materials? What do you like or dislike about them? Can you understand them well (are they too difficult or too easy for you)?
b. How do you think of the classroom activities in this class? What do you like or dislike about them? Can you learn the knowledge you need from doing tasks? Have you met any difficulty in the process of carrying out the tasks?

II. A review of learning in this class

a. What do you think you have learned from today's class?
b. Is there anything you have learned in this class that helps you know more about research paper writing which you think will probably be used in future study or career development?
c. How do you like the new teaching method of "presenting models – analyzing models – producing new products"?

III. Understanding genre and language specific features

a. How did you understand the concept of genre in academic writing as explained by the teacher?
b. Can you understand the CARS model covered in the course? Can you explain in detail?
c. Can you identify the general and specific language features of the introduction section, such as the (move-specific) lexical phrases in the RA model in class?
d. How much did the brainstorm and discussion activity help you understand the lexical phrases specifically for the move?
e. Which phrases did you specially note down in mind? Can you tell me without looking at the handouts?

Yun-yin Huang, Hsiao-Hui Wu
Toward better English for research publication purposes practices through the lens of activity theory: A case study of a cross-disciplinary graduate writing course in Taiwan

Abstract: In this chapter, we describe and analyze the challenges of *English-for-Research-Publication-Purposes* (ERPP) in a research university in Taiwan. Targeting a graduate writing course and ERPP issues faced by department faculties, writing instructors, and graduate students, we conducted focus group interviews with these stakeholders. Furthermore, we employed *Activity Theory* (AT) to structure the interviews and developed adapted AT models based on the interview data to illustrate the ERPP practices of each group. We identified contradictions in each AT model, including a lack of teaching and learning resources, limited knowledge, great diversity among genres, and unaccommodating and inconsistent administrative or pedagogical support. Thus, we propose an integrated pedagogical approach, incorporating co-teaching, blended pedagogy, and individual corpus to address these contradictions and relevant institutional issues in this context. The proposed approach is specifically derived from and designed for higher education in Taiwan and could shed light on similar Asian EFL contexts.

Keywords: Activity Theory (AT), individual corpus, co-teaching, blended pedagogy, English-for-Research-Publication-Purposes (ERPP)

1 Introduction

In the publish-or-perish era, researchers worldwide are eager to write up and submit their findings to an accredited outlet. Following the trend of the internationalization of universities (Lillis and Curry 2010; Flowerdew 2013), this ever-growing pressure spread quickly, and has reached graduate students in all disciplines, especially those in non-English speaking countries (Farley 2018). For

Yun-yin Huang, National Tsing Hua University
Hsiao-Hui Wu, Tainan University of Technology

non-native English-speaking students, reporting scientific findings in appropriate and precise English is challenging and demanding. Given this increasing need, it is important that university administrators, departments, and language support units adopt the most appropriate and effective pedagogical model for students.

In response to the trend of publishing in English, universities across Asia have expended great effort and resources on preparing graduate students for this demand, such as by offering writing workshops, 18-week courses, or a comprehensive English for Academic Purposes (EAP) program. Among various instructional models and foci, these EAP instructions can be delineated into two branches: English for General Academic Purposes (EGAP) and English for Specific Academic Purposes (ESAP). While EGAP focuses on English language for students in all academic fields, ESAP is concerned with the language used in specific disciplines. In practice, graduate students are usually asked to take an EGAP course prior to an ESAP course, because EGAP knowledge tends to be more universal across disciplines and provides the foundation of advanced and specific language skills. However, given limited resources and other reasons, EGAP is often the only option available for students (as the case described in this chapter). In this case, EGAP courses may incorporate discipline-specific materials or tasks to include ESAP elements in class (Blue 1988; Flowerdew 2016).

Each EAP class is unique in terms of its learning objectives, instructional materials, pedagogical approach, and its cultural and social contexts. The target course described in this chapter does not fall clearly into either the EGAP or ESAP category, as students' compositions are highly heterogeneous and the instructional materials cannot be limited to a single field. However, the target students share a universal goal, which is to publish research findings in international peer-reviewed journals. Therefore, the objective of the target course is to help and prepare graduate students to report research findings in academically acceptable written English. Given this hybrid nature, the term *English for Research Purposes* (ERPP) is considered to better depict the context of the target course.

1.1 English for research publication purposes (ERPP)

With the growing pressure to publish research findings, especially in recent years, the demand for ERPP instruction has greatly increased. By definition, ERPP can be considered a branch of English for EAP. Specifically, ERPP targets postgraduate students and prepares them to write scientific research articles as one type of document written by scientists (Englander 2014) and those who need to publish in peer-reviewed international journals (Flowerdew 2015). As a specific genre in academic writing, ERPP covers various conventions and formats of research articles in different disciplines, and disciplinary writing knowledge or genre knowledge is considered a major challenge to effective ERPP practices (Corcoran 2015). As most research-oriented universities have embraced cross-disciplinary graduate writing programs, accommodating the diverse needs of students from different disciplines has remained a great challenge for graduate students and writing instructors. These courses are usually run by language support centers and taught by language instructors; however, language teaching staff do not have specialist training in specific disciplines (Flowerdew 2013), rendering the effectiveness of such courses uncertain.

1.2 Context of the study

Research-oriented universities in Taiwan have realized the internationalization of universities and English publication demand for graduate students, and thus established a Language Center (LC) and/or Writing Center (WC) to accommodate students' needs. However, scientific and technical writing classes or workshops for graduate students are taught by LC/WC writing instructors and language experts. The teaching responsibility of writing research articles rests on the WC or LC for one prevalent notion: higher English proficiency is believed to lead to better English writing, for example, of a research article. Therefore, scientific and technical writing courses have been regarded as part of second language instruction. However, this notion ignores the role of the disciplinary knowledge required to compose acceptable and appropriate scientific reports in specific fields. This widespread notion has been reinforced by the fact that English is a foreign language in Taiwan and the fact that many Taiwanese students are struggling with general English already.

The movement of Writing-Across-the-Curriculum (WAC) starting in the 1960s and 1970s ushered in the recognition of the important role of writing in learning and across disciplines, as effective writing skills are essential for quality learning as in keeping a journal or taking fields notes for academic purposes. Later, given the variety of disciplinary conventions and formats in research articles, courses and curriculums focused on writing inside/within specific disciplines, and Writing-in-the-Disciplines (WID) began to emerge (Brian 1992; McLeod 1992). The target course of this study, *Technical and Scientific English Writing,* is a relatively new course, as a response to the need to publish in English. Only recently have writing instructors in our university encountered various pedagogical challenges in addressing students' needs in different disciplinary backgrounds and gradually realized a need for a more WID-oriented approach.

A graduate requirement at almost every research university in Taiwan is that science and engineering doctoral students author at least one indexed journal article. This requirement is a daunting and frustrating task for novice and non-native English speaking students in Taiwan (Huang 2010). Taiwan as an EFL environment, most undergraduate and other graduate courses are taught in Mandarin. In other words, Mandarin Chinese mediates the development of graduate students' professional and disciplinary knowledge. However, once in graduate schools and all of sudden, students are required to describe and report their research and findings in formal written English. Our graduate students are undoubtedly overwhelmed. Furthermore, the guidance provided by disciplinary experts (students' advisors) in each department emphasizes research design and experimental set-ups rather than professional writing instruction. In terms of providing feedback on technical reports and manuscript writing, department faculties focus on the content, not the language. As a result, feedback on linguistic features is much needed for most EFL graduate students.

Similar to the case described in this chapter, most universities in Taiwan currently only offer EGAP courses for graduate students in all disciplines, and rarely teach discipline-specific knowledge and language skills. These common EGAP-oriented courses have two major restrictions. The first constraint is that the school authority seems to believe that these graduate writing courses are "merely" another EFL class; thus, it is reluctant to increase the budget for ESP writing professionals and other resources. The second constraint is the lack of qualified ESP experts to teach technical writing with a disciplinary focus to address the diverse needs of students in various fields. These two constraints have given rise to challenges for the three major groups of ERPP stakeholders: (1) department faculties that house the supervisors of graduate students, (2) EFL writing instructors of the target course, and (3) graduate students who need publications as a graduation requirement.

1.3 ERPP practices: Challenges and opportunities

We conducted a needs survey of 153 graduate students (mostly in science and engineering) in early 2017 to better understand the English language skills they need to achieve their academic goals across various disciplines. In the needs survey, over two thirds of the students stated that reporting their research findings is a "very important" skill, and also about two thirds reported that they took graduate English courses to improve their academic writing skills, as a graduate requirement in English proficiency, or to write for publication. The students realized that effective writing for academic purposes is a critical skill in higher education for both graduate students and future scholars. However, this goal is not easy to achieve. Research on non-native English-speaking writers found that difficulties in publishing in English could be at the sentence, discourse, or rhetorical level (e.g., Gosden 1996; Cho 2009). Flowerdew and Li (2007) revealed that non-native English-speaking novice writers would seek help with their language from three major sources in the process of manuscript preparation: supervisors, language professionals, and peers. Each of these human sources has strengths and weaknesses. For instance, supervisors (from department faculties) may be too busy to provide thorough and detailed feedback; writing instructors are not usually equipped with sufficient disciplinary knowledge for journal publication; and while fellow graduate students could provide valuable feedback, they might have unfavorable expectations such as co-authorship. While human sources are not always available or affordable, language support for ERPP could perhaps expand to corpus-based applications, interactive writing environments (IWE), or other non-human sources.

Other than the challenges regarding language use, factors influencing ERPP practices also include social and political issues, as ERPP practices involve more than writing and revising manuscripts, but also require knowledge and skills for negotiating for authorship and dealing with power relations with supervisors and journal editors (Li 2006). However, to become qualified and acknowledged members of their scientific communities, graduate students as novice writers are trying to get tickets (publications), and it is unlikely their work will be "accepted" in a short time or through one single course. The acquisition of academic writing skills involves scholarly formation and academic literacy development in the discipline, and often, the process and related issues are "broader and more complex" (Cargill and Burgess 2008) than classroom teaching.

1.4 Activity theory as an interpretive framework to understand ERPP practices

Adopting an action-research orientation, this study aimed to solve pedagogical challenges in the graduate writing courses in the target context. In the case described in this chapter and based on the relevant literature, the challenges are not confined to the classroom in terms of students' disciplinary differences in writing, but also in the relationships between the student and advisor, students and lab-mates, or students and co-authors. Most research articles are the collaborative effort of multiple contributors and sub-tasks including research design, data collection, and data analysis. The dynamics between every stakeholder and each step in the process is not just about writing, and we are tempted to understand all factors influencing students' writing and publishing process. Given the complex nature of ERPP practices and attempting to examine relevant issues in depth, Engeström's (2014) expanded Activity Theory (AT) model was adopted to analyze the dynamics in the process and activities of writing for publication in higher education.

Activity Theory (AT) is a theoretical framework for understanding and analyzing human actions and interactions. Its underlying concepts originated from Vygotsky's mediated action (1978), as depicted in the top-most triangle, and Leont'ev's idea of the collective nature of human activities (1981), which shifts the focus outside the individual mind. Later, Engeström expanded these ideas into a more comprehensive framework known as (second generation) AT (1987). Figure 1 shows the basic structure of the AT framework and the six components (elements) thereof, on which this case study is based. The two-way arrows suggest the interaction between each element. The six interconnected and interrelating elements of an AT model are *subject, object, tools (instrument, mediated artefact), rules (norms), community,* and *division of labor*. These elements in the system are interrelated and help to examine human activities (Yamagata-Lynch 2010). In an activity model, subjects take actions using tools while influenced by rules/norms, the community, and

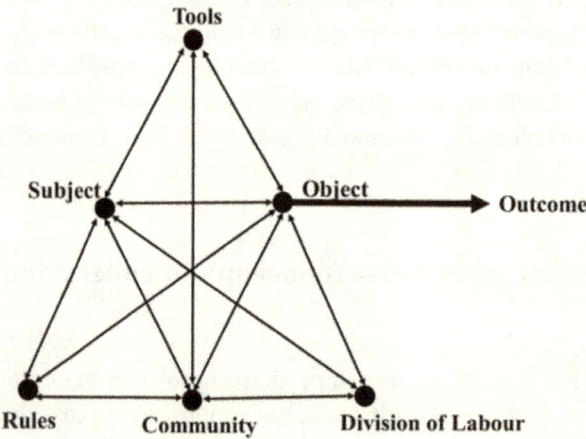

Figure 1: Activity theory (AT) model (Engeström, 1987, p.78).

division of labor to produce objects and eventually achieve outcomes. In reality, an activity does not always run smoothly, and any insufficient or malfunctioning component can cause tensions or conflicts in the system. For instance, even if the subject keeps the intended outcome in mind while carrying out actions, the intended outcome may not be achieved, as the object may not be transformed directly into the outcome. Alternatively, the community where the subject is situated might not be supportive, and the subject cannot receive sufficient scaffolding. Other possible contradictions in an AT model include an inappropriate or ineffective tool for producing objects, the subject's unfamiliarity with the rules, or an uneven division of labor.

In AT models, human activity is considered a collective endeavor and is driven by a certain need/goal. An individual (subject) utilizes means (tools) to create or produce something tangible (object) to achieve the goal (outcome), and actions taken throughout the process are affected by conventions and traditions (norms), stakeholders (community), and the contribution of each participant (division of labor) toward the goal. Given the collective nature of human activities, social norms would more or less confine even individual actions and activities, which would be influenced by his or her roles and others involved in the activity. Most previous studies and arguments on ERPP focus on the individual writing process or linguistic features of the writing product. However, ERPP practice is always "situated," and not only discipline-dependent, but also involves multiple decisions influenced by various cultural and social contexts from the first day of the brainstorming meeting to the submission of the manuscript. It is critical to understand and be aware of what contextual factors are influencing, as learning does not solely happen in an isolated classroom, but involves various individual, cultural, organizational, and systematic factors. Here, AT is particularly useful as an interpretive framework to analyze complex human behaviors in contexts such as ERPP practices.

AT was selected and applied as a theoretical framework given its openness and comprehensiveness. Therefore, through the lens of AT models, possible contradictions could be identified and relevant factors thoroughly examined. This can help us understand the current context and pedagogical challenges, and develop a more effective ERPP approach. In this study, three groups of stakeholders involved in ERPP activity systems were selected for analysis: department faculties, writing instructors, and graduate students, as these three groups were identified as the major human sources from which novice writers seek help (Flowerdew and Li 2007).

The second generation of activity theory (Engeström 2014) was adopted as the analytical framework for this study, because it provides a systematic approach to

data collection, analysis, and interpretation. Compared with the other two generations of AT models, the chosen AT model reflects a more collective nature with considerations of contextual elements, yet still focuses on individual entities (graduate students, department faculties, writing instructors) First, the six elements were employed to develop focus group interview prompts and questions, as the interviews explore the resources (tool), tasks and goal (objective), disciplinary norms and research writing conventions (rules), and possible stakeholders involved in the process (community) of participants' ERPP practices. Second, the interconnection between elements enabled the categorization of interview data and identification of conflicts/contradictions. Finally, the activity system serves as a practical means to analyze complex activity, as it provides a clear boundary of a case, and, yet flexible and open enough to include emerging themes (Creswell 2007). These aforementioned qualities of the AT framework were considered appropriate and used to guide the exploration of the following objectives:
– Identify the contradictions in current ERPP practices.
– Propose workable solutions to address the contradictions.
– Develop an ERPP approach from and for the context.

2 Method

With an exploratory nature, this study was not set to generalize or establish representativeness, but to explore theoretical issues and generate questions for further systematic study. The current study aimed to identify the difficulties experienced by (1) department faculties, (2) writing instructors, and (3) graduate students in guiding, teaching, and learning the reporting of research findings in English for journal publication, and to propose and develop an instructional approach to address the specific challenges and needs of the target population in this context. The target pedagogical context is a three-credit graduate course, *Technical and Scientific English Writing*, offered by the Language Center at the researchers' university. Potential students for this course include graduate students from master and doctoral programs in the nine colleges at the university (Science, Engineering, Computer Science and Electrical Engineering, Life Science, Humanities and Social Science, Arts, Technology Management, Nuclear Science, Teachers College), contributing to a diverse student composition and learning needs.

We conducted focus group interviews with department faculties, writing instructors, and graduate students to understand their perceptions and experiences of guiding, teaching, and learning how to write for publication. We used Activity Theory models as a framework to structure our interview questions and to analyze the transcripts. More details on the interviews and analysis procedures are described below.

2.1 Data sources and collection

We conducted eight focus group interviews. Due to time constraints and difficulties in recruiting department faculties to interview at the same time, we interviewed five separately. Each faculty interview included two to three writing instructors and focused on the situation and issues in the faculty's discipline/department. We conducted two focus group interviews with writing instructors, each with a different topic; both interviews had successfully recruited the same four writing instructors currently teaching the target courses. We conducted only one student interview, but with five graduate students with various backgrounds. All interviews were conducted in two consecutive semesters at a two to three-week interval. Each interview lasted roughly two hours, and was audio-recorded and transcribed for further analysis.

All participants were adults and were informed of the procedure and content of this study. Oral consent was obtained before each interview, and all participants were informed and well-noted that the interview data would be used for research purposes only and would remain anonymous. Please note that not every participant attended all the interviews due to their individual schedules and time constraints. The participants of this study were as follows:
(1) Five department faculties (Electrical Engineering, Chemical Engineering, Life Science, Engineering and System Science, and Education) that attended the interviews separately.
(2) Four writing instructors currently teaching the target graduate writing courses who attended the interviews twice altogether (not all five interviews with department faculties) to probe different aspects of their ERPP teaching.
(3) Five graduate students (Chemistry, Computer Science, Electrical Engineering, Life Science, and Education) who attended the interview together once.

The focus group interviews aimed to explore participants' guidance, instruction, and acquisition of English writing skills for publication. The aim was to comprehensively discover hidden difficulties in ERPP-related practices (contradictions in activities). Points of discussion in the interviews were structured and based on

six elements (subject, object, tool, rules, community, and division of labor). The prompting questions included the following:
- Why do you need journal publications as a graduate student? (Subject)
- As a supervisor, how do you guide your students to write up research findings, and what is your expectation regarding the quality of writing? (Subject)
- Do you apply any particular pedagogical method (e.g., peer feedback) in your class? (Subject)
- What online or offline instructional/learning resources do you use? (Tool)
- When guiding or teaching students to write for publication, have you experienced any difficulties?
- What is your expectation or requirement for your graduate advisees/students in class? For example, how do you measure the quality of writing? (Object, outcome)
- What are the common linguistic features or structure of research articles in your field? (Rules)
- How do you divide or assign research work (e.g., experiments, data analysis, writing reports, correspondence with collaborating partners) in your lab? Or: What lab work have you been assigned as a master/doctoral student? (Division of labor)
- Who are involved in fulfilling the publication requirement? What is his or her role in the process? (Community)

2.2 Data analysis

Data analysis was structured around the six elements of Engeström's expanded Activity Theory model (2014). Using a theoretical coding scheme, the six components in the AT model were applied as designated categories: *subject, object, tool, community, rule, division of labor*, and *outcome*. Examination and reflection of the interview data started immediately after the first interview, after which the following interview questions were revised to be more comprehensive. The researchers compared and contrasted data as more was obtained throughout the year. Emerging themes and conflicts between elements were identified and categorized into one of the AT components (categories). Interpretation and categorization of data were verified in the subsequent interviews until all interview data were salient (Yin 2009) and confirmed by researchers and later by the participating department faculties and writing instructors. Through this action-oriented and data-driven method, our analysis underwent consistent reflection, influencing elements, and possible contradictions in the system to finally construct the well informed adopted AT models.

3 Findings and discussion

The results of this study account for three adopted AT models of the ERPP practices of department faculties, writing instructors, and graduate students, as depicted in Figures 2–4. These adopted AT models were developed from the eight focus group interviews; each model presents the ERPP practices of one group of participants involved in ERPP practices in higher education, namely department faculties, writing instructors, and graduate students. The items and examples of each element shown in the figures emerged and were identified in the interviews. Through the interviews with the three stakeholder groups, the adopted AT model of ERPP practices confirmed that all six elements influence each other and ultimately contribute to whether the student can effectively produce an English manuscript for journal publication, which is the universal intended outcome of all three stakeholder groups. In the following sections, each adopted AT model and its elements are discussed. We aimed to address the challenges (identified contradictions in the activity systems) in the ERPP practices of each stakeholder group.

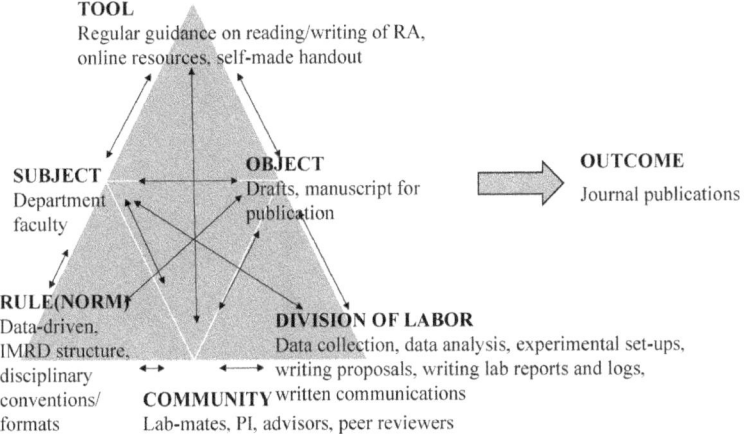

Figure 2: Adopted AT model of department faculties' ERPP practices.

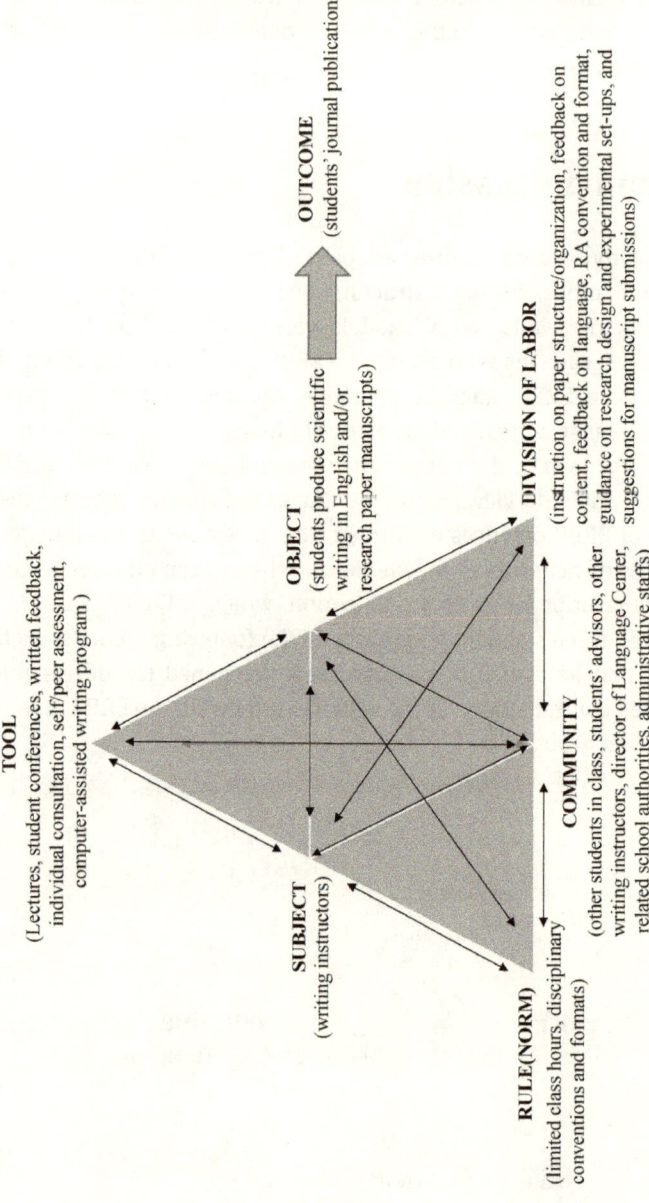

Figure 3: Adopted AT model of writing instructors' ERPP practices.

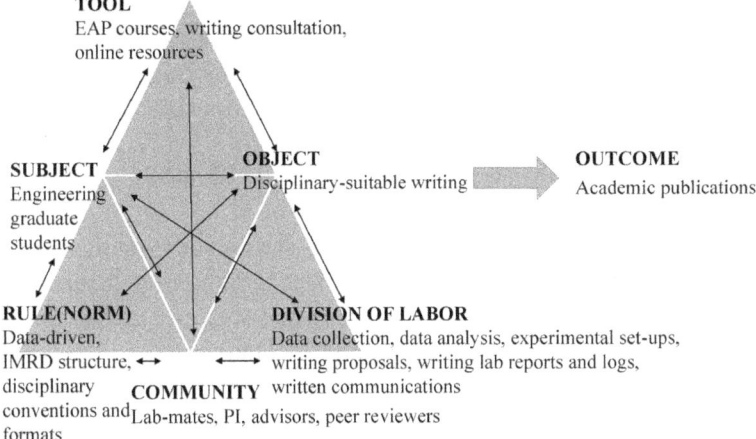

Figure 4: Adopted AT model of graduate students' ERPP practices.

3.1 Challenges for department faculties

In most departments in our school, graduate students are required to write their thesis or dissertation in English. The initial reason for this requirement is unknown, but many department faculties find the requirement disturbing. In the interviews, three of the five department faculties noted they would rather have the students write in Chinese so that they could better understand their ideas. Often, the supervising professors essentially rewrite a substantial part of the manuscript to make the writing readable. One faculty member reported that before submitting their manuscripts, instead of providing writing instruction, he asked students to read more research articles in the field, expecting them to pick up language use on their own. Another two participating faculties also reported providing only incidental guidance on disciplinary writing. All five participating faculties reported focusing only on the content (e.g., research design, accuracy of data presentation, and analysis), not language, because paying attention to the language takes too much time and is not their profession (*division of labor*). These reported choices and actions were consistent with those in Flowerdew and Li's (2007) study, which suggested that a lack of time or knowledge, or both led most department faculties to focus on the content of the writing only, not the language. As this scenario seems familiar and universal, it is not surprising that in our university, supervising professors would direct their advisees to the Language Center or the Writing Center for "language services," namely editing, revising, and even proofreading (*tool*). Given the fact that language professionals cannot possibly be familiar with detailed writing conventions and genres of all disciplines, guiding research writing for publication usually relies on disciplinary experts in each department, namely graduate students' advisors (Huang 2010). However, when department faculties consider language issues as outside their expertise, the burden falls on others.

Figure 2 illustrates the actions and interrelationships of the six elements in the ERPP activity system of *department faculties*.

- *Subject* refers to department faculties who supervise graduate students' research and learning in the discipline. Every faculty has different supervising styles, but all share one universal guiding objective: to assist graduate students to fulfill the publication requirement for graduation.
- *Object* refers to advisees' drafts and manuscripts for journal submission.
- *Tool* refers to the resources available to department faculties that can help them provide effective guidance on scientific writing in English, including group lab meetings, one-to-one meetings, written feedback, self-made handouts on disciplinary writing conventions and format, or assistance from senior students in the same lab.
- *Community* refers to the people involved in the guiding practices or who support students' writing, such as fellow students in the same lab, other faculty in the same department, writing instructors, the collaborating researcher, or peer reviewer of the journal manuscript.
- *Rule* refers to disciplinary conventions and formats regarding research articles, as well as contextual factors such as department regulations, lab norms, authorship, and ethical standards.
- *Division of labor* refers to every contribution in the ERPP process, including manuscript writing, research design, data collection and analysis, and whatever makes the study possible.
- *Outcome* refers to eventual publication in international indexed/recognized journals.

In the interviews, we asked about the structure and organization of research articles in each discipline. With variations in linguistic style and format, research papers in the five disciplines generally follow the IMRD structure. Participating department faculties recognized and agreed that IMRD illustrated how they present their research in their disciplines (*rule*). However, department faculties also indicated and expressed different opinions on language re-use, meaning the extent to which authors are allowed to borrow sentence patterns and structures from others' writing. Furthermore, although all department faculties agreed that they follow a general-to-specific pattern to draft their manuscripts, they expended various efforts on narrowing down to the specific study.

In other words, some detailed the relevant literature and produced a lengthy Introduction section, while others included only a few general statements and directed readers to the study immediately.

3.2 Challenges for writing instructors

The pressing need to report research findings in precise and concise written English is undoubtedly a tremendous burden on every EFL graduate student. Meanwhile, this growing need of graduate students to publish brings challenges to writing instructors, namely ERPP practitioners who should possess "specialized knowledge" but have a lower status than their counterparts in department faculties (Li, Flowerdew and Cargill 2018). Our university has nine distinct colleges, and one uniform scientific and technical writing class includes master and doctoral students from all these colleges and disciplines. One writing instructor reported in the interview that in addition to the differences across disciplines, the students have varying levels of English proficiency and disciplinary knowledge, making it extremely difficult for her to design the content of her class.

Figure 3 illustrates the actions and interrelationships of the six elements in the ERPP activity system of *writing instructors*.

- *Subject* refers to writing instructors in general who serve language centers or writing centers at universities. Writing instructors are usually applied linguists and TESOL experts.
- *Object* refers to facilitating students to generate appropriate and acceptable scientific reports in English.
- *Tool* refers to the resources available to writing instructors that help them provide effective instruction on scientific writing in English, including traditional lectures, peer review activities, individual guidance, written feedback, teacher-student conferences, new pedagogies, and educational technology,
- *Community* refers to the people involved in teaching practices, including students, students' advisors, other writing instructors, director of the LC, and other related school authorities.
- *Rule* refers to teaching fundamental concepts in (scientific) writing including coherence, flow, IMRD structure for research papers, and disciplinary conventions and formats. Rule also refers to contextual factors crucial to the quality of the aforementioned instruction, such as the class hours, teaching load of each writing instructor, and administrative support from the school.

- *Division of labor* refers to the responsibility of each stakeholder in the ERPP process, including providing feedback for content and/or language, guidance on research design and experimental set-ups, and suggestions for manuscript submissions.
- *Outcome* refers to publication in international indexed/recognized journals.

Regarding disciplinary differences, one emerging challenge identified in the interviews is that one single template cannot fit all (*rules*). In the classroom, on top of basic academic vocabulary and grammar, the writing instructor usually introduces the general concepts of writing such as organization, coherence, and templates of different sections of research articles. However, the uniform materials cannot address every student's disciplinary standards. For example, research articles in Chemistry often comprise an Introduction section followed directly by the Results/Findings section (experimental procedures are usually standardized and are reported in the appendix), not the typical Introduction-Method-Results-Discussion. Another exception is that in many engineering-related fields, the Results and Discussion sections are often combined, and thus require different linguistic features and styles (e.g., more passive voice and less interpretation of the data) (*object*). Owing to students' diverse backgrounds and disciplinary standards, these EGAP writing classes cover various disciplines and are pedagogically challenging for instructors. In reality, writing instructors spend extra hours on individual student conferences (*tools*) in addition to the limited class hours (*rules*). The writing instructors also suggested that the school authority could have provided support in the current situation, such as extra credit hours on written/oral feedback and professional development opportunities for disciplinary knowledge (*community*) for ESP/EAP writing instructors' professional development. One writing instructor reported that she had once encouraged her students to use an online corpus to assist their writing, but her students told her it was time-consuming and inconvenient (*tool*). Other instructors also indicated that they are still looking for more resources, either online tools or better pedagogies.

3.3 Challenges for graduate students

From the perspective of graduate students, ERPP can be taught as a skill set or socialization process, yet the reading and writing practices associated with ERPP should not be treated separately from writers' epistemology and identity (Barton and Hamilton 1998; Street 1995). As in most scientific and engineering research, the collaboration and effort of the whole research group is required, and thus *division of labor* and the people involved in the process (*community*) cannot be overlooked. However, the division of research work can be subjective and differs from lab to lab, not along different disciplines. Participating students noted that non-writing lab work took up most of their time and they could not find time for writing, let alone learning to write. However, this phenomenon seems to be the norm among graduate students. On the other hand, department faculties are relatively less affected by the division, because they usually decide the division, and graduate students receive work assignments.

Figure 4 illustrates the actions and interrelationships of the six elements in the ERPP activity system of *graduate students*.

- *Subject* refers to graduate students who deal with empirical data and are required to publish research findings in international (and indexed) journals, mostly in science and engineering.
- *Object* refers to the production of scientific writing in acceptable English, especially for reporting research findings, describing data collection, and forming arguments based on the findings.
- *Tool* refers to resources available to graduate students that help them produce scientific writing in English, including technical writing courses offered by the Language Center, individual writing consultation, online resources, and commercial editing services.
- *Community* refers to people involved in graduate students' research work, including classmates, lab-mates, supervisors, writing instructors, and journal submission peer reviewers.
- *Rule* refers to expectations regarding graduate students' writing, including an IMRD structure and disciplinary conventions and formats.
- *Division of labor* refers to the work related to the research assigned and completed by graduate students, such as the literature review, experimental set-ups, data analysis, and writing the research findings.
- *Outcome* refers to publication in international indexed/recognized journals.

Graduate students usually develop a close relationship with their supervising professors based on regular and frequent meetings and discussions on research and projects. However, with department faculties being the most valuable asset and resource in research and learning, participating students did not find their supervisors that helpful, partly because of limited time, attention, and knowledge regarding guiding their English writing, especially for language. Furthermore, in the interviews, we identified other contradictions in graduate students' ERPP practices. First, graduate students, especially junior ones, are not usually taught about the *rules/norms* in their discipline. Without a clear understanding of disciplinary expectations, they cannot effectively work toward the *outcome* or effectively apply *tools* and seek help from the *community*.- Second, the *tools* (resources) available at school are not sufficient, especially disciplinary-specific writing courses. The number of target courses offered seems insufficient, as the number of students always exceed the limit. Third, most science and engineering graduate students spend much time and effort on experiments, but not much on writing up the results. Graduate training seems to emphasize data collection and analysis, not constructing arguments and "telling a good story" (*division of labor*). We believe that resolving these three contradictions would enable graduate students (*subjects*) in this context to produce acceptable manuscripts (object) and publish their research findings successfully (*outcome*).

4 Conclusion and implications

It is critical that graduate students develop disciplinary knowledge and English writing skills, and combine them effectively to produce acceptable written products. In practical terms, increasing class hours, more qualified writing instructors, and/or offering academic writing courses for each department seem unrealistic in the current context. Therefore, this study attempted to provide insight into current ERPP practices in Taiwan through the lens of activity theory models.

The interview data and analysis clarified the challenges faced by department faculties, writing instructors, and graduate students in guiding, teaching, and learning English writing for publication purposes. First, tension and conflicts were found in all three AT models, suggesting that the ERPP practices of these stakeholder groups were not yet sufficiently effective and could be problematic. Major contradictions found in department faculties' ERPP practices include a lack of guidance on disciplinary writing and an unrealistic expectation of students' self-learning. Major contradictions found in writing instructors' ERPP practices were students' highly diverse needs and background, and a lack of disciplinary knowledge to provide ESP-oriented instruction. In consistence with what department faculties reported in the interviews, one contradiction found in graduate students' ERPP practices was a lack of guidance on disciplinary knowledge and the students did not know where to seek help. Another contradiction found in graduate students' practices is a lack of time specifically for writing up research findings.

As this study aims to develop an effective ERPP pedagogical approach to address disciplinary differences under the constraints of limited resources (ESP professionals, class hours, and diversity), we propose an integrated approach for ERPP practices based on the lessons learned from the interviews with department faculties and analysis through the lens of Activity Theory. This approach addresses the challenges of department faculties, writing instructors, and graduate students, especially for schools that offer scientific and technical writing courses for graduate students of various backgrounds, as in this case.

4.1 An integrated approach for ERPP instruction

The proposed integrated approach combines both the top-down Swales' move analysis, bottom-up corpus-based instruction, and team teaching to support graduate students in developing writing skills and promote autonomous learning throughout their scientific training. As writing for publication has become an integral part of scholar formation and graduate training, we believe that students will benefit the most when department faculties, writing instructors, and graduate students adopt this integrated approach.

4.1.1 For department faculties: Co-teaching

As department faculties are not familiar with writing instruction, it is recommended that they team teach technical writing with writing instructors, enabling students to benefit from both linguistic and disciplinary knowledge (Cheng 2007, 2008; Huang 2018). For example, students could receive feedback on the professional content, language, and organization and structure of the writing. The success of team teaching depends on careful preparation and mutual understanding. The co-teaching team must prepare the class together to tailor instruction for the specific discipline and adjust details based on students' needs and English proficiency (more on the language or more on the content). Furthermore, department faculties and writing instructors should communicate thoroughly in terms of course objectives and the division of labor of each side.

  Underlying this integrated approach is that ERPP instruction cannot be separated from disciplinary training on research design, experimental procedures, and data analysis. In addition, good writing helps convey the nuance of the research in clear and convincing manners. Co-teaching by disciplinary and language experts would be ideal for ERPP instruction; yet, successful co-teaching requires constant communication, planning, and the mutual understanding of both sides.

4.1.2 For writing instructors: A blended pedagogy

Writing instructors are recommended to adopt a blended pedagogy combining a top-down Swales' move analysis and bottom-up corpus-based instruction. Alongside teaching moves in each IMRD section, writing instructors should first ask students to analyze writing in their own field (moves) and encourage them to identify similarities and differences, helping them develop awareness of disciplinary differences and better understand their own field. Second, writing instructors should guide students to build their own individual corpus by critically analyzing their own reading and taking notes of frequently used phrases and sentence structures. This blended approach aims to give students an overview of the basic structure of research papers, and develops their disciplinary knowledge and self-learning ability for future improvement.

Furthermore, writing instructors work closely with department faculties on disciplinary differences regarding IMRD and other possible structures in research papers. It is critical that writing instructors receive continuous professional development regarding ESP pedagogies. Furthermore, ideally, writing instructors should work with content experts in certain fields for an extended period of time. This requires sufficient teaching personnel for the nine distinct colleges in our university and department faculties willing to devote extra time on this aspect of training.

4.1.3 For graduate students: Individual corpus

In addition to the input of both disciplinary and language experts, graduate students are encouraged to build an individual corpus by critically analyzing their own reading and taking notes on frequently used phrases and sentence structures. By constructing a discipline-specific database of frequently used sentence structures and phrases, graduate students could extend their range of lexico-grammatical knowledge and re-use the written English language effectively. We believe this could be a potential solution for disciplinary differences in class and promote autonomous learning. Specifically, graduate students could take notes and keep an ESP vocabulary/phrase log, and obtain genre knowledge from reading research articles regularly and critically.

An old-fashioned way of constructing an individual corpus using pen and paper is sufficient. Nevertheless, we envision that online tools such as interactive writing environments (IWE) could serve this learning purpose effectively, especially with the ability to process a large volume of linguistic data. Instead of using an overwhelming online corpus, a future individual data-driven tool could use students' own input of research articles' materials in their field for specific topics. Thus, the system could provide tailored and personalized suggestions on collocations and example sentences. Based on the interview analysis, writing instructors and graduate students are looking for ways to address disciplinary differences. A computer application customized for individual learners based on students' self-selected research paper sources in their fields may be one solution in this context. From the personalized sources of written language, ERPP learners can benefit from the same writing styles and conventions, more than general and vague concepts and sayings.

4.2 From tension to resolution and toward better ERPP practices

With considerations of the elements in each stakeholder's ERPP practices, this integrated approach aims to give students an overview and the basic structure of research papers. Students can develop their disciplinary knowledge and self-learning ability for continuous improvement. Through the actions taken for better ERPP practice proposed in this study, graduate students will benefit the most from the integrated approach to improve scientific writing skills, receive feedback on language and content, and have an opportunity to develop a personalized corpus. Participating students will benefit from class instruction and the interaction with peers from other disciplines, which helps develop an awareness of disciplinary differences. Through co-teaching, writing instructors and department faculties will also benefit from the new and effective approach to ERPP instruction, develop mutual understanding, and can apply the model to other ERPP-related training and education.

This proposed integrated approach utilizes the effort of department faculties, writing instructors, and graduate students themselves, and can serve as a pedagogical model for technology-integration and co-teaching in other courses alike. This ERPP approach also encourages the development of communities, in which every member benefit and learns, regardless of her role (Ding and Bruce 2017). Through the practices, mutual understanding, and collaboration between department faculties across disciplines and writing instructors can be promoted and flourish, which is crucial for a grounded community of teaching practices and faculties' professional development. ERPP training is an indispensable part of our mission to achieve excellence in advancing science and quality education. This proposed integrated approach is one effective and comprehensive method to realize these goals. This study hopes to shed light on current ERPP practices and inform relevant practitioners in similar contexts.

4.3 Limitations of the study

It should be noted that major contradictions (i.e., deficient knowledge in terms of disciplinary rules/norms, insufficient tools available at the school, and a lack of time spent on writing) were identified through the lens of AT model in the context of one research-oriented university in Taiwan. Thus, the findings may not be generalizable to all universities in the EFL context nationwide and worldwide. However, as mentioned, as the present study was exploratory in nature, it did not aim for generalization, but to provide insights for further research to develop effective ERPP instruction based on the challenges novice writers face in publishing research papers in indexed international journals. In addition, a limited number of department faculties participated in the focus group interviews, which might not represent all variations across disciplines. Last, the effectiveness and feasibility of the proposed integrated approach for ERPP practices should be fully examined within a short time.

References

Barton, David & Mary Hamilton. 1998. Local literacies: Reading and writing in one community. In David Barton (ed.), *Situated literacies*. London, Routledge.
Blue, George. 1988. Individualising academic writing tuition. In Pauline. Robinson (ed.), *Academic writing: Process and product*. London: Modern English Publications and the British Council.
Sutton, Brian. 1992. Writing in the disciplines, first-year composition, and the research paper. *Language and Learning Across the Disciplines* 2 (1). 46–57.
Cargill, Margaret, & Sally Burgess. 2008. Introduction to the special issue: English for Research Publication Purposes. *Journal of English for Academic Purposes* 7 (2). 75–138.
Cheng, An. 2007. Transferring generic features and recontextualizing genre awareness: Understanding writing performance in the ESP genre-based literacy framework. *English for Specific Purposes*. 26 (3). 287–307.
Cheng, An. 2008. Analyzing genre exemplars in preparation for writing: The case of an L2 graduate student in the ESP genre-based instructional framework of academic literacy. *Applied Linguistics* 29 (1). 50–71.
Cho, Dong Wan. 2009. Science journal paper writing in an EFL context: The case of Korea. *English for Specific Purposes* 28 (4). 230–239.
Corcoran, James N. 2015. *English as the International Language of Science: A case study of Mexican scientists' writing for publication*. Toronto, CA: University of Toronto doctoral dissertation.
Ding, Alex & Ian Bruce. (eds.). 2017. *The English for Academic Purposes practitioners: Operating on the edge of academia*. Switzerland: Palgrave Macmillan.
Creswell, John W. 2007. Qualitative inquiry and research design: Choosing among five approaches. Thousand Oaks, CA: Sage.
Engestrom, Y. (1987). Learning by expanding: An activity theoretical approach to developmental research. Helsinki, Finland: Orienta-Konsult.

Engeström, Yrjö. 2014. *Learning by expanding: An activity-theoretical approach to developmental research*. New York, NY: Cambridge University Press.
Englander, Karen. 2014. *Writing and Publishing Science Research Papers in English: A global perspective*. New York: Springer.
Farley, Fay A. 2018. NNES RAs: How ELF RAs inform literacy brokers and English for research publication instructors. *Journal of English for Academic Purposes* 33. 69–81.
Flowerdew, John. 2013. English for research publication purposes. In Brian Paltridge & Sue Starfield (eds.), *The Handbook of English for Specific Purposes*, 301–321. USA: John Wiley & Sons.
Flowerdew, John. 2015. Some thoughts on English for research publication purposes (ERPP) and related issues. *Language Teaching*. 48 (2). 250–262.
Flowerdew, John. 2016. English for Specific Academic Purposes (ESAP) Writing: Making the case. *Writing & Pedagogy*. 8 (1). 5–32.
Flowerdew, John & Yongyan Li. 2007. Language re-use among Chinese apprentice scientists writing for publication. *Applied Linguistics*. 28(3). 440–465.
Gosden, Hugh. 1996. Verbal reports of Japanese novices' research writing practices in English. *Journal of Second Language Writing*. 5 (2). 109–128.
Huang, Ju Chuan. 2010. Publishing and learning writing for publication in English: Perspectives of NNES PhD students in science. *Journal of English for Academic Purposes*. 9 (1). 33–44.
Huang, Ju Chuan. 2018. Teaching writing for publication in English to engineering students: Implications from a collaborative course in Taiwan. In Mary J. Curry & Theresa Lillis (eds.), *Global academic publishing: Policies, perspectives and pedagogies*, 217–232. Bristol, UK: Multilingual Matters.
Leont'ev, Aleksej N. 1981. *Problems of the development of the mind*. Moscow, Russia: Progress.
Li, Yongyan. 2006. Negotiating knowledge contribution to multiple discourse communities: A doctoral student of computer science writing for publication. *Journal of Second language Writing*. 15 (3). 159–178.
Li, Yongyan, John Flowerdew & Margaret Cargill. 2018. Teaching English for Research Publication Purposes to Chinese science students in China: A case study of an experienced teacher in the classroom. *Journal of English for Academic Purposes*. 35. 116–129. doi:10.1016/j.jeap.2018.07.006
Lillis, Theresa. & Mary J. Curry 2010. *Academic Writing in a Global Context: The politics and practices of publishing in English*. London: Routledge.
McLeod, Susan H. 1992. Writing Across the Curriculum: An Introduction. In Susan H. McLeod & Margot Soven (eds.), *Writing across the curriculum: A guide to developing programs*, 1–8. Newbury Park, CA: Sage Publications.
Street, Brian V. 1995. *Social literacies*. London, Longman.
Swales, John. 1990. *Genre Analysis: English in academic and research settings*. Cambridge: Cambridge University Press.
Vygotsky, Lev S. 1978. *Mind in society: Development of higher psychological processes*. Cambridge, England: Harvard University Press.
Warschauer, Mark. 1999. *Electronic literacies: Language, culture, and power in online education*. Mahwah, NJ: Lawrence Erlbaum Associates.
Yamagata-Lynch, Lisa. 2010. *Activity systems analysis methods: Understanding complex learning environments*. New York: Springer.
Yin, Robert. K. 2009. *Case study research: Design and methods*. LA: Sage.

Barry Lee Reynolds, Mark Feng Teng
Practice and future directions for developing Chinese speakers' English writing across different education levels

Abstract: We aim for this chapter to provide English writing educators and researchers a concise source of information on current innovative English writing classroom practices. This chapter further provides implications for the development of second language English writing instruction for Chinese speakers. We discuss current writing practices and propose future directions for teaching and researching writing in primary education, secondary education, university and graduate education. We also suggest how English writing teachers can make research-based decisions concerning their selection and implementation of instructional approaches (e.g., e-learning, metacognitive training, and genre instruction). By reviewing the studies in this book and also drawing on other sources, we aimed to reconceptualise English writing in terms of: integrating teaching approaches, incorporating e-learning, innovating process-oriented writing, introducing collaborative writing, instituting strategy-based instruction, encouraging the use of metacognitive strategies, examining washback effects, considering writing for international communication purposes, and teaching writing for publication purposes.

Keywords: English writing, Chinese speakers, writing pedagogy, writing instruction, writing enhancement

1 Introduction

We wrote chapter one with the aim of providing an overall view of teaching English writing to Chinese speakers. While we summarized the similarities and differences between the teaching of English writing in mainland China, Hong Kong SAR, Macau SAR, and Taiwan, we also highlighted areas that existing research literature has not fully explored. By contrast, our aim for this chapter was to provide our reflections on the research contributions in this book and to discuss some potential future avenues of inquiry. The order of the

Barry Lee Reynolds, Mark Feng Teng, University of Macau

https://doi.org/10.1515/9781501512643-011

chapters was not by happenstance; we have grouped them based on the educational level targeted by the authors: primary (chapter 2), secondary (chapter 3–5), university (chapter 6–8), and postgraduate (chapter 9–10).

2 Primary education

Researchers from Chinese speaking regions have focused their investigations on the teaching of English writing in primary schools much less than that of other educational levels (Reynolds and Teng 2019). We can also see a similar trend in the current volume with only one chapter focusing on this level of English writers. Many primary school teachers from Chinese speaking regions may shy away from teaching writing in the English as a foreign language classroom. This is due to particular educational policies put into place; policy makers have encouraged a focus on oral and aural skills in the early school years with literacy skills being the focus for later school years (Chern 2002).

Although most writing instructors will agree that process writing is a much better route to improving students' second language writing in comparison to more model-based or product-based approaches, process writing is not a panacea (Graham and Sandmel 2011). Instead, the use of process writing is only one of many innovative approaches that English writing teachers should incorporate into their writing classrooms. Writing teachers should continuously be evaluating their teaching contexts and consider how to combine innovative approaches or techniques that can best suit their particular learners' needs (Nation and Macalister 2010).

In chapter two, Anisa Cheung leads readers in understanding how to innovate the teaching of English writing by combining different teaching approaches. This is a good example of an innovative combination of approaches – the combining of process writing with e-learning. In chapter two, Cheung provides readers a description of a quasi-experimental study that compared the writing improvements of two groups of learners that received process-oriented writing instruction with the caveat of one group using e-learning tools to do their writing while the other group having used pencil and paper.

It seems that collaborative writing is a hot topic in second language writing circles (e.g. Eloa 2010; Storch 2005). E-learning could increase the potential for successful collaborative writing as it could encourage interaction between learners more easily than with pencil and paper approaches (Eloa 2010); this goes well beyond the often-cited criticism that technology is only effective for a short time due to its novelty effect (Wells et al. 2010). For example, Google docs allows learners to discuss and work on the same text regardless of the physical constraints of a classroom. Teachers can potentially utilize time better; a teacher does not need to move students around inside the classroom. Not surprisingly, Cheung reports that less time was spent on class management for teachers that used e-learning in comparison to teachers that used traditional paper-and-pencil approaches. Schools that have banned the use of mobile devices inside classroom should reconsider this policy; administrators fear an increase in e-learning technologies in the classroom could result in an increase in class management behavioural issues due to distraction. It seems counterproductive to limit the use of e-learning, especially in second language writing classrooms, as most people nowadays produce writing digitally (DeVoss, Eidman-Aadahl, and Hicks 2010).

When the accuracy of the language was examined, however, Cheung reports there was no significant difference between the group of learners that used e-learning and those that did not. Instead, there was a significant difference in the accuracy of the writing produced. It also appeared students that used e-learning also produced less text. Regardless of whether teachers are adding a new technology component or a new teaching activity into their classroom regime, there is bound to be a learning curve experienced by both the teachers and the learners – Cheung reported this attitude held by several key stakeholders. However, we believe it is short-sighted to consider this as a drawback to incorporating e-learning into second language writing classrooms. We understand why principals and English teachers would be reluctant to introduce particular technologies into classes without a guarantee that there is going to be payoffs. As Cheung admits, "the major obstacles of implementing e-learning appeared to lie within the mindset of the teachers themselves." Without having teachers involved in the research process and without having teachers that have successfully used the tools interact with novice or sceptical English writing teachers, then we think there will be little progress in tackling this obstacle.

We also admit that the challenges in fostering collaborative writing practices may be more pressing for teaching students in primary schools compared to other educational contexts. In teaching writing, young learners may not be willing or able to negotiate with peers or a tutor (Woo et al. 2011). Without asynchronous discussion of issues, problems, and viewpoints surrounding the writing topic, the efforts of conducting e-learning for writing may not be realized. One of the reasons is that students' English proficiency is always a predictor in the success of process-oriented writing (Teng and Huang 2019). Another challenge may come from the teachers, particularly for teachers from less prestigious schools; these teachers may report that they have no confidence and knowledge for conducting e-learning (Etherington 2008). English writing teachers and researchers should also consider how collaborative writing could encourage primary school learners to reflect critically on the process of learning to write. In addition, teachers of writing may also consider how web-based electronic learning environments can support the challenge of writing in a foreign language.

In future practice, we also feel there are two directions that interested researchers should consider pursuing. We like the idea of combining different innovative approaches into the teaching of second language writing. Some researchers may not like this idea as they may consider it muddling up their controlled research designs. However, we think to meet the needs of learners, teachers should integrate the use of e-learning tools with collaborative writing that encourages computer-mediated communication (Reynolds and Anderson 2015). The learners involved in Cheung's study communicated with most of their peers face-to-face; however, that is not always necessary, especially if the learners can continue work with their writing outside the regular classroom time. Furthermore, teachers may need to provide learners, even these younger learners, a good dose of metacognitive instruction and the teaching of how to apply metacognitive strategies and text structure knowledge when producing second language writing (Teng 2019a, 2020).

3 Secondary education

Asking learners to peer review classmates' writing without any guidance on how to go about it will result in subpar writing improvements. It is also a given that teachers need to provide learners with training prior to requesting students to give peer feedback (Lam 2010); however, we know less about how secondary school students feel about the peer feedback training they have been provided by English writing teachers. Moreover, we know very little about the intricate details on how students go about giving peer feedback after receiving the training. In other words, a lot of the research has looked at the results of peer feedback instead of examining the process of peer feedback (Huisman et al. 2019). In addition, secondary school learners should be taking a lead in their learning of English writing but it seems writing teachers are still very much in control, delivering very structured secondary level English lessons (e.g. Lee 1998; Liou 2001).

In chapter three, Amy Kong reports on a study in which secondary school teachers taught students peer review strategies before providing them with a checklist that could help guide the reciprocal process of peer review. Kong did more than ask learners to simply tick off items on a list – she wanted the learners to negotiate during the feedback process regardless of whether they were receiving or giving the feedback. Peer feedback should not foster a situation in which one learner is passively taking everything the other learner has to say about the piece of writing. Communication regarding the proposed changes must take place. English writing teachers should try to ensure that the learner receiving the feedback is retaining ownership over his or her writing. This feedback process benefits both students – one student does not minimize another student's role in the feedback process to that of an English editor. In addition, the students receiving the feedback will not have their own opinions stifled.

Another important point of Kong's study was that she aimed to uncovered how learners felt when receiving or giving peer feedback. The results of the study indicate that the training helped the students conduct the peer review, with the learners finding the metalanguage and peer feedback phrases provided by the teacher useful to the feedback and peer review process. However, sometimes the students still needed to use their first language to help them to finish the peer review. This happened when they came across terms they did not know in English. This indicates that learners are willing and able to use English during the peer feedback process, but teachers should not ban first language use during the feedback process. The task is to provide feedback on the writing and any oral language improvements will be incidental to the completion of the peer review.

Another finding relevant to English writing teachers that wish to incorporate peer feedback into their writing classes is the possibility of an overzealous peer reviewer. Specifically, one student in one of the pairs felt she needed to control the interactions in order to be able to give all the advice to her partner before she forgot. Unfortunately, this made the other student become quiet and feel intimidated. In addition, the student receiving the peer feedback explained that he would have felt more comfortable being paired up with someone of the same sex. This result further illustrates that for pair work, especially for adolescents, it may be best for teachers to allow students to form their own pairings. We advise English writing teachers to pay close attention to the interactions between student dyads and to provide students explanation on how to conduct mutually respectful peer review. For example, learners should try to refrain from dominating the conversation during the peer feedback process.

The limitation of this sort of study is that it is not longitudinal. It can only provide a snapshot of what happens during the peer review process. In addition, Kong was only able to focus on some specific types of instructed peer review guidance. If a longitudinal study is not possible, a future research that focuses on different types of peer review guidance for a larger number of dyads would be welcomed. Even qualitative studies like this one would benefit from having a few more pairs to gather a more robust sample of data that could allow for multiple case comparisons.

In another case study reported in chapter four, Wilson Cheong Hin Hong provides an account of his attempts to go against the advice of traditional grammar books that recommend distinguishing clause types during instruction. Instead, he advocates highlighting clause similarities for learners. He felt that reducing the metalanguage in the classroom helps speed up learners' English language acquisition. Hong investigated this assumption through a case study involving two pairs of low-level learners; however, he did not see any discernible differences between the two pairs of students in terms of the complexity of the clauses that the students were able to produce at the end of the three months of training.

We cannot assume that what teachers or researchers see when examining grammar is the same as the learners' experience. In addition, teachers need to understand that textbook authors do not write textbooks with particular learners in mind (Nation 2013). English teachers should always adapt their textbooks to help meet the needs of their own students. Unfortunately, from Hong's point of view, many teachers try their best to cover all the contents of the textbooks following the proposed approaches found within their pages. It seems that the English writing teachers in Chinese speaking regions should be more aware of the most common types of errors produced by Chinese speakers and try their best to target these errors in their instruction (Nation 2013). Focusing on common issues arising due to differences in the two languages at the sentence level would be a good start for writing instruction. Some research has even shown so-called advanced learners still struggle with producing grammatically correct sentences (Reynolds and Anderson 2015). Teachers could provide learners instruction that highlights these differences. This instruction might result in production of accurate sentences but that is only if students are ready for such complex structures. Hong offers a lot of advice about curriculum design to consider. Textbooks may raise consciousness about the existence of targeted structures but may not necessarily lead to accurate production of these structures in students' writing.

There really is not enough published on what is happening in Macao local schools (Reynolds and Teng 2019). Various aspects of English writing instruction in Macao is in need of attention from researchers. Hong's study further points out the need to gather more information about how teachers in Macao are teaching writing by looking into how they adopt or adapt textbooks for their instruction. In addition, we need to examine the connection between grammar instruction and writing instruction (Kao, Reynolds, and Teng 2019). Some research has indicated that grammar instruction is best delivered to students that can apply it to writing that is meaningful to the students (Kao, Reynolds, and Teng 2019; Kao and Reynolds 2017). In other words, grammar instruction should be more communicative. Similar large-scale studies would be welcome. Researchers in Macao may consider conducting quasi-experimental studies to draw conclusions that are more robust. A replication would be most welcomed.

In chapter five, Melissa H. Yu offers a bridge between secondary and tertiary education with the report of a study that used data collected on writing instruction and learning practices in Taiwanese secondary and tertiary education contexts. She was most interested in how teachers' instruction and students' learning has or has not focused on the teaching and learning of writing for international communication. Yu argues that the previous training teachers received in their teacher education programs and the environmental constraints of particular curriculum or school contexts could weigh heavily on whether teachers provide learners opportunities to learn English writing for communicative purposes. Most of the students in Yu's study reported that their secondary English education focused on exam preparation. While they also reported a change in English education's focus for tertiary education, there was still a sizeable emphasis on exams. Teachers did not prioritize the teaching of English writing in secondary schools or at the tertiary level. Instead, teachers seemed to prioritize grammar, vocabulary, and reading. Most teachers associated communicative competence with speaking and listening and not with writing, which could have something to do with the de-emphasis on writing for communicative purposes. English teachers focused more on the motivation of the learners; teachers considered selecting a writing textbook or one that emphasized writing as a way to demotivate English language learners. While there was some writing instruction in Taiwan, teachers focused mostly on writing for exam purposes with little to no peer review practice.

The limitation of a study as the one reported by Yu is the data source was only from one context. The English writing literature is in need of a large-scale questionnaire study aimed at collecting data from different geographical regions in Taiwan. This data could be analysed based on specific writing instruction focuses. Then, based on these results, researchers could collect additional qualitative data through interview and other qualitative data collection techniques to supplement the quantitative findings. We welcome such studies for all the Chinese-speaking regions discussed in this book.

4 University education

Chapter six written by Maggie Ma and Mark Feng Teng focuses on the metacognitive development of novice English writers in the Hong Kong university setting. There are parallels between the argument put forth by Cheung in chapter two and those of Ma and Teng in chapter six. Both chapters advocate not just process writing but process writing combined with metacognitive strategy instruction. Ma and Teng go a bit beyond discussing a need for peer feedback by focusing on how the individual writer needs to apply a number of self-regulatory strategies to improve their English writing. They also caution that teachers should administer such training delicately. Just because learners appear to be at the same language proficiency level does not necessarily mean that teachers should provide them the same type of instruction.

While they found the teaching of genre knowledge to be helpful to the learners, the learners may not have evaluated some feedback and instruction provided by the teacher. It is a common occurrence that some students seem to consider a teacher's advice as authoritative and all-knowing and thus not really reflect on what the teacher has suggested. Learner motivation to write in English could have influenced the way that learners interpreted the advice given by the teacher. This resulted in some learners seizing the opportunity to follow the teacher's advice but not really knowing why the teacher gave the advice. Teachers could remedy this problem by ensuring more communication channels are available between themselves and the students. Teachers need a better way to help students understand that the road to writing improvement is more than blindly following their suggestions.

It seems that the findings of this study reflect the three fundamental forms in self-regulated writing, i.e., environmental, behavioural, and covert or personal (Zimmerman and Risemberg 1997). As exhibited by Ma and Teng in their chapter, learners at the university level were far less aware of their need for high levels of self-regulation. Researchers have considered such personal awareness of self-regulation as a personality factor. In addition, the learners were not able to build awareness of readers' expectations for revising their drafts. The writer's environment involves "the rhetorical problem, written text as it evolves, writing tools, and external sources of information used during writing, such as a textbook" (Zimmerman and Risemberg 1997: 74). Hence, we argue that student writers have to build awareness of variations in their environmental, behavioural, and internal states to be able to remain self-regulatory in their production of English writing.

Dureshahwar Shari Lughmani and Dennis Foung also discussed metacognitive training in chapter seven; they described the meta-cognitive strategies used in a university-wide writing across the curriculum program in a Hong Kong university. They used data extracted from a learning management system to ascertain which strategies that learners used more often to complete assignments. This allowed the researchers to compare learners' writing performance to the execution of particular metacognitive strategies and draw conclusions about writing performance outcomes. The learners took advantage of the assignment guidelines and the reflections most often, finding the feedback reports the most helpful. The use of the assignment guidelines and checklists also seemed to have some relationship with students' writing performance. Future studies should try to encourage a more dynamic relationship between the teacher and the students so that feedback and the application of metacognitive strategies is also dynamic. The success in students' writing performance across the curriculum program in Hong Kong may suggest the effects of group feedback during metacognitive training. As argued by Teng (2019b), learners need to be stimulated through group feedback to "initiate writing tasks, monitor their writing progress, expand existing writing strategies with more effective ones, exchange feedback with their classmates, and make more informed choices, and gain a level of awareness beyond the subject matter" (p.14).

However, we also acknowledge there are challenges in facilitating metacognitive training for university students. As argued by Teng (2019c), Chinese university learners in such an examination-oriented culture as Hong Kong concentrate a lot on memorizing language structures for writing. Most learners do not understand what it means to write. Learners' lack of awareness to understand their own strengths and weaknesses directly affects their writing outcomes. In other words, such a lack of metacognitive knowledge becomes a significant factor in influencing their writing. In addition, students' English proficiency level, and other personal factors, e.g., time commitment on writing, familiarity with writing topics, and interest, also significantly affects students' writing performance (Teng and Huang 2019). For example, a previous study found that in spite of learners receiving training and exhibiting significant improvement in metacognitive regulation, they did not achieve significantly better performance in metacognitive knowledge (Teng 2016). Such findings raise a question that we feel is rather important. Is metacognition really a teachable skill that is central to other skill sets? However, in reading over the findings in this book, we have become more positive in our outlook. Learners who take conscious steps to understand the writing strategies and reflect on their process-oriented writing knowledge and process when they learn tend to be more successful student writers. We may need to think about the challenges in current metacognitive training practices, and future practices for adopting metacognitive training. We may need to adapt metacognitive training based on individuals' knowledge levels and cognitive abilities. English writing teachers should also familiarize learners with rhetorical knowledge, writing strategies, and genre knowledge for better metacognitive training.

In chapter eight, Anora Yu applied a narrative inquiry approach to investigate how washback of high and low stakes testing affected one instructor's teaching of English writing at a private university in Hong Kong. An urge to teach writing for communication when possible was uncovered; however, Yu also found that the teacher involved in the study changed her approach to teaching English writing. It went from more process-oriented to more product-oriented when students needed to prepare for high-stakes tests such as the IELTS. It appears that the teacher was considering the needs of the students and had to switch her teaching approach depending on the expectations of the students. There was also evidence that the type of feedback that the teacher provided differed depending on the individual differences of the learners. In other words, the teacher attempted to use "feedback forward" to promote learners to the next level. The teacher also praised these learners on what they had done well in order to help maintain a feeling of success. This study provided a rich description of the teaching practices of one teacher in Hong Kong. Future studies could build on this study by comparing what teachers say and what they actually do in the language classroom. This study also showed that a teacher's definition of high or low stakes could vary greatly from what research literature has defined as high or low stakes. English language teaching experts require more results from similar studies in order to understand how teacher beliefs shape classroom teaching in the English writing classroom.

5 Postgraduate education

In chapter nine, (Luna) Jing Cai, reports on the combination of two innovative approaches aimed at the teaching of English research article writing. As has been exemplified by many of the chapters in this volume, teachers must strive to integrate approaches with the aim of finding the most suitable combination for their targeted learners. The use of two genre-based pedagogies requiring students to focus on bottom up strategies to build up their own articles seemed to have a very positive effect on the postgraduate writers. The instruction included three stages requiring learners to prepare for reading, read and rewrite, joint rewriting, and sentence making. The students felt that the instruction was helpful as it was successful in improving their understanding of the genre structure, lexical bundles, and specific language features of academic journal articles. We felt that this course encouraged a strong reading to write culture. An interesting finding was that the students started to question the fixedness of the genre taught as well as the moves that they could incorporate into their own written work. This course was successful in raising learners' awareness of the genre, encouraging them to become more careful and critical readers; their metacognitive awareness had also been raised. The first step in becoming a good writer is becoming a good reader. All of this awareness raising and practice is bound to have made some great improvements on the students' academic writing but we do not have such a clear picture of how the learners' writing actually improved after the course or whether they were successful in producing a solid piece of writing for publication. An interesting next step would be to see how the training received in their class transformed into actual production of academic articles or theses written in English. Until we have some empirical evidence, we must keep an open mind. Hyland (2003), for example, argued that the explicit teaching of genres "imposes restrictive formulae which can straightjacket creativity through conformity and prescriptivism" (p.26). In future practice, teachers can guide learners to investigate the texts and contexts of writing situations, encourage learners to reflect on writing practices, and exploit genre sets. Instruction of genre knowledge does not mean to use a teacher-centred teaching mode to replace communicative practices.

In chapter ten, Yun-yin Huang and Hsiao-Hui Wu also report on a graduate course aimed at preparing students to publish English research articles. They also recommend an integrated approach to the teaching of English for research publication purposes. The reality is that good English writing is necessary for all academics, as English has become the language of published knowledge (Reynolds 2013). There is no equal playing field for second language writers and writing teachers can only do so much to help these students (Flowerdew 2000). The same goes for the academic supervisors that are not trained in how to deal with academic writing (Reynolds 2013). Although the researchers could not say why the learning context discussed in the chapter required their students to write their theses in English, using Chinese to write the theses would not solve the real problem that students were experiencing with production of solid written English texts. That would not be treating the problem and instead just be treating the symptoms. Of course, it would allow the supervisors to understand the ideas of the students but it would not prepare these students to become academics able to write scholarly English articles. Huang and Wu do offer up some suggestions for tackling this issue such as co-teaching between content experts and English writing instructors as well as the development of an individualized corpus for use by students to aid in their writing. Of course, the next steps would be to try to figure out whether either of these suggestions could result in successful scholarly writing produced by the graduate students. It seems highly unlikely that content experts and English writing teachers will team up to co-teach courses; however, the suggestion of building up an individualized corpus surely seems like a very good alternative. Most likely it will be up to the English writing teachers to shoulder this burden and assist their learners in harnessing corpus technology to assist in a more bottom up approach in producing texts that are more suitable for publication (Friginal 2018). Still, it is not the only approach and as Huang and Wu stated in the beginning of the chapter, an integrated approach is necessary. A study following a group of graduate students in the compilation and use of such a corpus would be welcome.

6 Conclusion

This book has offered up several examples of innovative approaches to the teaching of English writing across different levels of education. Looking back over the chapters, it is clear to us that its theme has been the integration of different approaches to meet specific learner needs. We have found the use of peer review and peer review training in connection with collaborative writing and metacognitive instruction very inspiring. We hope to see future studies that also integrate e-learning into instruction; we are sure there will be more studies conducted aimed at helping teachers to harness technology to assist in integrating innovative approaches, not just for a novelty effect. Most of the chapters in the current volume used qualitative approaches for data collection and analysis. We hope to see more mixed-methods studies that allow for data analyses and interpretations that are both wide and deep. Lastly, there needs to be more research conducted at both "ends" of education. We know much less about the teaching of writing to primary school learners and postgraduate students. We are looking forward to seeing how the authors of the chapters in this volume as well as other researchers and English writing teachers continue to pursue these endeavours.

References

Chern, Chiou-lan. 2002. English language teaching in Taiwan today. *Asia Pacific Journal of Education 22* (2). 97–105.

DeVoss, Danielle Nicole, Elyse Eidman-Aadahl, & Troy Hicks. 2010. *Because digital writing matters: Improving student writing in online and multimedia environments*. San Francisco, CA: John Wiley & Sons.

Eloa, Idoia. 2010. Collaborative writing: Fostering foreign language and writing conventions development. *Language Learning & Technology 14* (3). 51–71.

Etherington, Matthew. 2008. E-Learning pedagogy in the primary school classroom: The McDonaldization of education. *Australian Journal of Teacher Education 33* (5) 29–54.

Flowerdew, John. 2000. Discourse community, legitimate peripheral participation, and the nonnative-English-speaking scholar. *TESOL Quarterly 34* (1). 127–150.

Friginal, Eric. 2018. *Corpus linguistics for English teachers: New tools, online resources, and classroom activities*. New York: Routledge.

Graham, Steve & Karin Sandmel. 2011. The process writing approach: A meta-analysis. *The Journal of Educational Research* 104 (6). 396–407.

Huisman, Bart, Saab Nadira, Paul van den Broek & Jan van Driel. 2019. The impact of formative peer feedback on higher education students' academic writing : a meta-analysis. *Assessment & Evaluation in Higher Education* 44 (6). 863–880.

Hyland, Ken. 2003. Genre-based pedagogies: A social response to process. *Journal of second language writing* 12 (1). 17–29.

Kao, Chian-Wen & Barry Lee Reynolds. 2017. A study on the relationship among Taiwanese college students' EFL writing strategy use, writing ability and writing difficulty. *English Teaching & Learning* 41 (4). 31–64.

Kao, Chian-Wen, Barry Lee Reynolds, & Mark Feng Teng. (2019). What we need to know about student writers' grammar learning and correction. *Applied Linguistics Review*. doi:10.1515/applirev-2019-0016

Lam, Ricky. (2010). A peer review training workshop: Coaching students to give and evaluate peer feedback. *TESL Canada Journal* 27(2). 114–127.

Lee, Icy. (1998). Writing in the Hong Kong secondary classroom: Teachers' beliefs and practices. *Hong Kong Journal of Applied Linguistics* 3(1). 61–75.

Liou, H.-C. 2001. Reflective practice in a pre-service teacher education program for high school English teachers in Taiwan, ROC. *System* 29(2). 197–208.

Nation, Paul. 2013. *What should every EFL teacher know?* Tokyo, Japan: Compass Publishing.

Nation, Paul & John Macalister. 2010. *Language Curriculum Design*. New York: Routledge.

Reynolds, Barry Lee. 2013. A web-based EFL writing environment as a bridge between academic advisers and junior researchers: A pilot study. *British Journal of Educational Technology* 44(3). E77–E80.

Reynolds, Barry Lee & Tom A. F. Anderson. 2015. Extra-dimensional in-class communications: Action research exploring text chat support of face-to-face writing. *Computers and Composition* 35 (1). 52–64.

Reynolds, Barry Lee & Mark Feng Teng. 2019. *English Literacy Instruction for Chinese Speakers*. Singapore: Palgrave Macmillan.

Storch, Neomy. 2005. Collaborative writing: Product, process, and students' reflections. *Journal of Second Language Writing* 14 (3). 153–173.

Teng, Feng Mark. 2016. Immediate and delayed effects of embedded metacognitive instruction on Chinese EFL students' English writing and regulation of cognition. *Thinking Skills & Creativity* 22 (1). 289–302.

Teng, Feng Mark. 2019a. A comparison of text structure and self-regulated strategy instruction for elementary school students' writing. *English Teaching: Practice and Critique* 18 (3). 281–297.

Teng, Feng Mark. 2019b. Tertiary-level students' English writing performance and metacognitive awareness: A group metacognitive support perspective. *Scandinavian Journal of Educational Research* 63 (1). 1–18.

Teng, Feng Mark. 2019c. The role of metacognitive knowledge and regulation in mediating university EFL learners' writing performance. *Innovation in Language Learning and Teaching*. doi:10.1080/17501229.2019.1615493

Teng, Feng Mark & Jing Huang. 2019. Predictive effects of writing strategies for self-regulated learning on secondary school learners' EFL writing proficiency. *TESOL Quarterly 53* (1). 232–247.

Teng, Feng Mark. 2020. Young learners' reading and writing performance: Exploring collaborative modeling of text structure as an additional component of self-regulated strategy development. *Studies in Educational Evaluation*. Doi: 10.1016/j.stueduc.2020.100870

Wells, D. John, Damon E. Campbell, Joseph S. Valacich, & Mauricio Featherman. 2010. The effect of perceived novelty on the adoption of information technology innovations: A risk/reward perspective. *Decision Sciences 41*(4) 813–843.

Woo, Matsuko, Samuel Kai-Wah Chu, Andrew Ho, & Xuanxi Li. 2011. Using a wiki to scaffold primary-school students' collaborative writing. *Journal of Educational Technology & Society* 14 (1). 43–54.

Zimmerman, J. Barry & Rafael Risemberg. 1997. Becoming a self-regulated writer: A social cognitive perspective. *Contemporary Educational Psychology 22* (1), 73–101.

Index

academic writing 9, 122–123, 130–131, 134, 137, 188, 208–209, 211, 218, 220–222, 225, 229, 231, 235, 237, 250, 267
Activity Theory 43, 233, 238, 241–242, 251
assessment 4, 7–8, 45, 69, 108, 121, 124, 156–157, 179–184, 186, 188–189, 191, 193–196, 200–201, 219 *See* test

backwash 4, 184, 186–187

case study 47, 58, 67, 107–108, 110, 189, 233, 238, 262
Chinese 1–2, 3, 4, 5, 7, 12–13, 23, 25, 32–34, 58, 71, 86–88, 97, 112, 120–121, 134, 145, 155, 166, 169, 189, 207–208, 210, 215, 222, 236, 245, 257–258, 262–263, 265, 267
Chinese speaker 2–3, 13, 257, 262
clause 67–68, 70–71, 74–77, 79, 81–83, 86–88, 262
corpus 10–11, 74, 157, 162, 169, 211, 214–215, 219, 233, 237, 248, 251–253, 267
Co-teaching 251, 267
course evaluation 104, 207, 220
curriculum 6–7, 8, 9, 10, 91–92, 94–95, 97, 101–103, 106, 109, 116, 145–146, 169, 183, 187–188, 208, 213, 217, 228, 235, 262–264

EFL 2, 4, 13, 20, 22–23, 25, 58, 67, 70–74, 87–88, 117–123, 134–136, 139, 209–210, 225, 236, 247, 254
e-learning 8, 19, 21–25, 27, 29–38, 40, 258–260, 268
ELF 92–94, 99–101, 103, 106–109
English as a foreign language *See* EFL
English for research publication purposes *See* ERPP
English for Research Publication *See* ERPP
Enhancement 8, 60, 128, 190, 257
ERPP 233–234, 236–241, 243–251, 253–254
error 10, 23, 67, 73–76, 79–88, 154, 163–164, 167, 262

genre-based 169, 207–212, 215, 225, 266
graduate student 207, 213–214, 233–237, 239–241, 243, 245–253, 267–268
grammar 5–6, 11, 25, 27, 31, 35–36, 66–68, 70–72, 75, 77–79, 86–88, 100–101, 104, 158, 163, 186, 188, 196, 213, 222, 224, 248, 262–263

higher education 179–180, 185–186, 189–191, 199, 201, 237–238, 243
high-stake 37, 179–180, 184–189, 191, 194–199, 201, 266

innovation 8, 92–93, 107, 189
instruction 2–3, 4, 5, 6, 7, 8, 9, 10, 11, 12, 20–21, 37, 44–45, 48, 67–68, 70–72, 78, 86, 88, 117–118, 120–123, 128, 134, 136, 140, 145, 147–150, 155, 167, 169, 188, 196, 209, 212–213, 218–219, 221, 234, 240, 242, 257–258, 260, 262–264, 266, 268

lexical 71, 196, 207, 210–211, 214–215, 217, 219, 221, 224–225, 231, 266
low-stake 179–180, 184–186, 189, 191, 193–194, 197, 199, 201

Metacognition 44, 119–120, 145, 149, 265

narrative inquiry 179–180, 184, 188–189, 191–192, 199, 201, 265
novice 35, 169, 207–209, 225, 236–237, 239, 254, 259, 263

pedagogy 4, 13, 19–20, 94, 99–101, 103, 109, 117–118, 120, 140, 209–210, 212, 215–216, 225, 233, 252, 257
peer review 43–46, 47, 48, 49, 50, 51, 52, 53, 54, 55, 56, 57, 58, 59, 60, 124, 246–247, 249, 260–261, 263, 268
perception 11, 20, 24, 44–49, 51, 97, 130, 138, 157, 162, 165–166, 169, 184, 186, 189, 240

performance 2, 25, 32, 59, 126, 145–146, 148, 151, 156–157, 159, 164–169, 185, 188, 193, 198, 200, 264–265
phrase 50, 70, 73–74, 77, 158, 199, 207, 210–211, 214–219, 221, 224–225, 231, 252, 261
policy 7–8, 10, 12, 38, 155, 258–259
primary school 6, 8, 11, 19–20, 24–25, 37, 48, 57, 258–259, 268
process writing 8, 19–20, 21, 22, 24, 31, 35, 37, 40, 117–118, 120–121, 123–124, 134–140, 149, 258, 264
proficiency 4–5, 7, 11, 19, 45, 71, 77, 117–118, 120–121, 123, 125, 129–130, 134, 138–139, 155, 188–189, 197, 199, 208, 215, 219, 235, 237, 247, 251, 259, 264–265

research article 70, 207–208, 210–211, 215, 225, 234–235, 238, 242, 245–246, 248, 252–253, 266
revision 13, 22, 26, 45, 75, 118, 120–121, 124, 126–129, 133–138, 145, 150, 152, 156, 160, 187

secondary school 1, 6–7, 9, 11, 36–37, 44, 48, 57–59, 68, 88, 98–99, 101, 108, 123, 186, 189, 260
skill 2, 7, 9, 19–20, 35, 38, 44, 52, 91, 93–98, 100–109, 116, 119–120, 122, 135, 148–149, 153, 157, 163–164, 167–168, 187, 193, 197, 208, 210, 226, 237, 248, 265
stance 44–48, 51, 53–54, 56, 58–59

strategy 2, 6, 8, 20, 36–37, 44–45, 47–52, 58, 86, 101, 109, 117–121, 123–125, 127, 132–133, 135, 137–140, 143, 145, 147–155, 157–159, 161–162, 164–169, 185, 188–189, 196, 199, 260, 264–266

technology 6, 10–11, 21–22, 224, 247, 253, 258–259, 267–268
tertiary 2, 7, 9–10, 11, 12, 57, 91, 96, 98–100, 106–108, 208, 263
test 4, 9, 13, 27, 30, 32, 36–37, 68, 72, 77, 179–180, 184–189, 191, 193–201, 221 *See* assessment
tool 19–21, 22, 24–25, 27, 29–35, 37–38, 40, 46, 53, 146–147, 149–150, 152, 155–159, 161, 164, 166–169, 185, 210, 222, 238–240, 242, 245, 248, 250, 252, 254, 258–260, 264 *See* EFL
train 4, 8, 23, 25, 27, 29, 36, 44–49, 50, 51, 52, 53, 54, 56–60, 68, 72, 86, 93, 95–96, 98–101, 103–109, 115–116, 124, 149–150, 155, 157, 216, 222, 235, 250–253, 260–265, 267–268

vocabulary 5, 11, 25–26, 31, 41, 63, 100, 196, 211–212, 221–222, 248, 252, 263

WAC 145–146, 155, 159, 168–169, 264
washback 12, 179–180, 184–189, 191, 195, 197–198, 200–201, 265
Writing Across the Curriculum *See* WAC

www.ingramcontent.com/pod-product-compliance
Lightning Source LLC
Chambersburg PA
CBHW031423150426
43191CB00006B/375